TRANSFIGURED NEW YORK

Interviews with Experimental Artists and Musicians, 1980–1990

BROOKE WENTZ

Columbia University Press

New York

Columbia University Press
Publishers Since 1893
New York   Chichester, West Sussex
cup.columbia.edu

Library of Congress Cataloging-in-Publication Data
Names: Wentz, Brooke, interviewer.
Title: Transfigured New York : interviews with experimental artists and musicians,
1980–1990 / [interviews by] Brooke Wentz.
Description: [1.] | New York : Columbia University Press, 2023. | Includes index.
Identifiers: LCCN 2023020591 | ISBN 9780231210881 (hardback) |
ISBN 9780231558631 (ebook)
Subjects: LCSH: Music—New York (State)—New York—20th century—History and
criticism. | Avant-garde (Music)—New York (State)—New York—History—20th century.
| Musicians—Interviews. | LCGFT: Interviews.
Classification: LCC ML200.8.N5 T6 2023 | DDC 780.9747/10904—dc23/eng/20230526
LC record available at https://lccn.loc.gov/2023020591

Printed in the United States of America

Cover design: Noah Arlow
Cover photo: Christian Marclay, 1987. Photo by Sokhi Wagner. © Sokhi Wagner.

Dedicated to all the young people who follow their

passions and remain curious . . .

CONTENTS

PART III. THE COMPOSERS: NOTABLE CONTRIBUTORS OF CONTEMPORARY MUSICAL REPERTOIRE

PART IV. THE ICONOCLASTS: ECCENTRIC THOUGHT-PROVOKING PERFORMERS

PART V. THE VOCALISTS: EXPERIMENTERS WITH VOICE AND WORDS

PART VI. THE DISSENTERS: MODERN JAZZ INNOVATORS

LEE RANALDO ON THE SCENE

The scene in NYC in the late seventies / early eighties had so many fascinating pockets of activity that it's almost hard to pick just one or two. The ramifications of No Wave were heavy in the downtown community—the bands from the *No New York* album, of course, and other offshoots. Perhaps most fascinating, most radical, at the time was the music being made by Glenn Branca, Rhys Chatham, and like-minded "rock minimalists"—sort of polar opposites yet doppelgangers to what was going on with Steve Reich and Phil Glass. At that time it seemed like Glenn's music, in particular (I was a member of his ensemble and, later, orchestra, from 1980–1984) was pretty much the most incredible new development going. His compositions for electric guitar, first with his Ascension Band sextet (4 gtr/bs/dr) and later with his larger orchestras and personally developed instruments, were extreme and unlike anything anyone else was doing—channeling, on the one hand, the three-chord fury of the Who or the Ramones and yet compositionally reaching for everything from [Anton] Bruckner to [Krzysztof] Penderecki or [György] Ligeti. Rhys Chatham's music was similar in its reach, and his signature piece—"Guitar Trio"—was minimalist in the same way that early Terry Riley, La Monte Young, or Reich's music was, and yet also coming out of and reflecting the nascent art/music scene to be found at Max's Kansas City or CBGB.

In those pre-internet days, when no magazines were covering this music and Manhattan seemed an isolated island "off the coast of America," this music was blowing minds and blowing up the clubs and art spaces—but if you didn't live in NYC then to witness it, its ripples were very tiny outside the district below Fourteenth Street.

Meantime, Laurie Anderson was performing her early staged pieces (and had an underground hit with "O Superman"), and improvisers like John Zorn and Elliott Sharp were creating their own new recombinant genres on the Lower East Side, carrying on a creative tradition downtown that stretched from at least the '40s and '50s, if not earlier, when free jazz was the music to challenge listeners old ways.

Shortly after arriving in NYC (1979) I moved into an old factory loft in Tribeca, which seemed like the heart of the downtown community at the time. The local clubs were Tier 3 [aka TR3] and the Mudd Club, with Max's, CBGBs, The Kitchen, and Club 57 in the East Village not far off. It seemed like the whole world of music that mattered took place in these venues at the time. Moving to Tribeca, just a few blocks from both Mudd Club and TR3, seemed like being dropped into the center of the universe.

Pretty much every aspect of my working life was influenced by what was going on in the downtown community at that time. It was a unique moment—you had all these young people moving to Manhattan, when it was still cheap enough to do so (if, at times, dangerous as well). These were not teenage garage-rockers out of high school, but rather middle-class kids (for the most part) who'd been to college, were steeped in the ways of modern cultural practice and the radical movements in the arts of the twentieth century—young persons who came to NYC to be filmmakers, painters (I had a degree in studio art), writers, dramatists, or dancers. Everyone ended up in the clubs—it was the place to exchange ideas and meet each other, and it was at the time easier to get a gig at one of the local clubs than to get a gallery show or funding for your feature film. So everyone—trained in culture and grown up on pop music—started bands, applying the devices of contemporary culture—minimalism, appropriation, etc.—to the music they were making. You didn't have to be proficient on your instrument to have an impact, you just needed a vision and some chutzpah. It was a heady time out of which many of our cultural heroes came. Much of who I am today as an artist/musician came out of the experiences of living in Manhattan in the eighties, before things made it out into the wider world.

ACKNOWLEDGMENTS

P iled in the basement of my San Francisco home are numerous quarter-inch magnetic tapes of interviews and radio productions. I have carried these tapes from a loft space in New York City to a cottage in Connecticut to a house in Hancock Park and, finally, to the cement basement of my 1895 Victorian. Something had to be done so they wouldn't wilt into a heap of resin. So in 2018, I asked the audio engineer Bill Storkson to give them a "bake." Baking allowed him to restore the tapes safely so he could transfer them to disc format.

Then, during lockdown, I realized I had numerous cassette tapes of interviews and radio shows needing upgrades. I reached out to Paul Grippaldi, founder and CEO of Digital Revolution, for assistance, and his wonderful team member Justin McElfresh transferred the warbly audio to USB sticks. Next, the transcriber extraordinaire Monique Tavian made written sense of all these difficult audio files, the most difficult being the Ravi Shankar interview, which had decayed the worst over time.

Finally, a compendium of archival interviews was audible. I reached out to my publishing maven colleague, Julie Grau, who introduced me to the wonderfully talented editor Lee Smith. His work on Josh Hammer's book *The Bad-Ass Librarians of Timbuktu* immediately won me over. A huge thanks to Lee's ability to see the significance of my interviews despite my being a twenty something college radio host. He supplemented the chapters with deeper context and artist details that had eluded even me. The writer Devin Fuller assisted with photo research and approvals. Indexical's executive director, Andrew Smith, introduced me to the University of California Santa Cruz musicology PhD candidate Joseph Finkel, who assisted with archival research. Then my dear friend Lauren Oliver contributed some final edits, chapter titling, and finessing, and Brian Bacchus, Marisa Fox, and Andy Caploe helped unearth the names and places from cobwebs of the past.

But what would this book be without the time and sleuthing generosity of colleagues and many artists? Howard Mandel dug up photos from the Lona Foote estate. Mimi Johnson from Arts Services; Alex Waterman from the Kitchen; David Weinstein from Roulette; Louie Fleck from the Brooklyn Academy of Music; and Seth Cluett and Nick Patterson at Columbia University's Computer Music Center and Music and Arts Library all contributed immensely. And, of course, the talented artists who contributed their words and archival photos helped bring to light the scene: Fast Forward, David Moss, Christian Marclay, Martin Bisi, Rhys Chatham, Shelley Hirsch, Ned Sublette, Gerry Hemingway, Yale Evelev, Robert Dick, Ikue Mori, Craig Harris, Melvin Gibbs, Brandon Ross, Zeena Parkins, Margaret Leng Tan, Joan La Barbara, Frank London, Don Byron, Ned Rothenberg, Phill Niblock, Meredith Monk, Mark De Gil Antoni, Charlie Morrow, and Elliott Sharp.

Last, but not least, I am deeply grateful to Eric Schwartz of Columbia University Press for ushering in this time capsule with his incredibly supportive and creative team—Lowell Frye and Noah Arlow. Enjoy this wild ride of creative voices, all made possible by the passionate contributions of numerous people.

TRANSFIGURED
NEW YORK

INTRODUCTION

I found my place in the world hosting a radio show at one a.m. in New York City in the 1980s. I had just started school at Barnard when I showed up at Columbia's WKCR-FM. The new music director, Mark Abbott, was explaining the late-night show *Transfigured Night* and had name-dropped the new wave outfit Tuxedo Moon. "Pinheads on the Move!" I shouted, referring to one of the group's most well-known songs. *Count me in!* The program was billed as "explorations into the world of new music" and encompassed everything from avant-garde and fringe to classical, pop, experimental, and jazz. The station allowed me to broadcast anything I wanted to twelve million souls in the tristate area: the Residents, Philip Glass, esoteric rock like Henry Cow, Krautrock like Can and Faust, and atonal postpunks the Raincoats. I sometimes snuck in a bit of Traffic and the Beatles just to keep things surprising. It was true freeform radio. And I considered it a public service to promote the panoply of amazing music performed throughout the city each week and that got little support outside of radio stations like ours.

Three months later, the program was featured in the *Village Voice* as one of the city's top independent radio shows. *Transfigured Night* became a platform for emerging artists, who would venture up to the humid and disheveled station in Ferris Booth Hall (now Lerner Hall) at 116th Street and Broadway to promote their upcoming shows and new releases. Our conversations attracted an eclectic mix of late-night listeners—students, taxi drivers, chefs, and lobster-shift workers.

Working at the station gave me a pass to attend most any show in town. I'd take the 1 train downtown to clubs like Hurrah's, CBGB, The Kitchen, A7, Mudd Club, and to concert halls like the Brooklyn Academy of Music, Town Hall, and even the Metropolitan Opera. Venues were close to one another, so it was easy to move about town. Although Manhattan could be a bit dangerous in those days, I'd still walk through the Lower East Side, passing dilapidated buildings, large empty lots, and needles on the pavement to go see Curlew, the George Cartwright, Fred Frith, and Tom Cora trio. It was both intimidating and exciting. After a show, I'd stop at Sweet Basil's and talk to the bartender, Joe, while hearing Sun Ra Arkestra, Olu Dara, or Steve Coleman before heading back uptown. It was a wondrous place and time for sonic exploration!

At the station, encounters with visiting musicians were always intriguing. Seeing Cecil Taylor, Sonny Sharrock, John Zorn, Diamanda Galás, Anton Fier, and Don Cherry was common in the 1980s. Once, an interview with the drummer Andrew Cyrille had to be cut short because John Cage had just arrived. Another time, Ned Sublette played live out on the street, rigged into the studio. Christian Marclay brought his turntables up and scratched live on air. Eric Bogosian recited monologues. Anything could happen.

The show allowed me to get closer to the artists, their process, their passions, and their struggles. I wanted to understand everything about them. My show wasn't about finding the weirdest, most jarring thing I could. My mission as a programmer was to gradually guide listeners into this wild new music scene. And that desire has never faded.

● ● ●

So how did an overly curious, post-hippie kid from San Francisco end up turning pro? My native Californian father absorbed himself in literature, music, and the newest ideas via the playwright Harold Pinter, the longshoreman philosopher Eric Hoffer, and our neighbor, the actor and author Sterling Hayden. Although classical music from Prokofiev, Dvořák, and Astor Piazzolla provided the household's soundtrack, my father was also obsessed with Wendy Carlos's *Switched-On Bach*, *Abbey Road*, *Revolver*, and the "Theme from *Shaft*." He insisted I join him at the San Francisco Symphony every Friday night, where I would generally fall asleep, but there would be a strawberry sundae from Blum's on Polk Street afterward. Saturday nights often found us at the Silver Theater to see silent movies accompanied by a live Wurlitzer organ.

My mother loved playing standards on the piano. "Sentimental Journey" was her favorite. She was a trailblazing physician who escaped a small town in Minnesota to complete her residency at the Mayo Clinic, and she specialized in internal medicine and rheumatology. San Francisco seemed to be the only place hiring women physicians in the fifties, so off she went.

In the early sixties, my father bought a reel-to-reel tape recorder. He loved documenting his world. He enjoyed pulling out the microphone to record piano recitals and conversations. He often recorded my brother and me talking about what we wanted to be when we grew up. Boxes of tapes soon filled the stereo cabinet's drawers, similar to how I would later document my radio shows and interviews for this book.

My bedroom was directly above my parents', so headphones became a friend as I listened to my records late into the night. I scored a coveted Marantz receiver and started building a stereo system that matched my enthusiasm. I would spend hours at Tower Records on Columbus Avenue running my fingers over the record spines. *Whipped Cream* by Herb Alpert and the Tijuana Brass was, at the time, ubiquitous. I grew up on Led Zeppelin, Cat Stevens's *Catch Bull at Four*, the *White Album* by the Beatles, *Greatest Hits* by Sly and the Family Stone, and of course, *Silk Degrees* by San Francisco local Boz Scaggs. My brother was, meanwhile, deep diving into Black soul—Isley Brothers, the Commodores, and Barry White—rebelling against the grating innuendo of my father's insistence on the supremacy of European classical music.

I attended a private all-girls middle school, where teachers allowed us to play whatever records we wanted before class began. Our art teacher loved the Rolling Stones and once left *Sticky Fingers* splayed out in the classroom. Andy Warhol's cover with a man's close-up crotch zipper was quite a sight for a twelve-year-old!

My self-esteem, however, went out the window with a scoliosis diagnosis. I was forced to wear an awkward torso brace twenty-three hours a day from age fourteen to eighteen, covered with loose clothing purchased in the boys section of department stores. I felt regarded as a cripple, an outsider, and a freak whenever I left the safety of my room. My headphones became my best friend. Music was my respite from rejection, and I built an extensive inner world around my music. Each album took me down a different path to a place where no one could judge me. My ears became more sophisticated to the nuances of each instrument, voice, and the art of studio production. I picked up on the Latin rhythms I heard in mainstream releases by Chicago or Paul Simon or the electronic twinkles I was hearing in albums by Yes. I diligently read every word of the liner notes and credits on the gatefold sleeves, becoming familiar with the producers, session musicians, and photographers and graphic artists who made the cover art.

My world was mine alone. I listened to the progressive FM station KSAN and often went to Bill Graham's Day on the Green concerts in Oakland. I had my first kiss in front of the venerable Fairmont Hotel before seeing Ella Fitzgerald at the Venetian Room. But when two like-minded classmates introduced me to the Mabuhay Gardens, San Francisco's punk rock club in Broadway's strip-joint district, I found a new point of departure.

The dark and damp club, lovingly called the Fab Mab, was founded by the impresario Dirk Dirkson and the Filipino restaurateur Ness Aquino. We'd go to see bands almost every week: the Nuns, the Dils, the Mutants, Dead Kennedys, Crime, SVT, Z'EV, Pearl Harbor and the Explosions, and more. I saw guitarist Robert Fripp play solo at Mabuhay and metal man Z'EV bang his wares on stage. Soon I was a regular at the Deaf Club, Savoy Tivoli, and later, the I-Beam, seeing acts like Gang of Four, Patti Smith, and Jim Carroll. People might recall the tragic history of the Jim Jones Temple on Geary Street yet may not remember the cult rented out their space for punk shows!

But most of all, I wanted to be Patti Smith, the high priestess of underground cool! She, Blondie, and Elvis Costello were all making the scene in New York. As soon as the brace came off, I was on a plane headed east.

* * *

The interviews in this book were conducted between 1980 and 1990 for broadcast on WKCR-FM or a syndicated National Public Radio show or for print publication. This was a time when a polarizing Republican Party dominated the White House. Antiapartheid protests were popping up on universities around the country, the AIDS crisis threatened an emerging culture, and the stock market boom fueled excesses of every persuasion.

Music in New York City blurred the lines between highbrow and lowbrow, between fringe and mainstream. Composers manipulated tapes and brought computers on stage for the first time. Punk-inflected pop, called new wave, was inescapable in the clubs and radio, yet the avant-garde downtown sounds, called no wave and minimalism, were being defined. Black rock bands and experimental jazz were also carving new inroads in the industry, and one could hear it all just walking from one block to the next.

I came across cassettes and reel-to-reel tapes in my basement from this period that I felt necessary to safeguard. During this time, I produced radio festivals featuring John Cage, La Monte Young, and Fred Frith, and along the way met countless amazing musicians and artists. Looking back, this work became the basis and impetus for my career as a music supervisor. My lifelong curiosity and passion have not waned; I continue this exploration by supporting international artists via my company, Seven Seas Music. I support new music venues Roulette, Indexical, Other Minds, BAM, The Kitchen, and others.

I chose this small selection of the hundreds of interviews I conducted in these years because they best convey the character, struggles, and creative process of each artist. All are revered for their contribution to their art forms; many were on the road to fortune and accolades. All were provocateurs of some sort, champions of a moment in time—their moment and a moment of New York's music history. They remain aspirational figures, among many others not included in this book, for many young experimental composers and musicians today. These artists are champions in their genres and are looked up to by so many of today's pop, contemporary, and world music artists—Steve Reich by Radiohead's Jonny Greenwood; John Cage by Wilco's Glenn Kotche; Morton Subotnick by Daft Punk and Four Tet; Laurie Anderson by St. Vincent; and Joan La Barbara by Jóhann Jóhannsson.

I truly hope you enjoy reading these interviews as much as I did unearthing and making them available to you.

PART I

THE FOUNDING THEORISTS

Influential Figures
of Contemporary
Thought and Music
Composition

FIGURE 1.1 JOHN CAGE
SOURCE: MARION ETTLINGER

1

JOHN CAGE

August 14, 1982, and July 23, 1987

No composer had as great an impact on music in the twentieth century as John Cage. He viewed the 1952 composition "4'33"" as his most important work. Essentially four and a half minutes of silence, it was an expression of Cage's revolutionary idea that any sound can be heard as music. "Until I die there will be sounds," he wrote in his famous collection of essays, *Silence*, "and they will continue after my death. One should not fear about the future of music. Any sounds may occur in any combination and in any continuity."[1]

I met Cage at the large Chelsea loft he shared with his longtime partner, the dance choreographer Merce Cunningham. The windows were open wide, and one could clearly hear the horns and sirens on the streets below. I asked him about the striking prints hanging on the walls. They were the work of his friends Bob (Robert Rauschenberg) and Jasper (Jasper Johns), and Cage said he was now working with an artist's press to make prints of his own.

Merce was mulling about in the kitchen while Cage and I sat down to chat. Wearing a blue painter's coat, he spoke slowly, seemingly so I could understand every word, and made double entendres of almost everything he said. He told me he believed one of the strangest instruments was the oboe because of its funny, high-pitched sound and that he wanted to compose a live piece at our station for an on-air celebration of his upcoming seventy fifth birthday. He was keen to access the station's opera collection so he could produce a composition using his "chance operations" derived from the *I Ching*. The birthday celebration I hosted ultimately became a seventy-five-hour marathon of Cage's music. The interest in his work ran that deep.

B. WENTZ: I read that, as a boy in Los Angeles, you studied piano with a teacher who didn't approve of Bach and Beethoven.

JOHN CAGE: The teacher was my Aunt Phoebe. She had a book called *Piano Music the Whole World Loves to Play*, which was on almost every piano in the 1920s. It was all music from the nineteenth century, but it very carefully avoided the most important composers. That is to say, it avoided Bach and Beethoven. So I became fascinated with the music of Norwegian composer Edvard Grieg— whose work did appear in that book.

B. WENTZ: Years later you studied with Arnold Schoenberg, who pioneered the method of composing music with twelve tones that are related to one another. When did you first hear his music?

JOHN CAGE: When I dropped out of college and went to Europe in 1930, I became aware first of modern painting and then of modern music. I went to a piano recital where I heard the music of Russian composer Igor Stravinsky, and it struck me that if twentieth-century music sounded that way, then I could write it. So I began writing music without knowing how to do it. At the same time, I was painting pictures because I had a similar reaction to modern painting. I continued that way for a year and a half until I came back to the United States where I met some people who knew their modern art: the Arensbergs, who were the patrons of Marcel Duchamp, and Galka Scheyer, who brought [Wassily] Kandinsky and [Paul] Klee to America. Around the same time, I met the pianist Richard Buhlig, who was the first in the world to play Schoenberg's Opus 11. And Buhlig was more interested in my music than the Arensbergs or Scheyer were interested in my painting, so I decided to devote myself to music. At that time, if you explored music, you came to the conclusion that there was Stravinsky and there was Schoenberg, and I chose Schoenberg—I was experimenting at the time with twenty-five-tone compositions. So I went to New York to prepare to study with him.

B. WENTZ: When you asked Schoenberg to teach you, he said, "You can't afford my price." You replied, "Don't mention it. I don't have any money." Then he asked if you were willing to devote your life to music. When you said, "Yes," he offered to teach you free of charge.

JOHN CAGE: Yes. I got free lessons. But he was a slavedriver. You couldn't satisfy the man. You could cover a paper with exercises, and he'd say, "Why don't you do more?"

B. WENTZ: How long did you study with him?

JOHN CAGE: Two years. By that point it became clear to both of us that I had no feeling for harmony. He said I'd never be able to write music, that I would come to a wall and wouldn't be able to get through it.

B. WENTZ: Years later he said you are not a composer but an inventor—of genius.

JOHN CAGE: He didn't say that to me. He said it to another composer. I like that because my father was an inventor. But genius isn't so important really because so many people have it.

B. WENTZ: Not long after you parted ways with Schoenberg you began experimenting with percussion music, using various objects for instruments. How did that come about?

JOHN CAGE: It came about through the trouble I had with harmony and through my deciding to work with noises. I didn't like the distinction between noises and musical tones. Around that time you could hear the noise music of the Italian futurists, and that whole thing was inspiring to me.

The filmmaker Oskar Fischinger was the one who encouraged me to hit things. I was working as his assistant to write music for one of his films, and he said everything in the world has its own spirit and that spirit is made evident when you set the thing into vibration. So I was hitting everything and listening to it. I began organizing groups to play percussion music, and we used things that we found, like flowerpots and brake drums, automobile parts. I'd go to junk yards and pick things up and get pots and pans or pieces of wood. It was during the Depression and I didn't have much money, but when I could afford it I would sometimes rent a gong or a timpani.

B. WENTZ: Soon after that, you were offered a job in Seattle at the Cornish School, where you created something you called macrocosmic rhythmic structure. Can you explain what that is and what led to your discovery?

JOHN CAGE: When I studied with Schoenberg, he emphasized the importance of structure in music—that is to say, the division of a whole into parts. And he said that this should be accomplished with tonality and changes from one key to another. But if you're working with noises that have no relation to tonality, then you need a different kind of structure. So I examined the nature of sound and saw that it had pitch, duration, overtone structure, and amplitude. And of those four, the only one that silence had was duration. Because silence didn't have pitch, didn't have overtone structure, and didn't have amplitude. So I figured that the most important structure for music, or certainly for music that would involve noises, was one based on duration. So the first structure I thought of was a square root structure. If I had one hundred measures, I could divide it into ten tens, then I could divide each ten measures in the same way that I would divide the ten tens. That way, the large parts would have the same proportion to one another that the small parts had to each other. And that appealed to me in the same way that a crystal appeals to us through the perfection of its structure. So I wrote music for quite a while with that rhythmic structure based on this square root system. I called it macrocosmic rhythmic structure, meaning big/little, you see?

B. WENTZ: You ultimately made your way to New York City. While you were living there, you began, in the late 1940s, to take periodic teaching gigs at Black Mountain College, in North Carolina, where you staged the first so-called happening, which featured your lifelong partner, dancer Merce Cunningham, and your friend, painter Robert Rauschenberg.

JOHN CAGE: It was a marvelous place. The place where ideas were exchanged and where the people affected one another was not in the classrooms. It was at the meals because we all had our meals together. We had breakfast, lunch, and dinner, and people stayed at the tables for hours after eating, just carrying on conversations, and that's why the school was so very lively. People often want to know how to start Black Mountain over again, and I think the first thing they should do is have a community dining room. Food is very important, and it wasn't very good food at Black Mountain. At least, we didn't think it was good. All we wanted was meat, and there never was any!

B. WENTZ: It was around that time that you took a trip to Harvard. Can you tell that story?

JOHN CAGE: I don't know why I was going to Harvard. I drove there from Black Mountain in my old Model T Ford. Nice car. At Harvard, I visited an anechoic chamber, which is an extremely soundproofed room. I went in there expecting to hear silence, but I heard two sounds, like there was something wrong, so I called the engineer, and he asked me to describe them to him. I said one sound was high and one was low. He said the high-pitched one was the sound of your nervous system in operation, and the lower one was of your blood circulating. So that made me realize that I was at the crossroads, not between the sound of silence, which I had thought, but I was at the crossroads between sounds that were intentional and unintentional. All silence is sounds that are not intended. So that meant that I had to write music nonintentionally.

B. WENTZ: You once said music is all around us. There is no need for concert halls if a man could only enjoy the sounds that envelop him. But when we hear music and we're in a concert hall, we hear an arrangement of sounds, and I find that one perhaps is more conscious of certain sounds because of the ways you juxtapose the sounds rather than in everyday life where you hear cars going by because it happens all the time.

JOHN CAGE: I am devoted to music, and I spend most of my time writing it. On the other hand, I love the sounds around me, and I hear them as music. The traffic here on Sixth Avenue is extraordinary. I'm not so fond of the sound of the fan in my apartment because that doesn't change, whereas the traffic changes all the time. I call that traffic silence because I don't intend it, and if you said that it was intended, you would have to have so many intentions being thought of. All the drivers of all those cars, all the various intentions would wipe one another out as intention, so that it really is a kind of nonintentional sound that takes place. I want my mind to become nonintentional. Not nonintentional stupidly but nonintentional attentively. I actually listen to all those changes of sound, and that's how I want my music to be.

B. WENTZ: Your experience at Harvard and your ideas about nonintentional sounds ultimately led to the composition of "4'33'," in which not a single note is played. It's clearly your most famous work—it's always referenced when people write about you.

JOHN CAGE: I don't mind that. Because I enjoy these sounds from Sixth Avenue myself. And that's what "4'33'" is. It's listening to the world around you.

B. WENTZ: Around this time you began collaborating with pianist David Tudor. How did you meet?

JOHN CAGE: We got to know one another through the composer Morton Feldman. I went to hear the New York Philharmonic perform Anton Webern's Symphony, Opus 21. Afterward, there was a piece by Sergei Rachmaninoff, but I didn't want to hear it after being so overwhelmed by Webern's piece, so I walked out. In the lobby, I met Morton Feldman, who had walked out for the same reason. So we became friends almost immediately.

I had been in Paris, it was the late forties, and I had brought back the second piano sonata of French composer Pierre Boulez, which was considered unplayable. When I showed it to Morty, he said there is only one person who can play this: David Tudor. I showed it to David, and he immediately became fascinated by it. He learned French in order to read the poetry that Boulez had been reading when he wrote that music. Can you believe it? I've known David ever since.

B. WENTZ: You wrote "Music of Changes" specifically for David to perform on piano. That was the first piece you composed using chance operations—asking questions of the *I Ching* to help shape your approach rather than making choices yourself.

JOHN CAGE: I started to write "Music of Changes" because I was working systematically with chance operations. I could tell almost, if not to the day, then I could tell to the week, how much work I had to do. I had very little money at the time, and you couldn't get work easily in the years following the war. So I wrote a little blurb about the piece, and I sent it to a lot of people. I said, "Would you like to be rich when you're dead?" The idea was that I would give them shares in "The Music of Changes." David didn't have any money back then, but he sent me some.

B. WENTZ: You became a friend and mentor to Yoko Ono in the late 1950s, through her husband at the time, Japanese composer Toshi Ichiyanagi, who was a student of yours.

JOHN CAGE: Yoko put on these events at their loft downtown, where pieces by [composer and artist] La Monte Young and [artist and musician] Henry Flynt and others were done. It was quite marvelous. You'd climb all these stairs, and then you'd see Yoko sitting at the table ready to take the money for the tickets. She was so elegant-looking with that straight black hair. The performances excited a great deal of interest. People would come from great distances to go to one of those concerts.

B. WENTZ: Years later, through Yoko, you received some handwritten lyrics from John Lennon?

JOHN CAGE: That was for a collection of manuscripts that I made in the mid-1960s. Everywhere I would go, every performance I saw, whether or not I liked the music, I would ask the composer to give me a manuscript. It didn't have to be a whole score, it could be a page or a sketch or anything they wanted. And everyone agreed. The collection is now at Northwestern University.

B. WENTZ: You gathered scores from hundreds of composers, including Aaron Copland, Igor Stravinsky, and Pierre Boulez. How did the Beatles respond?

JOHN CAGE: When I asked them for a manuscript, they didn't send me music. They sent me lyrics. I don't think they really had scores.

B. WENTZ: Those were mostly lyrics for songs that appeared on the album *Revolver*.

JOHN CAGE: When they sent them to me, I was teaching at the University of Illinois, in Champaign-Urbana. Everyone there, especially the teenagers, were flabbergasted that I received anything from the Beatles. They were terribly popular at the time.

B. WENTZ: Did you ever listen to their music?

JOHN CAGE: Oh, sure. I don't think you could get around back then without hearing it. They were marvelous.

B. WENTZ: Recently, you composed a piece based on James Joyce's *Finnegans Wake*. It's called "Roaratorio." What does that mean?

JOHN CAGE: So an oratorio is a church piece, and roaratorio, you might say, is an outside of the church piece. What I did was first to write mesostics on the name James Joyce through the *Wake*, and those mesostics begin with the first word in the wake that has a J in it that doesn't have an A, followed with a word that has an A but doesn't have an M, and so on. And it goes from the beginning to the end. It's not too long because I kept an index of the syllables I used and didn't permit repetition. So you can read the whole text in a little less than an hour. And when Klaus Schenning of the German radio in Cologne heard that I had done this, he asked me if I would read it over the radio, and I said I would, and then when I said that, he said, "Would you write music to go with it?" And I said yes, and I didn't know what I would do, but I decided to take this thing I had written and use it as a ruler, which could identify the pages and the lines. Then I would read through the *Wake* again and list the sounds that I heard in it. Like when Joyce mentioned a dog barking or something, anything that struck me as having a sound, I would jot it down, according to its page and line. Then we could make a recording of a dog barking and put it in where it belonged in relation to the text. Also, a book was published called *A Gazetteer of Finnegans Wake*, by Louis Mink, who teaches philosophy at Wesleyan. That listed all the places in the *Wake*. John Fileman and I made a trip to Ireland to record sounds in the places mentioned in the *Wake*, and likewise, we put them where they belonged in relation to page and line. So we worked for a whole month, and we came up with a piece having, I think, about sixty-seven layers of tape, and then on top of it, there's my reading, and it goes kind of like a circus, kind of Irish traditional music, with bodhran drumming, eolian pipes, flute, and fiddle. Oh, and the singing of Joe Heaney.

B. WENTZ: How do you go about composing these days? Does it tend to be systematic, like the chance operations were?

JOHN CAGE: No, I tend to do many different things. And I was back then, too. I did a preface to my catalog recently, and I studied, listed all my work, and I listed the different kinds of composition that engaged my attention, and I found that some of them I lost interest in, and others I haven't lost interest in, so that it's like layers. There are three, four, five things going on at once, and some of them die out, and others get started, and it continues. It's like a kind of stratification.

B. WENTZ: Do you tend to go back to some of the older ones?

JOHN CAGE: I don't tend to go back so much as to continue or to introduce new things. For instance, it wouldn't occur to me to write twelve-tone music now, the way I did at the beginning. It just wouldn't.

B. WENTZ: What is an element that all of your music has in common?

JOHN CAGE: I think the thing that is in common with all of them is that, one way or another, I free the sounds from my intentions. Either through chance operations or using astronomers' star maps to create the tones of an octave or through imperfections in the paper on which the music is written or one thing or another. Recently, I used templates, that's shapes, in cardboard that I can punch holes in. I can also mark the apexes of the templates, and I can place the templates on the manuscript paper through chance operations. So some of my recent compositions are graphically composed.

B. WENTZ: Through composing, you've returned to your roots as a visual artist.

JOHN CAGE: It began with the advent of magnetic tape following the war. When I started using tape, it became clear to me that there was an equivalence between space and time. On a professional recording reel, one second equals either fifteen inches of tape or seven and a half inches of tape. That brought about developments in music notation that we called graphic. And my score card, the piano card of the concert for piano and orchestra, is visually very attractive, so much so that the Stable Gallery in New York exhibited it in the late 1950s. Some other pieces of mine were exhibited at the Museum of Modern Art. When people interested in prints saw that my manuscripts were graphic, I was then invited to make lithographs and, more recently, etchings. Following Marcel Duchamp's death, I made a series of plexigrams and lithographs called *Not Wanting to Say Anything About Marcel.*

B. WENTZ: Were you good friends with him?

JOHN CAGE: Toward the end of his life, I saw him a great deal. He was interviewed once and asked what he thought of me. He was speaking in French, he said, "*Nous sommes copain.*" That means we're buddies! [laughs]

B. WENTZ: What does music mean to you?

JOHN CAGE: It means paying attention to signs. In the case of Bach, you're led by the music to pay attention not so much to the sounds as to the relationships. I think in Mozart there's another tendency that is different from Bach. In Bach, it's as though he wanted you to focus on the subject or, as Schoenberg would say, on the motive. And Schoenberg used to say all music is repetition and variation of a motive and that variation itself is a repetition. So it all gets boiled down to one motive. I think in Mozart there is another tendency, which is the tendency toward many or multiplicity. And I think that tendency toward multiplicity leads away from the fascination with relationships that is concentrated upon in the case of Bach and even in Beethoven. So I prefer Mozart. I find it livelier, and it leads me to the world around me, rather than a fixed idea about sounds.

B. WENTZ: What do you think of where music is headed today? Do you ever listen to rock music?

JOHN CAGE: You know, when we were traveling around—David Tutor and my partner Merce Cunningham—I remember David getting excited about rock and roll. And you know why? Because of the great volume. It was really loud. What I liked was that it was so loud that I couldn't hear the beat. It all sort of blurred together. It was the loudness that was really impressive.

B. WENTZ: What do you think of improvisation? A lot of people here in New York, like John Zorn, Fred Frith, and Joëlle Léandre, are doing improvisation nowadays.

JOHN CAGE: I'm much more interested in improvisation than I was years ago. I used to have a chip on my shoulder regarding improvisation. And the reason I had it was because so many people who improvise do it the same way each time because it's based on their taste and their memory. I have developed various ways now of getting other people to improvise that separates them from that taste and memory.

B. WENTZ: There's a whole generation of young musicians and composers— Brian Eno, Philip Glass, and Steve Reich, to name a few—that have been influenced by your work. Do you think the world has finally caught up to your music?

JOHN CAGE: My old work is less controversial now. I think many people who don't like my recent work begin by saying that my early work isn't so bad! But they don't like the recent work. And that there are some people who like the recent work. So it keeps going.

B. WENTZ: Maybe ten years from now they'll like your recent work.

JOHN CAGE: And maybe they won't like what I'm doing then. There's this octogenarian who writes such terrible music!

Meredith Monk
Composer and interdisciplinary artist

The 1980s in New York was an edgy, bright, brash decade. Permeating my memory is the emergence of the AIDS epidemic and all the brilliant, luminous friends that we lost. It was a time of extreme contrasts: I could perform in a club with beer bottles hitting the floor one night and Carnegie Hall the next.

FIGURE 2.1 LA MONTE YOUNG

SOURCE: BRIGITTE FRIEDRICH

2
LA MONTE YOUNG
July 10, 1984

The Tribeca neighborhood in Lower Manhattan had a desolate feel in the 1980s. There were few cabs to be found on the cobblestone streets lined with warehouses, and you could turn any corner and find yourself utterly alone, even in the middle of the day. But the area's solitude belied a vibrant cultural scene, as it was home to some of the city's hippest clubs, like the Franklin Furnace, Mudd Club, and Roulette. One of my favorite places to visit in Tribeca was the building at Six Harrison Street, home of La Monte Young and his wife Marian Zazeela, where they staged the sound and light installation *Dream House* with support from the Dia Art Foundation and where Young regularly performed everything from ragas to hours-long renditions of his masterpiece, *The Well-Tuned Piano*.

One Saturday morning, I ventured up the building's wide staircase to the second floor and entered a vast room with high ceilings and a plush mauve carpet. Visitors sprawled out while Young and Zazeela performed on a low platform at one end of the room. She softly pumped sound from a harmonium while Young overlaid vocals and piano. Sun rays beamed through the tall windows, and I just lay there and was lulled to sleep by Young's soothing harmonic tones.

Young grew up in Idaho and Los Angeles and attended UCLA, where he met and played saxophone with jazz pioneers like Don Cherry, Ornette Coleman, and Eric Dolphy. In the summer of 1959, he took a summer class in Germany with Karlheinz Stockhausen and met the pianist David Tudor, who introduced him to the music and theories of John Cage. He later studied with Schoenberg's disciple Leonard Stein at the University of California in Berkeley, where he bonded with a like-minded classmate named Terry Riley. Schoenberg's twelve-tone composition technique, along with Young's studies of Gamelan music and

Japanese and Indian classical music, would form the basis of his sustained tone theories, which, according to Young, "allow music to evolve to a higher level."[2]

After graduation, Young left for New York City and fell into the Fluxus art scene in the sixties. He organized concerts in Yoko Ono's loft in Tribeca and began experimenting with drone tones and Dadaist thought. A slight, short man with a soft, high-pitched voice, Young was wonderfully congenial, with a keen sense of humor, but he also could be acerbic about his critics.

I have always enjoyed my time and encounters with La Monte and Marian. Both are fastidious, keen-witted, and always curious. Because Young has influenced so many musicians, composers, and listeners, I decided to produce a twenty-four-hour retrospective of his music on WKCR-FM to celebrate his forty-ninth birthday in October 1984. With taped interviews with Yoko Ono and Tony Conrad and a live panel discussion with Terry Riley, Henry Flynt (founder of concept art), the New York poet Jackson McLow, and the Wesleyan musicologist Daniel James Wolf, the festival was a huge success.

B. WENTZ: How many concerts do you give a year? You've performed your piece, *The Well-Tuned Piano*, several times here at Six Harrison Street, where the Dia Art Foundation helped set up your continuous sound and light installation, *Dream House*, in 1979. But it seems you generally don't stage many concerts.

LA MONTE YOUNG: I don't do a set number a year. Most of the things that I perform live have become such big productions that it's very hard to get places that can afford to do it. And I have intentionally tried *not* to just come up with something that fits in the plaster-cast mold of a one-night-stand type of thing. Phil Glass used to tell me how proud he was of the fact that he can set up in two hours. It sounded good every time, and he could get in and out of the concert hall the same night. I realize the practicality of that.

And it's not that I don't want to do it, but the way I compose, and the way I work, I have always followed my intuition and my inspiration. For instance, when I do *The Well-Tuned Piano*, it usually consists of seven or eight concerts. Each concert is about a week apart because . . . Did you hear some of the *Well-Tuned Piano*? When did you hear it?

B. WENTZ: In October of '81, here at Harrison Street.

LA MONTE YOUNG: You probably heard part of the five-hour concert. You see, to do this, I rehearse and we tune the piano for a month or two before the concerts begin.

B WENTZ: Yes, this was one of the performances you did for your Gramavision recording. So, it must have been tuned "well."

LA MONTE YOUNG: Yes, then I perform once a week. I like to do at least seven or eight concerts so that people can see the growth and development of the piece. Each concert is somewhat different, even though the chord changes are the same, even though the thematic material is pretty much the same.

B WENTZ: The piece has seven major sections, starting with the "Opening Chord," and then multiple subsections or themes, including "The Romantic Court" and "The Shimmering Pool," but the piece doesn't seem to progress so much as gradually envelope the listener. The tuning of each note is slightly different, or off-center, than another, which means the intervals are replicated.

LA MONTE YOUNG: I begin with the "Opening Chord," and it develops and grows, and each performance takes its own shape and structure. I might spend two hours in "The Shimmering Pool" theme at one performance, and only an hour at another performance, and more time in "The Romantic Court" theme so that it becomes an organically alive thing. If I perform on Sundays, I have a tape playback on Wednesday so that people who want to can come hear the performance again. Also, I then get a chance to hear it and think about what I've done, and it influences my next performance.

Our original goal was to perform *The Well-Tuned Piano* here every year. And we were doing that in the first years that we were in this building because we have the space. But I don't want to play it unless I can record it on tape because I can't bear to put all of that into it and then just see it go up in the air like smoke, and it's gone forever.

B. WENTZ: Have you ever considered recording it on an album?

LA MONTE YOUNG: Yes. We're working now with a record company, and we plan to put it out next year. I am very anxious to get it out because I realize one of the gaps in my career is that there are no records available. The ones that were available, the Shandar disc [La Monte Young and Marian Zazeela, *The Theater of Eternal Music*, released in 1974] and the Edition X release [La Monte Young and Marian Zazeela, *31 VII 69 10:26–10:49 PM / 23 VIII 64 2:50:45–3:11 AM, the Volga Delta*, released in 1969], the black record, they've been out of print for a long time, and it's a big problem. Because not everybody in the world can come here to Six Harrison Street and hear what's going on.

B WENTZ: You began composing *The Well-Tuned Piano* in 1964, but it wasn't premiered live for an audience until ten years later, in Rome.

LA MONTE YOUNG: When I composed *The Well-Tuned Piano* in the sixties, I thought I would never get to do it live because it seemed too big to me, and I always presented it as a tape presentation. But then we did *Dream House* in Rome at the National Gallery of Modern and Contemporary Art, and

Fabio Sergenti, who had curated it, invited me to perform the following year at a festival in Rome. I initially suggested a tape concert of *The Well-Tuned Piano* and gave him some tapes. He heard it and said, "I really like it. Why don't you come and play it?"

B WENTZ: You play the piece on an Imperial Bosendorfer, which is larger than a standard grand piano and spans eight complete octaves. So I'm guessing he had one available in Rome?

LA MONTE YOUNG: He did. So I went to Rome and played the piece, and it was an instant success. They were crazy about it. Fabio bought the Bosendorfer I had used and gave it to me. It's a really beautiful instrument! It's here now at Six Harrison Street.

B. WENTZ: You mentioned earlier that your performances here at Dia can last for more than five hours. How can you play that long without a break?

LA MONTE YOUNG: I keep in very good physical shape. The performance is like an athletic event. I train, I prepare. No alcohol on the days before the concert. I've always had terrific stamina. Even in the sixties, when I was playing sopranino saxophone, I tended to play for a long time in concert.

Since I'm interested in this concept of continuity, of music that goes on, let's say, forever, I want to demonstrate what that concept could be as much as possible in my live performances. And I pride myself on my ability to deal with abstract structure and sound over an extended period of time. So that when you hear one of these *Well-Tuned Piano* performances, I'm not just daydreaming away and getting lost into this music. I'm really playing on a very high, inspired level, and I'm remembering what I played consciously or unconsciously, and it's influencing the entire development of the piece.

B. WENTZ: Let's stick with your work in the sixties for a moment. Around the time you left California for New York City, you wrote *Compositions 1960*, a series of text-based musical pieces that included instructions like "release a butterfly into the room" or "push a piano against a wall." How do you view those works today?

LA MONTE YOUNG: I still like them. Those pieces were written as a reaction to the academic scene I had been exposed to studying music theory as an undergraduate at UCLA and then at Berkeley. They were a social statement. They made a very strong statement about music and about the social scene that music took place in.

At that time, one of my thoughts was that it's more important that the work be *new* than anything else. There was just no need to continuously rehash things and try to relive the past. I was inspired by John Cage. I had just been to Darmstadt, Germany, in the summer of '59, and I had taken Stockhausen's advanced composition seminar, which I really liked and got a lot out of. While I was there, I heard Cage's "Concert for Piano and Orchestra" played by David Tutor. Plus, I had been reading Cage's lectures before that. They're my tribute to Cage, those early pieces, but at the same time, they're very La Monte Young because they have this focus on one event type of thing.

B. WENTZ: They're very short.

LA MONTE YOUNG: Yeah, they're like haiku. I had studied haiku in high school and in junior college, and I think that the Japanese contribution to culture is really a great one. So I still like them, and I still think they have their place. You won't find me writing pieces like that today. I mean, I won't go back. It's good to try to move on.

B. WENTZ: At Berkeley, you moved away from jazz, which you had played early on, and dedicated yourself to composition. It's also where you befriended Terry Riley and began experimenting with sounds. That must have been an interesting time.

LA MONTE YOUNG: Oh yeah. When I would do noon concerts outside, the architectural department would give me the entire architectural building to use as a sound source. It was really great. I had speakers on the roofs and people going around doing all kinds of unusual events. I was also able to get my entire music appreciation class to do a chamber opera performance of the 1960 compositions *Poem for Chairs, Tables and Benches*. It's really mind-blowing. We were in a hall, and I had a girl playing Beethoven on a piano, and I had a girl cooking bacon and eggs in a frying pan, and another girl was sleeping in an aisle in a sleeping bag. And the artist Bruce Conner took part in it. He had a cricket in his shoe—one of those things that when you walk, every step you take, it's clicking. He was going up and down the aisles doing something or other with each person. It was a big multimedia event. And my entire class was walking through the hall reading from music appreciation textbooks so that there were all of these simultaneous events going on. It was quite an affair!

And after I did one or two of those, they were really worried about me. Terry Riley and I had both won the Alfred Harris Memorial Scholarships after our second year at Berkeley when we graduated. They gave me the traveling one, sort of to get rid of me, I always felt. And they gave Terry the resident one to keep him there, just so we'd be split up. But really, I did love my time at Berkeley.

B. WENTZ: What was the inspiration for another piece you did around this time, 1960's "2 Sounds"? You called it "friction noise music." The British composer Cornelius Cardew called it the most horrible sound in the world.

LA MONTE YOUNG: That piece is a real screamer! It sounds electronic, but it's cans on windows. At the time, I was interested in long sustained tones. I was working with ways of producing sounds, sometimes even architecturally, with the walls of the space that we were working in or with the windows of the space. And in "2 Sounds," what Terry and I did was, there was a big glass door and a big glass window in this recording studio we were working in. So Terry took a big bucket and was scraping that on the glass door. I was doing cans on windows. It's quite a striking sound.

The other sound is a drumstick on a gong. I took a drumstick and did a circle on a gong continuously for the length of tape that I had available. That sound, too, is quite striking. But together, the two work very well. So that was "2 Sounds."

B. WENTZ: Around the time you arrived at Berkeley in 1958, you wrote *A Trio for Strings*, which was the first work made entirely of sustained tones and is considered the foundational piece of minimalism. You're still associated with that term, along with Terry Riley, Steve Reich, and Philip Glass. How do you feel about that label as it's used today? I see your sixties work as being more minimal.

LA MONTE YOUNG: More minimal than *The Well-Tuned Piano*, let's say, which is really a very grand work and so big in scale that it's difficult to think of it as minimal.

First of all, let's take the term *minimalism*. Minimalism is that which is created with a minimum of means. Therefore, a lot of my early work in the sixties, as you pointed out, is really very minimal. Like *Poem for Chairs, Tables and Benches*. *Trio for Strings* is, obviously, very much minimal in direction. But the term only applies to one aspect of my work.

Then there's what I'd call hardcore minimalism. It is a more rhythmic approach, as presented by Terry and Phil and Steve. This rhythmic approach in *Theater of Eternal Music* does exist in my music, like in the—did you hear any of the sopranino saxophone playing? Do you like it?

B. WENTZ: *The Tortoise, His Dreams and Journeys* is one of my favorite pieces.

LA MONTE YOUNG: Oh, great. Thank you.

B. WENTZ: That's one you should definitely record.

LA MONTE YOUNG: I do want to put that out. Is that the only one you heard of the saxophone playing?

B. WENTZ: There was another one. *Early Tuesday Morning Blues* and the *Fifth Day of the Hammer*.

LA MONTE YOUNG: So there I was doing fast rhythmic work, and also in some sections of *The Well-Tuned Piano*. But it's never presented quite in this simplistic, if I may use the term, way that Phil and Steve present theirs. One big difference between me and Phil and Steve, and I include Terry a little more with me in this particular respect, is that Terry and I are improvisers. Phil and Steve are not. Whatever they write on the page, that's the way it's going to be. They may build a little bit of flexibility into it, but beyond that, it's fixed. I feel that they [Phil and Steve] have their place, but their place doesn't have the potential for inspiration and feeling that can take place in an improvised performance.

B WENTZ: So would you say that you helped create minimalism?

LA MONTE YOUNG: There's no question in my mind that the entire minimalist movement did come out of my work. But I think of my work as much bigger. When you think of the other things that I have contributed to the history of music, such as my work in just-intonation [the tuning of musical intervals as whole number ratios of frequencies, such as 3:2 or 4:3].... Now, I'm not claiming I invented it—I know Harry Partch made a huge contribution.

I remember as a young boy when I was listening to Harry Partch, and I was thinking, this is real interesting and it's real far-out, yet it never grabbed me the way I would have liked it to. And I think that what my music has done for just-intonation, it's presented it in such a crystal-clear way because of the fact that there are these sustained sections because I have some knowledge of acoustics and I've been able to set it up so that these clouds generate in *The Well-Tuned Piano*. It has drawn people to just-intonation, and I predict more people will be tuning their pianos like I do. No one was doing this ten years ago. I think once the record comes out, you will see a whole generation of young composers start tuning pianos. I think it will be very influential.

Then I had a very strong influence on Terry Reilly at Berkeley when we were there together. As you know, Terry then created *In C*. In my mind, Steve and Phil, to this very day, are still rewriting *In C*. They have hardly come up with anything new that wasn't already suggested in the format of *In C*. I think it's a very important work, and I think Terry's role in minimalism can't be underplayed. I think that he definitely had a lot to do with establishing what we think of as really hardcore minimalism. This kind of rhythmically, pulsating, phase-changing type of music.

B WENTZ: Another aspect of your work is your interest in Indian classical music, which you've been studying under Hindustani singer Pandit Pran Nath since the 1970s.

LA MONTE YOUNG: Some people think I'm only studying with Pandit Pran Nath these days, which isn't true. I'm very much involved in my own work, but my life is sort of divided into two parts now. It's not that I do half as much of each, I do both about the same amount, and I just work twice as much.

We did four concerts with Pandit Pran Nath here at Dia. We may do some other performances with him this year. We've been doing his raga-cycle concerts every single year. I'm also composing some new works. I have something that will first go through a computer stage. We have a new synthesizer made by David Rayna, and it runs with a computer. This synthesizer is good for me because I can work in ratios so that I can continue my work in just-intonation and come up with intervals that really nobody has had a chance to hear before.

B. WENTZ: It's interesting to see you're using computers.

LA MONTE YOUNG: The synthesizer can play these tiny intervals that no one can easily sing and articulate. So I want to get them going and hear them. I will give the computer rules, and it can do a version improvising by itself. And then I would have a group also play with the computer using the tones as I suggested as background to guide the musicians to where the pitch is.

B. WENTZ: It will be working in real-time when you perform?

LA MONTE YOUNG: Yes, In real-time when we perform. Even when the computer works alone, it will be in real-time if I give it these rules for which notes can play together. So that's a new piece I'm working on. I hope to get it going.

B. WENTZ: It seems everybody's working with a computer nowadays. I was just talking with John Cage, and he's so excited because now, with a computer, he can do his mesostics perfectly.

LA MONTE YOUNG: That's the thing, they present some possibilities that just weren't there before!

There's a string trio in Europe that's very interested in commissioning a new work from me. One of the problems I have with commissions is that, since I'm working in just-intonation, most of what I want to write, other people can't play. And the only way I have found to solve that is to give them a set of electric tones in the background that they match up to, as I was doing in *Dream House*. And it makes it a big production all over again.

If I had wanted to be a commercial success, I would have done something else besides be a composer. I devoted my life to music because I'm crazy about music, and I really see it as my role in life, and the kind of music I want to do is the kind that's going to change the history of music, change the history of the world. So it puts me in a position that it's hard for me to compete with those who have something that, commercially, is more easy to do, more easy to get it out. And I almost don't try to compete with them. But I very much do want my music to get out to the public.

Shelley Hirsch
Artist

I met amazing people performing in Zorn's projects
including during *The Big Gundown*—[Fred] Frith,
[Arto] Lindsay, at BAM and I loved performing in
Christian Marclay's *Dead Stories*, which premiered
at the Performing Garage.

The first time I saw Jerry Hunt perform was
at Roulette when it was still in Tribeca at Jim
Staley's loft. It was one of the most inspiring
concerts I've ever seen. Jerry Hunt was a huge
inspiration for me! His performance stayed with
me for a very long time.

PS1 was a fantastic meeting place for Europeans,
especially Germans because they had studios
there. Everything was informative. . . . Going
to gallery shows, seeing experimental theater
like the Wooster Group, and seeing experimental
film was a big part of my life.

Maggie Smith presented a wonderful series
at the Tin Pan Alley Bar in midtown. I believe
strippers performed there too, but not at the
same time she held music events!

PART II

THE MATERIALS SCIENTISTS

Pioneers of Tape
and Electronic Music

FIGURE 3.1 DAVID BEHRMAN
SOURCE: TERRI HANLON

3
DAVID BEHRMAN
July 7, 1983

D avid Behrman was one of the first composers I met in New York who dabbled with computers as an instrument long before most of us even owned one. His fascination started in the 1970s, when Steve Jobs and Steve Wozniak were working on home computers in a garage. Born in Austria, the soft-spoken Behrman attended elite American schools—Philips Academy-Andover, and Harvard and Columbia Universities for his master of arts. His uncle was the world-renowned violinist Jascha Heifetz.

In 1959 he studied in Darmstadt, Germany, under the tutelage of pianist David Tudor during the same summer that La Monte Young and visual artist Nam June Paik attended. There, he worked directly with Karlheinz Stockhausen. Behrman returned to New York and worked at Columbia Records in the 1960s. Under the Columbia Masterworks series called Music of Our Time, he became the producer of Terry Riley's seminal work *In C.*

I would frequently see Behrman at shows in New York, not only because he would perform with various colleagues but also because he liked to go out and support fellow fringe composers. He created sound installations as well and frequently played with contemporaries Robert Ashley, Gordon Mumma, and Alvin Lucier, who together made up the Sonic Arts Union, which Behrman played in before creating his first electronic keyboard in 1977.

Behrman spoke to me about working on an Apple computer in the early 1980s. To own one was a feat in itself; to compose on it was audacious. Yet, Behrman always had an affinity for the nuances and subtlety of sounds that could emanate from interacting in real-time with computers. The music he created was so beautifully tonal and refined that he is many times categorized as a true minimalist composer.

B. WENTZ: Your compositions involve interactions between live musicians and computers. Can you explain how that works?

DAVID BEHRMAN: I think the main thing about these pieces is that the performers don't have scores. They have situations where there's a pitch sense of one kind or another waiting for them to do something. When a certain pitch is played on an acoustic instrument, that activates pitch-sensing circuits, or "ears," connected to a computer. The computer then reacts by sending harmony-changing messages to various synthesizers. The pieces are made with computer programs governing the interaction between the performers and the electronics, but the performers have options rather than instructions or a score. The whole system is really waiting for some wonderful performer on an acoustic instrument to collaborate with.

B. WENTZ: So you're saying that the musicians just interact with a certain program?

DAVID BEHRMAN: Usually, the piece has a bunch of different programs that are like sections. And usually, the performer can go from one section to the next whenever he or she wants. So it's sort of almost like making sports equipment rather than a fixed music object. I think of it like I'm building skis, and then a good skier can have a good time on the skis.

B. WENTZ: We have here a copy of your latest album, called *Leapday Night*. The first side is the composition "Interspecies Smalltalk," an interactive piece you created with the Japanese violinist and former Fluxus artist Takehisa Kosugi for Merce Cunningham's dance company.

DAVID BEHRMAN: Kosugi is a marvelous composer and performer. So he's sort of an ideal collaborator on these pieces.

B WENTZ: The combination of the wood tones of the violin with your electronics creates a surprisingly warm sound. The album's B-side is the title piece, with Ben Neill and Rhys Chatham, which sounds more jazzy, in part because of the horns.

DAVID BEHRMAN: Ben has a wonderful instrument that he designed himself called the mutantrumpet, which is a trumpet with three bells and mutable slides. The instrument allows him to change timbres instantaneously in a very nice way, so it seemed to work well in these situations.

B. WENTZ: These pieces are rooted in improvised sounds and chance interactions with a computer. So what is it like recording them? Do they tend to sound similar every time they're performed?

DAVID BEHRMAN: No, they sound different. Actually, with this Kosugi recording, it was not easy to choose one take because they were all quite different. But I like the recording. And Steve Cellum recorded these pieces very beautifully.

In a way, it's a contradiction, but on the other hand, it's like what Mike Stahl once said, "Records are like frozen radio."

B. WENTZ: That's an interesting way of putting it. You produced a series of records in the late 1960s for Columbia Masterworks called Music of Our Time. This was just a few years after you finished your master's at Columbia University. How did that come about?

DAVID BEHRMAN: I joined Columbia Records at just the right moment. The label was doing very well, there was a lot of extra money. Goddard Lieberson, the president of Columbia, was himself a composer, and he had a real interest in helping composers. Music was changing, and no one could quite figure out how. So I was given the opportunity to try some things.

B. WENTZ: You were quite the critic of that period—the series produced some landmark pieces. You worked on Terry Riley's legendary first recording of *In C*, for one. And you produced Steve Reich's influential civil rights-era tape-loop piece, "Come Out," which featured the voice of a Black man who'd been beaten by the police. What was the reaction when that was initially released in 1966?

DAVID BEHRMAN: It was controversial. It was kind of a shocking piece, and it had a really new sound. But a lot of people really liked it.

B. WENTZ: You left New York in the mid-seventies to teach at Mills College in Oakland, California. That was an auspicious time for computers, especially in the Bay Area.

DAVID BEHRMAN: Actually, that was where I got my start with computers because I was never interested in them when they were big and expensive, and you had to go to some clean room to work with them. But around 1977, tiny, cheap ones became available. There were some that you could buy for two or three or four hundred dollars and take home with you. And then you could start fiddling around with them. So people in California were among the first to work with those.

B. WENTZ: Your first album, 1978's *On the Other Ocean*, was created using a microcomputer called the KIM-1, or Keyboard Input Monitor, which interacted with acoustic instruments like cello and bassoon. You've maintained an interest in computers ever since. Is it difficult to keep up with the advances in technology?

DAVID BEHRMAN: It's impossible. It's hopeless. But you do your best. I mean, you're in a situation with these things where you have to throw them out every couple of years. You're lucky if it's two years because the things you're working with, for one reason or another, become awkward and obsolete compared with what's new. Maybe it's settling down. Probably not.

B. WENTZ: What do you think will happen now that people can make music on their own little Apples at home?

DAVID BEHRMAN: It's a million times easier than it used to be, of course, and everybody's doing it. There are a lot of different ways of working with them now. You can go to a music store and buy all kinds of miraculous things that are not very expensive. Samplers where you can record sounds and alter them. Synthesizers where you can get factory sounds of great variety or make your own.

B. WENTZ: You recently performed at the Experimental Intermedia Foundation here in New York. There were little dogs barking across computer screens, along with umbrellas and eggs and beautiful little symbols. And then there was music. How do the visuals relate to what you're doing?

DAVID BEHRMAN: That project was the result of a collaborative grant Angela Green and I got to make a piece that would combine real-time computer graphics with real-time computer music. She's an artist who's very gifted at creating computer graphics. We met about four years ago when we were both working at Children's Television Workshop. I was there designing children's computer games. So we tried out this project. It took a long time just to get the technological sides of it solved. In fact, they got solved only about eleven hours before the performance.

I think there are a lot of ways that imaginative graphics can enhance a musical experience. I think, mostly, as a kind of playful notation for nonmusicians, I think that's an interesting direction to take it. Because there's really no reason you should have to know music notation in order to make music. It should be possible to just get information some other way about a music system. So the idea of that performance was to have a computer sensing music and then have another computer doing graphics animation.

B. WENTZ: Lately, you've been creating computer-controlled sound installations that also have nonmusicians in mind. Your two most recent installations are collaborations with George Lewis, another composer who works with electronics and computers. Can you explain how these pieces work?

DAVID BEHRMAN: The idea behind those pieces is to make it easy and intriguing for anybody, including nonmusicians, to make music. These are pieces that are waiting for somebody to come up and interact with them. Anybody can do that by playing these little instruments that are Americanized mbira, which is a name for African thumb pianos. These simple, easy-to-play instruments are attached to computer systems, which respond to the slightest touch on the mbira and create various sounds or music.

B. WENTZ: How long have you and George been working together on this?

DAVID BEHRMAN: We worked for about three years on the first one. It's called Mbirascope, which is a word we made up. We finished it last year, and it's now at the La Villette Museum in Paris. That experience gave us some new ideas to create another one, called A Map of the Known World. That one is more elaborate. It's up for the summer at the deCordova Museum in Lincoln, Massachusetts, which is a very nice place that isn't too easy to get to.

B. WENTZ: I can't get over how these machines respond to the smallest things that you play.

DAVID BEHRMAN: At great human cost. I spend a lot of time working on the programs.

B. WENTZ: I've been to concerts where the machines have broken down, and the musicians just don't know what to do. Has that ever happened to you?

DAVID BEHRMAN: Oh yeah. I remember one concert I did where the computer wouldn't load at intermission, and the *New York Times* reviewer walked out because it was like a twenty-five-minute intermission.

B. WENTZ: Did you get a review?

DAVID BEHRMAN: No.

B. WENTZ: Well, maybe next time.

DAVID BEHRMAN: Next time, that's right!

Martin Bisi
Record producer

There were many genres and subcultures of music—I was of none, but of all.

The proximity of venues played a part; Danceteria and Mudd Club had subscenes—you'd have hardcore on one floor, an art opening of Fab Five [Freddy] on another, and dance music in the middle.

FIGURE 4.1 ALVIN CURRAN

SOURCE: LONA FOOTE

4

ALVIN CURRAN

July 12, 1983

The charming and charismatic American electronic composer/sound artist Alvin Curran absorbs surrounding sounds with an acute sense of playfulness. He listens attentively, takes in pensively, and reconfigures electronically for audiences to enjoy. His legacy stems from being the cofounder of the live improvisational acoustic/electronic group Musica Elettronica Viva (MEV) from 1966–1971 with Richard Teitelbaum and Frederick Rzewski, yet numerous other artists such as Steve Lacy, Garrett List, and George Lewis were all a part.

Born in Providence, Rhode Island, Curran worked as a young man in a Greek dance band that played Las Vegas and the Catskills. He settled and attended Brown and then Yale School of Music, where he studied with forward-thinking composers Elliott Carter and Mel Powell. He moved to Rome in 1965, where he met Teitelbaum and Rzewski and became ensconced in the avant-garde theater scene. Rome has been his home ever since.

A huge mentee of John Cage and his work with found sounds—for example, fog horns—Curran has also been fascinated by nature sounds and incorporating them into electronics and instruments. He has also performed in nature at parks, in caves, and on the edges of lakes. Meeting him for a show at the Anchorage space in New York, he said, "It's poetic license for me. . . . I couldn't pass up a concert at the Brooklyn Bridge . . . it's one of my favorite instruments." I have seen him perform solo with electronics on a table and in a group collaborating as a conductor with other artists. He's worked with dance companies such as Trisha Brown, the Living Theater, and Margaret Jenkins to collaborations with John Cage, Fred Frith, Shelley Hirsch, Pauline Oliveros, Evan Parker, and Joan La Barbara, and many others.

B. WENTZ: You're visiting from Italy to perform one of your pieces at the Anchorage, a catacomb-like vault beneath the Brooklyn Bridge. What drew you to travel to New York to play a concert under a bridge?

ALVIN CURRAN: It's a trip that had to be done. I couldn't pass up a concert at the Brooklyn Bridge. It's one of my favorite locations in the whole world. It's also one of my favorite musical instruments.

Strangely enough, in the piece I'll be playing, I don't even use the sound of the bridge. But on the other hand, you don't have to because it's always there. You can't escape it. And when they close the door to the vault and you're inside, you can hear the vibrations of the traffic above. I've been recording the sounds of the Brooklyn Bridge for years now. I've worked them into another piece of mine, which uses the sound of the bridge in conjunction with a small chamber chorus, my own voice, piano, and brass instruments. Because the sound of that bridge really does sound like a human chorus sometimes, especially at a distance.

B. WENTZ: You've been living since the mid-sixties in Rome, where you founded the experimental group Musica Elettronica Viva, which blended synthesizers with nonmusical objects, like panes of glass and tin cans. Is MEV still together?

ALVIN CURRAN: Musica Elettronica Viva exists when anyone calls us up to give us a gig! We'll always play it. We get about one a year now. Some sentimental, knowledgeable people remember MEV and say, you know, we have to have them play. And they don't realize that we're not a working group anymore. But we do get together and play. And the group now consists of myself, Frederick Rzewski, Richard Teitelbaum, Steve Lacy, and Garrett List. We still can improvise very well.

B. WENTZ: How long have you been working with electronics?

ALVIN CURRAN: Electronics were initially my nemesis. Richard Teitelbaum was studying in Rome when he brought the first Moog synthesizer to Europe. I despise that instrument. To me, it was like the devil. It was this fancy thing with beautiful, mysterious knobs and black panels and all kinds of funny names like envelope generators and three-way oscillators—I just decided right then and there that I was never going to have anything to do with electronics. At the time, I was playing an amplified tin can and an old beat-up trumpet, which I didn't even know how to play.

But when the MEV group dissolved in the early seventies, I found myself alone in Rome, and I needed to make a living. And electronics actually became that living. I got myself a little synthesizer and found myself making a lot of film and theater music with it because, at the time, I was one of the few people around with a synthesizer.

But even though I have this long history which dates back to the late sixties with electronics, I still don't know a transistor from a resistor. And I don't really care about that problem.

I also don't care really much for electronics—that is, electronic music in itself. Because as you know, most of my music is made using natural sounds combined with acoustic sounds and occasionally synthesizer sounds. So to me, it's just another instrument. I mean, I'd just as soon play a conch shell.

B. WENTZ: Have you mainly played solo since MEV ended?

ALVIN CURRAN: Yeah, I'm a loner in many ways. I don't lend myself easily to collaborate with other people. In the aftermath of MEV, I had to find a way to make my own music alone, without depending on a group. And so those solo pieces were born then. The whole movement of solo performance really began in the late sixties and early seventies and had its big boom in that period. And it was an attractive way of becoming a musician with dignity—that is, being your own musician, playing your own music, creating it, and realizing it at the same time.

B. WENTZ: Do you find it difficult trying to incorporate found sounds, like the sounds of the Brooklyn Bridge, with a live piano? That's a lot going on at once.

ALVIN CURRAN: Yeah, that's a problem of mine. I tend to put too much in, but in a way, it's like making assemblage. I take some of this, and I take some of that, and I put them into this container. And I try to really make them live together, to make a harmony out of these elements.

It also has a lot to do with the skill of arranging. And in particular, the sense of orchestration. Because if I'm using the sound of some bullfrogs and then I start mixing in some pile drivers, those are two things that have two kinds of rhythm. I mean, frogs very often make a kind of larger rhythm or even smaller rhythms. And pile drivers have a very specific rhythm. Or a pinball machine has no rhythm. It has a kind of random sound.

So these choices are really about dealing with the sounds at a very fundamental level, as you would if you were dealing with orchestrating something in 2/4 time with something else in no/4 time. To me, it's the same problem.

B. WENTZ: It's sort of like mixing. When I saw you perform at Roulette, I noticed how you were mixing the found, recorded sounds with live electronics.

ALVIN CURRAN: A critic for the Italian weekly *Espresso* once called me the Big Mixer. And in a way, this is really the heart of my work. When I make tape loops, I'm mixing many elements, and much of my music is mixed very, very slowly, so things fade in and fade away without even sometimes being noticed. The art of mixing is the technique I use.

B. WENTZ: Have you always incorporated found sounds—like the sounds made by everyday objects or the sound of traffic—with live sounds?

ALVIN CURRAN: Yeah, this really goes back to your question about electronics. I'm not a synthesizer freak, but I am a freak about tape recorders and even more so about microphones. I first encountered these tools in the early sixties when I studied for a year in Berlin. They helped me discover this whole world of found sounds, which I immediately identified as music. That is, almost anything I heard or recorded became music to me.

B WENTZ: In Berlin, where you studied under Elliott Carter, one of your fellow students was Frederic Rzewski, with whom you would go on to form MEV. Rzewski had previously worked with John Cage in the U.S. Did Cage's ideas influence your interest in sounds?

ALVIN CURRAN: I didn't have any real push in this direction from anyone. I didn't know Cage's music back then, nor did I know much about how he had opened up this whole world by using natural sound as an instrument. It was a kind of private discovery for me and one that was in the air at the time. And since then, it's really become my hallmark. I mean, it's something I live with every day. I'm always looking for sounds. I'm always thinking of projects like hanging from a balloon off the East Coast of America and recording the entire coast. Impossible pieces—and then some real possible ones too, ones that involve satellite mixing from different continents and different cities, and pieces that will expand the whole microcosm I developed while using specific sounds. I haven't nearly exhausted everything I want to do in that area at all.

B. WENTZ: Do you have a library of different sounds?

ALVIN CURRAN: I have a huge library. It's my shrine. It's my sacred church. I pray to it every day.

B. WENTZ: And pray that nothing ever happens to them.

ALVIN CURRAN: Even if something did, most of those sounds are always there. The commonplace ones will always be there. And new ones are always on the horizon. To me, it's my natural, cosmic orchestra. Whenever I need inspiration, I turn to those sounds, and I usually find something. There are tons of them I haven't even used yet.

B. WENTZ: Someone once said you're consciously involved in microtonality. Do you feel this is something that someone can be conscious of as they do it?

ALVIN CURRAN: The people who said that are right.

B. WENTZ: How did microtonality shape your 1983 piece *Canti Illuminati*? That work includes a whole range of sounds: snippets from James Joyce's *Finnegans Wake*, foghorns, electronic feedback, as well as your own singing.

ALVIN CURRAN: Originally, that whole piece was a study on a single note. And it really became my first vocal piece. I used a system, which Terry Riley had been using for many years, of making a continuous tape loop by threading a tape through two tape recorders and being able to record over yourself continuously. And therefore, perform with your own sound, which is delayed by the distance between the two tape recorders.

So being that it's impossible to sing in real unison in any circumstances, the natural structure of this piece, which became the attempt to sing in unison with myself, led immediately to the discovery of microtonality. That is, I didn't aim to do that, but when it became apparent that that's what was happening, the whole character of that piece became a study on the impossibility to sing or to play in unison.

La Monte Young often works in this direction, as well as Phill Niblock, although La Monte probably believes that a unison is possible. I think he's almost achieved it at times, quite magically too.

B. WENTZ: Overtones?

ALVIN CURRAN: Not just the overtones, I mean, the insistence on really zeroing in on unison with your voice that you're able to not even waver a microtone, in a way.

But the beauty of working with unisons, of course, is that you present this almost theoretically impossible situation to yourself so that a whole world of other music develops from it. Be it the overtones, which are produced, and the interferences between just the slight imperfections of your own intonation, and all of the rhythms, these little internal rhythms, which appear through all of the beating processes of the imperfections of your own tuning.

So again, *Canti Illuminati* really is about microtonality. I don't stick with that for too long, though. I mean, the initial part of the piece stays on the one tone, and then that tone becomes blurred. I let the whole structure just improvisationally go where it will. So that piece can take me anywhere, and it usually does.

B. WENTZ: What are you experimenting with nowadays?

ALVIN CURRAN: There's a part of my work that's a big departure from my solo music. It hearkens back to some of the experiments that MEV did in the late sixties when we were in our more radical political orientation. I'm talking about music for huge groups of people. In a way, the piece I'm doing at the Anchorage at the Brooklyn Bridge, which is called "Safe for Only 25 Men at One Time," is a version of this kind of piece. I say a *version* because, basically, the piece was to have been an invitation to the city of New York to come to the Anchorage and play with me and with everyone else. But in practice, this won't be possible because the size of the space is too small. But there will be many, many people playing together. It is not a free improvisation. It's not just bring your horn and play. But for people who read music and play any instrument, they can come into the central hall of the Anchorage, and they'll find four hundred feet of music written on the walls. And they can walk around and play whatever they see in front of them. The music is extremely simple and accessible to anybody, so there's no fear of making any mistakes. In any case, in my music, there are no mistakes, so that's not possible.

For people who don't have an instrument, if they like, they can bring a simple, battery-operated cassette tape recorder, and they will be given a cassette to play, and they can walk around with that cassette, which will just play for you. But by walking around, you can move the music wherever you want. So the music will be moving around. People will be moving around playing, and the sound will be moving and changing all the time in density, in every way.

There will be other elements, too. There will be some conch shells, there will be some orchestral chimes, but these will be manned, more or less, by people who've already been orchestrated into the piece. But by and large, any instrument is welcome, any portable instrument. There's no transposing to be done, so you needn't fear what's written on the walls. It can be played by any instrument.

This is not just a concert either. It's a piece of music, which is a piece of film music because, at the same time, there will be four or five film loops about the bridge itself made by Jacob Burkhardt, a young New York filmmaker and a colleague of mine.

B WENTZ: You seem to enjoy working with large groups of people.

ALVIN CURRAN: This is a recent tendency of mine, on the one hand, to explore large groups of people and also to explore large, real spaces. So taking my whole natural sound concept and bringing it out of the concert hall.

To give a simple example, I'm planning a series of pieces called *Maritime Rites*. One of them is for a simple chorus of human voices placed in rowboats on a quiet lake. This piece has been done several times around the world now. Another of the *Maritime Rites* pieces is only for ships' horns. The first version was performed in the bay of La Spezia in Italy last summer. And the second version will be done in the port of Amsterdam at the end of August. I'll be using between twenty and thirty ships' horns, just where they are, and using a simple score, which is played by people who can read a time score.

And then this fall in Rome, I'm planning a large piece, larger than the Brooklyn Bridge piece, which will have more than two thousand people performing. That will be a real test. It will test everyone's patience.

Fast Forward
Artist

Rhys Chatham once said to me at Danceteria, "Fast, Welcome to New York." And I said, "It seems a little too late?" Rhys replied, "It's never too late!"

8BC that was the most euphoric, public performance situation that I experienced at that time. It was like heroin. . . . Everything about that place that Cornelius Conboy [cofounder] put together there—the structure of the place and the illegality of it. It had a vibe where you could be there until the early hours of morning. The performance space was about eight to ten feet up above the audience.

FIGURE 5.1 MARIO DAVIDOVSKY
SOURCE: COLUMBIA UNIVERSITY

5

MARIO DAVIDOVSKY

March 11, 1987

The Columbia-Princeton Electronic Music Center was founded by Columbia professors Vladimir Ussachevsky and Otto Luening, and Princeton professors Milton Babbitt and Roger Sessions. It all started with an Ampex tape machine that was delivered to Columbia University around 1952, which Ussachevsky described as "opening Pandora's box." The thought of making music from cutting and looping tape—as opposed to using the machine to record music—seemed like an endless possibility.

These tinkering madmen received an official stamp of approval to create the center with a 1958 Rockefeller grant. Soon after came a delivery of an RCA Mark II Sound Synthesizer. From the 1960s to the 1980s, various composers—Edgard Varese, Charles Wuorinen, Chow Wen-Chung, Charles Dodge, Pril Smiley, Wendy Carlos, and Lucio Berio—either studied or worked at the center. Ussachevsky helmed the center until 1980 when the Argentinian-born Mario Davidovsky took over the department.

Davidovsky began his music education at the age of seven, studying violin in Buenos Aires and then moving over to composition while attending the University of Buenos Aires. In 1958, at age nineteen, he landed a summer program at the Tanglewood Music Center with Aaron Copeland and Columbia-Princeton Electronic Music Center founder Milton Babbitt. Both composers encouraged him to continue his studies as he became fascinated with electro-acoustic music and electronics.

Heeding their advice, Davidosky moved to New York and delved into composing. He eventually came to the center to tinker with the RCA machine. A wonderfully erudite yet personable professor, Davidosky taught composition at the Manhattan School of Music, Yale University, and City College of

New York before he was asked to run the center. I had the honor of speaking to him at his home. During our interview, which took place for a feature piece for *Columbia Magazine* and WKCR, Davidovsky was beaming with excitement, thrilled to talk about the curriculum and facility and the center's history. He spoke about the effects of his discipline, where the computer was going to be used in ten to fifteen years, and how the computer and electronics would be the pinnacle of importance as we marched into the future.

B. WENTZ: What was the response to electronic music in the 1960s? Were you guys still considered spacemen, as Vladimir Ussachevsky says?

MARIO DAVIDOVSKY: First of all, I learned about the existence of electronic music when I was still a composer in Buenos Aires, Argentina. And the recordings that we had available then were coming from Europe. Some of them were from the studio for electronic music in Cologne, Germany, like Stockhausen, and some were done in the studio in Milan, Italy. We also heard recordings of concrete music coming from French radio.

I came to the United States in 1958 to study with Aaron Copland and Milton Babbitt at Tanglewood, where Babbitt told me about the imminent creation of what would become the Electronic Music Center. There was a consortium between Columbia University and Princeton, and they had a Rockefeller grant. So at Copland's suggestion, I returned to the U.S. in 1960 and settled in New York City. When I came to Columbia, what I found, basically, was one complete studio on campus, another studio being developed on 125th Street, and the very first RCA synthesizer, which at the time was on some kind of permanent loan to the university.

But there wasn't much going on except for Ussechevsky doing a few pieces and some experiments by himself or with Otto Luening. The real development started once all these studios were established, around 1959, which happened soon after I came. Babbitt was working in the RCA room. There was a very fine composer from Turkey called Bülent Arel, who wrote and recorded two major works at the center. I had come from Argentina, and of course, Ussachevsky and Luening were already working there. So between 1960 and 1961, we were more or less the steady, full-time devotees of electronic music in New York, as well as some Columbia students, Charles Wuorinen and Harvey Sollberger.

Basically, when I came, the studio was what would be known now as a tape studio. Most of the equipment was not designed for making music. There was a collection of pieces of equipment that were put together very intelligently to resemble some kind of a special music instrument. But from the point of view of working, we could not create any kind of continuity, in terms of music continuity, because we couldn't program on that equipment.

So what we had to do was make music in a way in which every single event would have to be done one by one, so to say, and then piece it together. So if we were to make something similar to a melody, we would have to make every single separate note, shape the release of the note, give it a proper timbre value, you know, the proper value in loudness, and then just splice together a melody on tape.

This was very exciting for me because we had to find, through our own ingenuity, ways of dealing with the sounds that the technology wasn't able to do. Of course, by doing the type of research and work that we were doing in this very simple environment, we began to learn what kind of a device we needed to do that kind of thing or this other kind of thing, if such a device could be developed.

And we had very brilliant engineers, and we started to design devices that would enable us to do something very specific, something very simple, and would make the production of sound and the elaboration of sound less cumbersome.

In the early sixties, Robert Moog was an engineering major at Columbia, minoring in music. And what he learned from the compound experience of the composers working in the tape studio and the possibility of developing devices, voltage control devices, basically gave him the whole philosophical basis of how to design a device that would encompass enough elasticity and offer an extensive variability of possibilities to different composers. And that's really the beginning of what became, during the late sixties and early seventies, the Moog synthesizer.

And eventually, synthesizers afforded the possibility of creating continuity, musical continuity, without having to splice and build every single note of our pieces from scratch. Instead, we could program the synthesizer to do five notes, or a stretch of ten seconds of music, or a stretch of one minute of music. Then around the early seventies, computers arrived in the field of music. Charles Dodge, a young professor at Columbia teaching composition, got very involved with the computer program. And he helped establish the first facility with computer music.

So from the early sixties to the middle seventies, we went through the whole trajectory of technology, starting from an almost primitive state where we were doing things by hand and by our wits. And because of that kind of experience, we were able to develop rationales for devices, and slowly the devices became more and more sophisticated to the point that, now, technologically, things are simply amazing, almost frightening sometimes.

B. WENTZ: Do people still use the RCA synthesizer?

MARIO DAVIDOVSKY: No, the RCA synthesizer was mostly used by Milton Babbitt. His last piece that used electronic sounds was "Reflections (For Piano and Synthesized Tape)," in 1974, and since then, he's been writing for conventional ensembles.

Right now, we are in the process of completing in the Electronic Music Center two new studios. One studio is going to represent all of the center's history. In other words, under one roof, we are going to have a very elaborate facility where you will be able to use the most advanced technology, like digital synthesizers, or the most primitive technology, like basic tape decks.

We still use the more primitive technology because it has enormous technological value for graduate students or other people that like to work. And then we are also completing a computer facility at Columbia, which will probably be the most advanced computer facility in, well, at least in Manhattan. And we got a very substantial grant from the university for the basic equipment, and we have a formal promise of a budget for the next couple of years in order to keep updating the equipment there. So that's going to be a very, very capable facility.

B. WENTZ: Do you get a lot of students who are interested in coming to Columbia simply because of the Electronic Music Center?

MARIO DAVIDOVSKY: No question about it. Especially during the seventies, we found that probably—I don't know the percentages, but a very high percentage of the students were coming to work in the Electronic Music Center. I think the literary output, in terms of the compositions, that have come out of the center—I don't want to sound presumptuous, but I think the totality of the literature that we produce is probably the most impressive of any such center in the world.

And one of the reasons that happened is because its directors, Ussachevsky and Luening, kept the place very open, and there were not any kind of prerequisites as far as what kind of music you write. Stylistically, we don't care. We just wanted you to come and work in the most professional conditions possible. And somehow, what happened in the beginning is that composers came to us because they were going to open up their own laboratories . . . because we were the first really professionally organized studio within the context of a university.

So everybody from the West Coast to the North, to the South came to the studio just to see what kind of equipment we were working on. At first, we had a lot of Latin American composers and Italian composers—[Luciano] Berio was working in the studio. We had Romanian composers, French composers, Japanese composers, Chinese composers, and the early wave of North American composers. And the openness of the place, and the nearly limitless access to studios, made it possible for a lot of people to write a lot of pieces. And so we created an enormous amount of literature, and though the music that came out of the center was stylistically very different, there was a common ground among those works because there was a certain technical philosophy on how to produce sound and how to process sound, and that became the trademark of Columbia University, really.

B. WENTZ: Some centers or some electronic composers now seem to focus on the idea of live interaction when a person plays an instrument, for example, Boulez's *Répons*, which premiered in 1981.

MARIO DAVIDOVSKY: We did this ourselves in the early sixties. Varèse had already done something similar in the early 1950s when he composed "Déserts" for brass instruments and electronic interpolations. The technology at that time was still very primitive. We are talking about a twenty-year difference. Then there was also a series of pieces that Luening and Ussachevsky did for orchestra and electronic recorded sound.

Most of my work, starting in '61, involved developing a technique to integrate both the space of the acoustical instrument and the space of the electronic sound into a single space—the whole idea of embedding one into the other. That was done in the early sixties. What happened is that probably Boulez, because of his popularity, seemed to reach a greater audience, and people think that he discovered it and it's a new process. It's not; it's twenty-five years old.

B. WENTZ: What does the program focus on today?

MARIO DAVIDOVSKY: We offer basically everything. We offer courses in the literature of electronic music and the history of the technique. And we offer courses for composers that are interested in working with more old-fashioned synthesizers to digital synthesizers to purely digital technology in the computer center, which now is almost complete.

If they want to write, for example, music for instruments and electronic sound, whether the electronic sound is recorded, whether the electronic sound comes from a synthesizer or is played live, or whether the electronic sound might come, like in the case of Boulez that you mentioned, from the computer recording the sounds and reprocessing them. All these technologies are available.

B. WENTZ: What do you think has been the center's greatest contribution to electronic music?

MARIO DAVIDOVSKY: I think it's literature. We have probably produced in the Electronic Music Center around twenty compositions that are now part of the classical literature of contemporary music. These are compositions that are now played all of the time, all over the world. I'm talking about twenty very successful pieces, but there are probably forty to fifty pieces that are part of the repertoire. Whether they involve a combination of electronic sounds with instruments or purely electronic pieces. And, of course, there was also a very substantial contribution to the development of the technology.

In the beginning, the Electronic Music Center was seminal and fundamental to developing electronic music in the States. And then once the technology exploded and it became a matter of public accessibility—the Yamahas and the Buchla and the Moogs were mass-produced, and now universities could afford to buy more advanced technology and even develop their own. What we did at Columbia, especially the body of literature in the beginning, was crucial. I mean, absolutely crucial to the development of electronic music in the United States.

B. WENTZ: Do you think that we'll see more electronics being used in contemporary music?

MARIO DAVIDOVSKY: Definitely. I see, for example, the computer facility not only as a facility for composers to write music or for audio engineers to study ways of processing sound, but I see the computer becoming pervasive in the music department. Even for graduate students in the theory program, the computer will become a tool of enormous value. The computer is becoming a pervasive kind of Esperanto language, affecting all the disciplines. It's going to affect ethnomusicology and musical history. So ten or fifteen years from now, I see the Electronic Music Center as a place where all the disciplines of music, getting together in the facility, and very interesting things will happen.

Rhys Chatham
Artist and Kitchen curator from 1971–1973

When I saw Terry Riley at the Electric Circus, I walked in as a postserialist composer, and walked out as a minimalist.

The first person I asked to play The Kitchen was Milton Babbitt. He asked me how old I was. I was nineteen; I lied; I was twenty-two. The next person I asked to perform was Philip Glass but he turned us down.

I then asked La Monte [Young]. We gave him 100 percent of the door. Mariam sold records since La Monte had just put out the black album, with "Tortoise Dream." The Kitchen was packed, and they sold lots of records and made their grocery money. One of my biggest regrets was not programming John Zorn and Elliott Sharp at The Kitchen.

FIGURE 6.1 OTTO LUENING
SOURCE: NANCY RICA SCHIFF

6
OTTO LUENING
May 1985

Otto Luening was an opera conductor and trained flutist who veered into experimental music because of his interest in magnetic tape. He was one of the first composers from the stable of what would become known as the Columbia-Princeton Electronic Center geniuses that I met when I came to New York City in the early 1980s. It was a joy to sit down with him in his Morningside apartment. At eighty-five, Luening was well past retirement when I interviewed him. Slightly hunched over, open, and ready to talk, he offered tea and shuffled me into his living room. Cozying up with my tape recorder teetering on the edge of one of his super soft chairs, we chatted for almost two hours about his wide-ranging career.

Tremendously humble, Luening explained how at the age of twelve, he and his family moved from Wisconsin to Europe, landing first in Germany and then escaping World War I by moving to Switzerland, where Luening studied at the University of Zurich's conservatory. At twenty-four, he returned to the United States and began conducting operas, utilizing the theatrical training he received abroad. He ultimately conducted one of the greatest American operas to date, Virgil Thompson's *The Mother of Us All*, about Susan B. Anthony, with a libretto by Gertrude Stein. The opera premiered at Columbia University in 1947. A few years later, Luening conducted yet another modern masterpiece—Gian Carlo Menotti's *The Medium*. He continued living and working at universities in New York City, where he met fellow composer Vladimir Ussachevsky at Columbia and began experimenting with tape and electronics. Together, they wrote and premiered *Tape Music an Historic Concert*, one of the first concerts for tape recorders, at the Museum of Modern Art, in 1952. One piece for flute and tape manipulation titled "Fantasy in Space" established Luening and Ussachevsky as pioneers in electronic music and led to the founding of the now legendary Electronic Music Center.

B. WENTZ: Your father was a composer and conductor, and your mother sang. How did they shape your interest in music early on?

OTTO LUENING: When I was very young, the natural thing at the time in my family was to start with singing. We had a nice piano, my father was a very fine pianist, so I sort of went along with that. I was about nine years old when my mother bought me a piccolo because she wanted me to play an orchestral instrument. So I learned how to play it myself; I wasn't anything sensational. When my family moved a few years later to Munich from Wisconsin, I went over to the flute and actually studied flute and piano in Munich at the Royal Academy.

B. WENTZ: You had mentioned somewhere that when you were a small boy, your father became interested in Thaddeus Cahill's dynamophone, an early electric organ. Were you intrigued by it as well?

OTTO LUENING: We lived at the time on a little farm outside of Milwaukee, but there was an enormous amount of publicity surrounding the instrument in the magazines on our coffee table. My father was always interested in those sorts of things. He said, you know, this is going to be a new world of music.

So, of course, that really interested my brothers and me. My brothers had a phonograph, called talking machines in those days. And they immediately began fooling around with the horn, stuffing pillows in the horn, and then trying to run it backwards, and playing it without a horn, and getting different kinds of sounds, trying to speed it up, or running it by hand-cranking. That was a very experimental moment. I had the same sort of inclination to experiment as my brothers did—one of whom ended up going to MIT—but then those thoughts went to sleep for a long time.

B. WENTZ: When you were studying in Munich in the early 1900s, Arnold Schoenberg was in Germany completing some of his most revolutionary atonal compositions. What was your initial reaction to him? You said at one time you thought he was very strange, even mad.

OTTO LUENING: When my family arrived in Munich, I was twelve years old. Schoenberg had just come into a sort of scandalous prominence. He had published his book, *Theory of Harmony*, and several compositions. So my father told me to go get that book and the scores. And as we looked at Schoenberg's work, my father said, "Oh he's a great master. I don't understand what he's doing, but he's a great master."

The story about his being "mad" happened when I went to the conservatory in Zurich a few years later. My professor there decided that Schoenberg was just crazy. He said, "Well, there's this man in Munich, Schoenberg. He just scribbles anything on a piece of paper and thinks it's okay." That was the attitude about him around 1914.

But when I read Schoenberg's book, it opened me up considerably, and I began having a private life as a composer that had nothing to do with what I did at the academy at all. I had a completely private exploration that I did secretly; I never showed it to anybody, including my father, because I was afraid that he would thumb it down.

B. WENTZ: So your father had a lot of influence on you and your work.

OTTO LUENING: He believed you had to learn the foundation, that you had to have a tradition behind you, and that you were supposed to learn much of that by yourself. Father always said, "You have to go forward into new paths, but they must be on a solid background. It must be evolutionary and not revolutionary." He was very forward-thinking in that respect but a very tough customer to handle.

B. WENTZ: At the conservatory in Zurich, you studied with French composer Philipp Jarnach and the great Italian master Ferruccio Busoni. Which of them had more influence on your theories about music?

OTTO LUENING: I would say Busoni. He was a man of enormous genius and great kindness. I was only eighteen when I came into his orbit. Jarnach was Busoni's main disciple. He was also his musical secretary—he made piano scores of Busoni's operas for him. After I produced a couple works, Jarnach said I should show them to Busoni, so I went to see him. Here's this great world figure who's invited me to his house to talk about my work, and even though I was only eighteen, he treated me like a real artist—like an adult. From that time on, I've tried to act like one, with limited degrees of success.

But that was a great experience. He said that any time I had a new piece, I could show it to him. So he probably saw about four works I did before I left the conservatory two years later, and he was very meticulous in the way he studied those things. The story was that he would spend whole afternoons and evenings studying these pieces to see what was going on. Of course, that was if he was interested. You got in only if he thought you had talent. He was very supportive—and very stern. He would give you an assignment or some suggestions, and you would have plenty to do to get ready for the next visit. Oddly enough, one of the pieces I wrote when I was eighteen, which was one of the first things Busoni saw, laid around for quite a while. The piece was played a few times, and for years nothing happened. Then, five years ago, it was performed and well-reviewed. I just heard that somebody sent it back to Zurich, where I wrote it at that time, and they're going to play it there, and they don't even know that I wrote it when I was studying there. It's very funny.

B. WENTZ: What piece is it?

OTTO LUENING: My "Sextet" [for flute, clarinet, and horn—recorded in 1919]. It's a very good piece. I was a very good young pro, but that's the thing you have to be when you're with Busoni. He demanded that you know your stuff, and so you learned it.

B. WENTZ: When you finished school in Zurich, you came back to America. Is that where you met Mrs. McCormick?

OTTO LUENING: I met her years earlier in Zurich. I had left Germany for Switzerland because of the First World War. When my sister and I got to Zurich, we had no money, so I asked the director of the conservatory for a job. I was sixteen years old. He offered me a position as fourth flutist in the symphony orchestra, but he said I should have more training. I replied, "I know, but I need money." So he introduced me to Mrs. Rockefeller McCormick, a socialite from Chicago who was in Zurich at the time studying with Carl Jung. When I went to see her, I looked pretty bad: I weighed one hundred pounds, wore ragged clothes, it was a real refugee deal. She said she would be willing to back my studies in Zurich, but I had to focus on composing because the United States at the time had very few composers. She also said that she wanted me to live in Chicago when I finished my studies, so that's what I did. She introduced me to all the leading musicians in Chicago when I moved there. She was also the patroness of James Joyce and of Philipp Jarnach. She helped a lot of painters too. Very nice lady.

B. WENTZ: You performed your first string quartet in Chicago in the early twenties, and it didn't go over well. Your second string quartet was written around the same time, but it didn't receive critical acclaim until the sixties. Why do you think that happened?

OTTO LUENING: That's happened with quite a few of my works. When my third quarter, which I wrote in 1927, was played, it was torn apart. The reviews said it was the most abstract, awful, hideous thing. Then about ten years ago, when it was recorded in Munich and put on an album, the reviews were a complete turnaround, very positive people change—sometimes you're not on the same wavelength with them. I don't bother much about it. One day you're in and the next you're out. You just enjoy it while you've got it.

B. WENTZ: When you began your career in the twenties, did many people go out to hear live performances? Or was most of it recorded?

OTTO LUENING: In the twenties, there was not only very little live performance but no recordings at all because the record labels wouldn't waste money on contemporary concert music. That came much later. In those days, there were few people in Chicago who could play contemporary music. They could play either the standard symphony repertoire or the standard opera repertoire. There was no audience for contemporary music. That was pioneer work then, and you got cudgeled by the critics.

B. WENTZ: After a few years in Chicago, you took a post overseeing the opera department at the Eastman School in Rochester, New York. But, paradoxically enough, you didn't compose your only opera, *Evangeline*, until shortly after you left the school for New York City.

OTTO LUENING: Well, it was a very strange thing, a sort of accident of fate. When I was in Rochester, I helped found an opera company that wound up being based in New York City. I was here hanging around, and so they commissioned me to write an opera. Commissioning in those days meant you write the opera and we'll get the parts copied and play it. No money exchanged hands. What I wanted was a libretto rooted in the history of the United States, a story that everyone knew, and finally, I hit upon Henry Wadsworth Longfellow's poem *Evangeline*, about an Acadian girl who searches for her lost love in eighteenth-century America. It was very inspiring, and I got very interested in the music of the Acadians. Thanks to a Guggenheim Fellowship, I was able to go to Nova Scotia and Louisiana and live with the modern-day Acadian peasants and study their culture. That fellowship was a lucky break, which you have to have in life.

B. WENTZ: So when you returned to New York, it was the middle of the Great Depression.

OTTO LUENING: Those were hard times. I was married to a very fine singer at that time, Ethel Codd. We would go on these auditions and get great ratings, but there were no jobs. So the only opening in the entire United States was this job at Arizona State University. We moved there because you have to eat. The school's music department wasn't accomplished in terms of theory and composition, but there was a lot of natural talent around the place. And the opportunity there for me, which I picked up from Busoni, was to give those students as much training as I could, so they can get jobs that they have to do, and then teach them as much about the art of music and how to be themselves so they can stand on their own feet and get through this jungle without getting damaged too much. That's what I learned there, so it was a very good experience.

B. WENTZ: Did Composers Recording Inc. come out of the American Music Center?

OTTO LUENING: CRI is another story. I picked up the *New Music Quarterly* publication recordings when I was on the faculty at Bennington in the mid-1930s, and I got a cooperative to run it to see what would happen. It was on a subscription basis, and after two years, the faculty said they wouldn't go on with it anymore. I got the Eastman School's publication, *Arrowpress*, to say, we'll join forces, and maybe then we can kind of get through shared expenses and make it happen. And that started the thing. I ended up running it for twenty years.

B. WENTZ: You moved onto Columbia University in the mid-1940s. When did Edgar Varese join you there?

OTTO LUENING: I knew him long before he came to Columbia. Varese was a protege of Busoni in 1906, ten years before I knew Busoni, and he came to the U.S. around 1915. Varese was an early supporter of mine. A lot of his early music was lost in Europe. I think it was lost in a fire. And for nineteen years, he didn't really write anything. He was stymied. He had prophesied electronic music, based on Busoni hearing the Cahill organ, and made a statement about it in a little book called *The New Aesthetic of Music*, which came out in the early twentieth century. Thanks to Busoni, I also had been very excited about the possibilities of electronic music. So we shared that. But Varese couldn't compose anything electronically until the 1950s when the technology began to catch up to the ideas we had. That's when Varese began writing again.

B. WENTZ: At some point, you and Ussachevsky began experimenting with voices and flute on tape?

OTTO LUENING: I experimented with my own voice, and flute because I played flute. And he [Ussachevsky] played the piano. But we were aiming toward the extension of the resonance of existing instruments. We opened the door for future composers.

B. WENTZ: What do you think about the development of electronic music today?

OTTO LUENING: When I worked with Varese and Ussachevsky, we were the first and only electronic music studio; now they're all over the place. So a new horizon has opened. There's a big repertory. Some of it you could classify as being junk, I suppose, and a lot of it as masterpieces because they have stood the test of time.

Ned Sublette
Artist

Things changed radically in 1983 with the
appearance of AIDS, which was the death of the
downtown scene. But then there was a sharp,
permanent turn in my musical focus one night in
June 1985 when I walked into the Village Gate
(only nine blocks west from CBGB on Bleecker
Street), where the Monday night Salsa Meets
Jazz series was featuring El Gran Combo de
Puerto Rico. It blew everything else away. I was
there almost every Monday until the series shut
down in 1993. The clave revelation reoriented
everything I was doing musically.

I have a certain fondness recalling the hangs
at all-night restaurants after leaving the
clubs—Dave's Corner at Canal and Broadway or
103 Second Avenue. Once I started hanging out
in the salsa world, it was exciting to get to
know the great musicians one by one. And the
food changed.

New York's recording studio culture was at
its peak. There were so many studios, with an
emphasis on audio quality that did not carry
over into the home-studio era, and there was a
universe of world-class players who ran from one
to the other. I spent a lot of the eighties in
studios, much of it with Peter Gordon, and the
variety of musicians available to tromp through
the tracks was an endless source of wonder to me.
It was an expensive habit, though.

FIGURE 7.1 ROGER REYNOLDS
SOURCE: REYNOLDS ARCHIVE

7

ROGER REYNOLDS

April 23, 1984

R oger Reynolds joined me at the WKCR studio to talk about his upcoming performance at the New York Philharmonic's New Horizons Series. Reynolds, a Pulitzer prize–winning composer whose early sixties mixed-media theatrical dramatization of Wallace Stevens's poem "The Emperor of Ice-Cream" earned him the recognition of critics, grew up in Detroit and studied piano at the suggestion of his father. But he was drawn to physics at the University of Michigan and seemed headed for a career in engineering before he fell in with the school's budding art scene. He founded a kind of new music collective with colleagues Robert Ashley and Gordon Mumma called the ONCE Group. While at Michigan, he also discovered avant-garde composers Milton Babbitt, Edgard Varèse, Nadia Boulanger, and John Cage. Intrigued, he left for Europe after graduation and worked at the West German Radio's electronic music center in Köln, a hub of experimentation.

When he returned to the United States, a friend lured him to Southern California, where he founded the Center for Music Experiment and Related Research (now the Center for Research in Computing and the Arts) in San Diego. It's become his home. Passionate about poetry and literature, Reynolds based his early pieces on works such as *The Odyssey* and later his Pulitzer prize-winning piece *Whispers Out of Time*. In 1984, his piece "Transfigured Wind" for flute and computer premiered at the New Horizon Series at Lincoln Center. Although his aesthetic has been characterized as being influenced by contemporary American composers like Cage and Ives, his comfort around computers stems from his engineering background, and he continues to experiment in new and inventive ways.

B. WENTZ: How did you get involved in the New Horizons Series?

ROGER REYNOLDS: The series got a great deal of press last year, in 1983, and when the original planning for that event was being done, I was in Paris at Pierre Boulez's Institute, IRCAM, doing research on music and acoustics. That was when I heard about the notion of the New York Philharmonic putting on a large and really imposing presentation of contemporary music.

The additional and very gratifying surprise was that the philharmonic decided to do it again a second year. And rather than simply emulate the program or the philosophical stance that they had taken in the first year, they chose what I guess now is being touted as a broader view. And it is a great deal broader than it was last year. I find that very gratifying.

B. WENTZ: And for how long have you been working with the series's director, Jacob Druckman?

ROGER REYNOLDS: I first talked to Jacob about including some series of programs or events that would explore the history and interaction of the computer with musicians in August of last year. It happened that Charles Wuorinen was visiting the University of California, San Diego, where I teach from time to time, and he was pursuing a long-term interest he had in computers via Bell Telephone Laboratories. Charles wanted to allow these ideas to flower into a full-scale composition and knew that he had to go to a facility that was sophisticated and would allow not only technical insights but also musical results. And so he came at my invitation to San Diego, where he completed the tape components of a work that will be premiered at the festival.

So Charles and I were talking about the extraordinary impact the computer has had on music and how we hoped that the impact would be a healthy one. That is to say that the impact of digital technology would not simply facilitate doing easy things fast but rather would suggest to people doing new and more difficult and more intriguing things in spite of the, let's say, rather arduous path that is entailed if you try to use large computer systems to make music.

In any case, Charles and I were talking in August in La Jolla, overlooking the ocean, and we thought wouldn't it be marvelous if there could be an actual festival, not simply a program devoted to, for example, music written for orchestra and computer-generated sound? So we committed ourselves to the idea. And the notion of approaching Jacob to see whether this would be in some way in keeping with his plans and those of the philharmonic, that simply fell out of that more general discussion that Charles and I were having about attempting to do such a thing in New York.

Around that same time, I raised the idea of such a set of programs with Jacob in New York, and eventually, he and the philharmonic embraced it. There surely is no example anywhere in the world, and certainly most assuredly in this country, of a major cultural institution like the New York Philharmonic taking such an adventuresome and broad-based approach to the presentation of this new musical activity—the composer in association with computers and exploring new aspects of vocal and instrumental virtuosity. There is a really quite breathtaking range to this festival, and I think the philharmonic, and Jacob in particular, ought to be commended for their adventurous spirits.

B. WENTZ: Tell me about the performances you have planned.

ROGER REYNOLDS: There are three concerts associated with the computer. One of primarily tape or tape with one instrument music. One for a small ensemble and computer and another for orchestra and computer. Then, appended to the two recitals that are subtitled "The New Virtuosity," there will be two other sorts of infestations of computer-related music. These will be real-time systems that will actually be on stage, including a new work by George Lewis.

And on the second New Virtuosity program, Salvatore Martirano will be doing an improvisation for his extraordinary SAL-MAR Construction, a self-produced computer that is dedicated to the production of a whole family of instrumental activity. Sal can set this machine up, and it will continue to improvise according to certain conditions that he specifies. Over the past decade, I've spent several evenings at his house eating supper while the machine plays, and it does some rather astonishing things. Every once in a while, he'll excuse himself from the table and go touch a few dots, and it heads off in another direction. There will be five concerts produced directly by computers or in association with them.

B. WENTZ: For a person who knows nothing about computer music, how will these performances be set up physically? Will there be large or small computers, like the ones we have at home? The idea of computers on stage at the New York Philharmonic seems rather awesome!

ROGER REYNOLDS: It could be awesome in the sense that one can imagine a scenario where large devices are wheeled onto the stage and hum and buzz and flash and so on. This is not what will happen: Complex machines are fairly sensitive to their environments, and you neither want to bounce them about too much or to subject them to extremes of temperature, as they're made to be extremely precise and extremely rapid and, therefore, like any sophisticated and delicate device, they require care and proper attention.

So, in general, there will not be on stage, or even in the proximity of the Lincoln Center, the machines that have created most of the music that is played. In fact, digital devices of various sorts are widely used, so if you're speaking about computer music, I think it's wise to step back for a moment and consider what one really means. And I think that can mean at least two things. In a general sense, of course, you mean any music that has been produced with the aid of some sort of digital processing. That may include everything from electric organs and various kinds of processing devices that are used by rock groups to the use of extremely large and sophisticated research computer installations like at IRCAM or MIT or Stanford or that have been created to explore sound and produce music.

B. WENTZ: So most of it will be recorded.

ROGER REYNOLDS: Most of it will be on tape—two forms of tape: analog and digital. Digital is capable of producing considerably enhanced clarity and reduction of noise over analog recordings.

The two that I mentioned that will actually involve computers on stage will be George Lewis's presentation, which will involve, I believe, four Apples and three Yamahas. The other will be Martirano's, which he calls the SAL-MAR Construction, which is a special-purpose computer which he designed in collaboration with engineers at the University of Illinois. It's designed exclusively to produce music.

As I mentioned, the field has been operative for more than twenty years. The earliest experiments were done at Bell Telephone Laboratories in the late fifties and early sixties, and so the idea of using computers, that is to say, devices that represent music by means of lists of numbers, has been around for a while, and it's constantly been promising us miracles. And indeed, it is now clear, as it never has been before, that those promises can, in fact, be delivered.

And I hope that the programs that we're presenting will at least raise a very clear flag that says we have a major new ally in structural, expressive, and imaginative extensions of what we have understood as music.

B. WENTZ: Have the Group for Contemporary Music and the American Composer's Orchestra worked much with computers before? Will they be playing off of the music the tape-generated music? I see there are two programs—one for contemporary music and one for the American composer.

ROGER REYNOLDS: Oh, well, those are two of the three full programs. On June third, there's a program called Music from Computers, and this includes work by (McNabb, Schpieglewasa, Dodge, and Schoning). And they are, with small exceptions, to be presentations on quadraphonic tape, not with live instrumentalists. And that evening, there is a performance by the Group for Contemporary Music with works by (Senacchi, Salinski, and Heller).

And in those cases, of course, the composers have written out scores and, of course, copyists have made parts for the instrumentalists, and the conductor has the responsibility of coordinating the fixed elements of the work, which are produced by computer and stored on tape, with those elements produced by the live musicians in the concert.

Certainly, this is one of the ways in which the computer has been able to make its most important early, let's say, interventions into the field of normal performed music. As I say, it's difficult to move a large and sophisticated device around. People don't maltreat machines, perhaps, as much as they do other kinds of creatures, and so it has come to be the habit to put sound on tape. And there are, of course, much larger number of places in which tape can be played appropriately and synchronized with cooperative musicians and produce an extended palette of sound, of movements and space, of articulative speed and precision, and so on. There are simply some things that machines can do that go beyond normal limits of human performance capability.

So it really is, I believe, while compressed given the enormous amount of activity all over the world in using digital devices and processing and so on for musical purposes, it does give a, I think, fairly wide gamut of ideas for a listening public as to the early experiments in using computers, more recent developments, and some prognostication about what the future holds.

B. WENTZ: How long have you been working with computers?

ROGER REYNOLDS: Since around 1977. I worked initially at the electronic music studio in Stockholm that is run by the Swedish government. Later I went to Stanford where I did the tape portions of two works, one that involved digital processing of sound, called "The Palace," and this is part of a set called Voicespace. And "The Palace" involves taking a poem of [Jorge Luis] Borges, read by a vocalist, and using the spoken words to create an orchestral-sized accompaniment against which the same vocalist sings. The computer was able to create a kind of tonal palette by analyzing and extending the qualities of the spoken voice, which I found a very exciting foil for, I couldn't say a normal singing part, but for songful activity.

The other piece that I wrote at the same time was on one of the other side of what the computer can do, and that was the direct synthesis of sound. Not the alteration or processing of prerecorded materials but rather the creation of sounds entirely out of physical modeling or out of ideas about the way numbers relate to sound. And that was the tape for a work that is called "The Serpent-Snapping Eye" for trumpet and percussion and piano.

So that was how I got started. From there, I started working at UCSD. I was invited to come to IRCAM and do a two-year project there. So I've been active at most of the major centers at one time or another. I studied engineering as a student before going into music, so while I can't say that I am by any means expert in these areas, I at least learned in my engineering education a certain, let's say, relaxed attitude in the presence of machines, which is an advantage that's not shared by all musicians.

B. WENTZ: What can be expected of "Transfigured Wind I" [1984 for solo flute]? Is that going to be an alteration or created?

ROGER REYNOLDS: It's an effort to take the idea of musical variation and extend it. I wrote, while at IRCAM, a piece called "Archipelago." And "Archipelago" was an effort to look at how much we could do with recorded instrumental sound to distance it from the original, as to make it unlike the thing that was originally recorded, and yet still allow it to retain some kind of kernel of association that allowed you to make links between things. I call it "Archipelago" because archipelago is the name for chains of islands in the sea, and my notion was to have a simultaneous mosaic of fifteen sets of themes and variations going on at the same time.

It's a fairly ambitious piece at thirty-two minutes long, and it explores the idea of transformation, of transfiguration, in a way that I find goes beyond what is a fairly patterned and constrained concept of musical variation. If one aspect of a theme is altered, there tends to be a synchronous alteration of all aspects. For example, the idea of the melody, the harmony, the rhythmic structure, the formal structure changing from variation to variation in an independent way is unthinkable. You always keep the entire structure coordinated with itself.

It seemed to me clear that, while this is very helpful to live musicians when they have the task of playing together, when you have powerful machines, you can go far, far beyond these normal limits of synchronous behavior or categorical behavior. You may change, for example, pitch by transposition, but once the transposition is affected, you remain at that key until that variation is over, and then you may make another kind of transposition or return to an original, and so on.

In any case, the idea is that the composer can rethink in a very fundamental way what it means to vary musical materials. For example, perhaps even go inside the sound itself. One has always thought of a sound, for example, like that of the oboe, as being an inseparable, inviolate thing. I would think, well, actually, we could think of the oboe sonority of being constructed of a number of partial components and that if we had access to those partial components, we could actually split the sonority of the oboe apart in space physically, literally, and have a part oboe playing on the left and another part oboe playing on the right. And while they would still add up to the whole if you wiggled and jiggled and smeared, and so on, that left- or right-hand oboe part, you could create, as, for example, I did in "Archipelago," a situation where you could hear a holistic oboe, and within it coordinated, but still independent, you could hear the sound of, for example, a female voice and a clarinet that existed within this larger image of the oboe. So these kinds of processes, finding access to musical opportunities that we might always have imagined but could never have actually hoped to realize, is one of the things that is so exciting about using the computer.

Now, in "Transfigured Wind," I've taken this idea of variation and extrapolation even further, where one attempts to so distance the processed result from the original that you actually change the whole kind of emotional or imagistic impact that the sound has on you as a listener. This is a fairly extended work, and the computer-processed parts of it are more than twenty-five minutes of the piece, which is thirty-five minutes long.

There are four proposals, as I call them, rather than themes, by the soloist, who is Harvey Sollberger, and the person with whom I collaborated in making this piece. These four proposals are performed solo, and then the orchestra, with the computer-processed sound on tape, responds to the proposals. And the responses and the proposals get more and more complex and cover a wider and wider range of materials and emotions and so on as the piece goes on. And the idea is that these initially modest proposals are enlarged, enlarged, and enlarged to the point where they become considerably more than we would originally have anticipated.

I hope that in incorporating the computer into my plans, where I can move the sound in auditory space where I can separate the, as I said, partial components of individual sounds to create from an instrument which is relatively weak in, let's say, timbric variety as the flute is, twenty-five-minute quadraphonic tape was a fairly demanding sort of task and one that I found most enjoyable. I believe that I accomplished the task in a way that satisfies me very much, and I think that it will be of considerable interest to listeners to hear just how far you can move away from the expected sound of the flute, let's say, while not losing that fluteyness or that sense that the instrument that the wind that drives the instrument, continues to be at the root of everything that happens.

David Moss
Artist

The early eighties was a time of intense
individuality and eccentric discovery combined
with powerful ambitions fusing (and sometimes
fighting) with a desire for collaboration
and connectedness. The scene as I remember it
contained about two hundred musicians, performers,
sound artists. We were all probably wishing for
a role model while committed to personal style.
I found myself most intrigued with vocalists in
general—singers from around the world who offered
insight into abstract sound and/or song-making,
like Demetria Stratos, Diamanda Galás, Arto
Lindsay, etc.

EIF (Experimental Intermedia Foundation),
The Kitchen; and especially NMDS (New Music
Distribution Service)—that loft on 500 Broadway
was filled with thousands of LPs of very new
music, improvisation, world music, experimental
pop. With the expert (and opinionated!) help of
Yale Evelev (who ran the place), one could find
new unexpected people, music, ideas.

Fond memories include: Singing in Christian
Marclay's *Dead Stories* mini-opera; playing
gigs at 8BC, a condemned building on Eighth St
between Ave. B & Ave. C in which the audience
stood in the basement looking up to the first
floor stage ten feet above towards the back

(i.e., most of the first floor had simply
disappeared, and we, on stage, looked down onto
the heads of the audience in the basement), plus
there was a family of rabbits roaming loose on
stage with us. . . . And finally, several solos
and group gigs at EIF where John Cage sat in
the audience, always nodding and laughing his
recognizable laugh!

FIGURE 8.1 PRIL SMILEY
SOURCE: COLUMBIA UNIVERSITY

8

PRIL SMILEY

Unknown date, 1987

P ril Smiley was one of the original instructors at the Columbia-Princeton Electronic Music Center in the late 1960s. She is considered a pioneer of electronic music, alongside her colleagues Vladimir Ussachevsky and Mario Davidovsky. One of only two women at the center during its first iteration, Smiley fell into working at the center's studio after doing a summer internship with Vladimir Ussachevsky, who invited her back after she graduated from Bennington College. She later held a teaching position at the center and eventually served as its director. Much like her female composer colleagues Joan La Barbara, Laurie Spiegel, Maryanne Amacher, Alice Shields, and Pauline Oliveros, Smiley quickly made her mark in electronic music, working in theater productions at the newly-opened Lincoln Center. In 1975, she received an NEA grant and Guggenheim Fellow Award for Music Composition.

Smiley and I met at the Electronic Music Center on the west side of Harlem, on 125th Street. The computer music laboratory, housed in Prentice Hall next door, has terminals on which faculty and students create their instruments and pieces (the terminals were linked to the university's mainframe). A digital-to-analog converter transforms the tapes produced by the mainframe into a form playable on the lab's stereo system. Speaking with her, surrounded by wall-to-wall equipment, I felt like I was getting an education in how electronic music gets made.

B. WENTZ: You came to the Columbia-Princeton Electronic Music Center in the 1960s. Who was teaching at the time? What was the direction?

PRIL SMILEY: I initially came to the center around the end of 1962. At the time, I was a sophomore at Bennington College, majoring in composition. I was studying with composer Henry Brant, who had done some interesting things at Columbia with Vladimir Ussachevsky. The center, at that point, had been in existence officially fewer than five years. Bennington has what's called a winter term, where you take a break from classes and do an internship or a job. I asked Brant where I should go, and he suggested I do an internship with Ussachevsky.

Ussachevsky happened to be doing exciting things at the time. He was working on a score for a film adaptation of Sartre's play *No Exit*, and had been working on a theater score for *King Lear*. I just learned the best way you can learn, which is standing at someone's side and doing it. He had me do a splicing exercise on tape, with five hundred brass instrument sounds he created, and had me label them on reels. He quickly realized I could be adept on the equipment.

B. WENTZ: Did you already know you wanted to work in electronic music?

PRIL SMILEY: No. I was writing instrumental music as a student at Bennington, and this was just a great job opportunity in a whole new field that we had barely heard about. Otto Luening, who cofounded the center, had been an instrumental part of forming the Bennington College Music Department. So Ussachevsky and Luening were our friends. They had done their original tape manipulation experiments together at Bennington's summer composer's conference in 1952. So there was a connection between Bennington and Columbia, and it was a natural place for me to come and work with interesting composers.

And the work was addictive. So even when school was back in session, I would come down on weekends to Columbia just to be part of the process of working with Ussachevsky and to learn things. I would often stay up half the night working as his technician. I would do everything from answering the phone to tape work. At some point, he started paying me two dollars an hour.

I came down for the rest of my college years, and I began working on my own little studies. Mario Davidovsky was here then, too, and he would stop in and listen to what I was working on and informally coach me. I never did take a music course at Columbia because, at that time, classes weren't even being offered in electronic music. I just learned by doing. By the time I graduated from Bennington, we had organized courses for graduate composers here at Columbia. They were required to take at least a year off of electronic music as part of their program. So I kind of walked into a teaching assistant job because the courses had just gotten off the ground and there weren't that many people who had done electronic music at Columbia, or anywhere else, that could be an assistant to the person teaching the class. Graduate students need hands-on instruction, and that has to happen one-on-one because you can't do that in a whole class full of students. So I—and later Alice Shields—we were the ones who worked closely with the students. And for me, it was also a way to learn since I was able to experiment through them. I could say something like, "Let's record these percussion sounds and see what we can do with them."

At the time, I was beginning my career writing music for theater. Ussachevsky and Davidovsky were both very good mentors not only to people like me who were composing our first electronic pieces but to students in general. They made sure we got performances. They took tapes of our compositions with them to lectures around the country. They sent our tapes along with their own to studios in Europe and other places.

We're talking now about the later sixties and early seventies. There were more electronic music concerts in New York and around the world. People were writing to us every week asking for pieces. And audiences were willing to sit through an entire concert of electronic music, sometimes even works that were all for tape alone with no performers on stage, which is not the fashion now. People will get bored fast if there's not something happening onstage.

B. WENTZ: So, what type of concerts are you producing today?

PRIL SMILEY: Right now at Columbia, we're waiting for a theater to be renovated, so we didn't have any concerts this year. But Mario Davidovsky, who came on as full-time director after Ussachevsky retired, wanted to have a studio, create a little more excitement, and at least be the equivalent of the feeling of the concerts that we had back in the sixties where we really worked hard to put good quality concerts on at McMillin Theater.

So we aimed to create a concert series consisting of commissioned electronic works, either in the computer area or analog area. And each of our concerts would feature a different New York performing group, so we would have variety that way. But mostly, the point of the performances is just to generate a sense of excitement, let people know that we're still alive and healthy and doing interesting things. Which is very important when you've been around for decades like we have. Ours was one of the first and one of the biggest electronic music studios, and it's so easy to rest on your laurels and get complacent after a while.

Another way we're trying to stay current is to keep up with the latest equipment. So, right now, you and I are sitting in a new studio that's probably one-of-a-kind in the United States. It's a hybrid of analog and digital equipment. Most of the newly built studios I've seen in other parts of the country are completely digital. Most of them have Yamaha synthesizers or Synclaviers or a few tape recorders, but not the amount of analog equipment we have. We're trying to keep the best of the older analog equipment that we've all enjoyed composing on but teaching ourselves how to use the new digital equipment, and merging the two in the same studio, and also connecting into our computer studio, which we're also trying to upgrade.

This will help change the way we teach our students. Students now show a knowledge about synthesizers because they all have them in their living rooms. So we try to teach them analogy techniques that they have never heard of and things like a splicing block.

B. WENTZ: You said kids have a lot of equipment at home and more knowledge about computers and synthesizers. What do you find is their attitude when they come to the studio today?

PRIL SMILEY: The students who come in now, they've already had a lot of exposure to electronic music, especially in the last five or ten years. There's so much of it out there now, in rock groups or jingles for advertisements. And many of the students have synthesizers at home. But they've been using equipment that's relatively primitive in terms of the kind of sounds it can create. The students that are enrolling in our courses are graduate composers, and they may know some of the electronic technology, but from our point of view, they're in kindergarten in terms of how you'd apply that technology as a composer and try to use the equipment to express yourself as a composer. And so our biggest battle is to get students away from the keyboards that most synthesizers now come with, where they really act more like glorified performers than as conceptual composers. That's why we force them to use the tape splicing block, and have them ignore the equipment for a while, and learn the electronic vocabulary in their heads and not just to have it so readily available because you push keys on a synthesizer keyboard.

B. WENTZ: What sort of reputation does the Columbia-Princeton Electronic Music Center have now?

PRIL SMILEY: I think it's very solid. In some corners of New York City, we might be viewed as those "academics" uptown, especially compared to other kinds of music happening in New York City. But in other places I've been around the country, we're thought of as the most solid, long-lasting electronic music studio in this part of the eastern U.S.

B. WENTZ: Where do you think electronic music or composition is heading today?

PRIL SMILEY: It's going in a lot of different directions. As far as students coming out of our studios at Columbia, many of them will go and teach at a college or university level. So they're learning in order to be teachers and administrators, more than perhaps composers. As far as outside of our studio, I see electronic music moving more into commercial areas. That's where the equipment is going to be used. It's going to replace traditional instruments. The Local 802 Musicians Union in New York is very, very worried about that. It worries some of us who, as composers, studied traditional instruments and played them. And a lot of the technology used to create electronic music will go in a digital direction. Students are signing up for computer courses right and left.

B. WENTZ: Where is your music headed?

PRIL SMILEY: My music is a little bit on the shelf, wondering what to do next. I'm mostly waiting for the new studio to be finished, and then I'll learn how to use some of the new digital synthesizers and incorporate them into my music. And I'll merge the old analog techniques [tape, synthesizers] that I've used for more than two decades with the new digital technology [computers].

B. WENTZ: What is the advantage of digital over analog?

PRIL SMILEY: Good music is good music; it doesn't matter whether it's made by digital means or analog. It used to be more of a definite sound. You could say that definitely is a computer sound, meaning *digital*, or that's definitely a tape studio sound, meaning old-fashioned *analog*. The two have very much gotten merged now, and a listener can't necessarily tell what the source was.

Some of us who worked with old analog techniques like the more direct hands-on techniques. Although digital can be more precisely controlled, some of that controlling involves more parameters of what you're controlling. And with analog, you can compose directly by ear, hence more like a performer.

B. WENTZ: Your most recent composition, "Forty-Three," was performed here at Columbia. It sounds like a lot is going on in the piece. Can you explain it a bit?

PRIL SMILEY: "Forty-Three" is composed for tape alone, and it combines the sounds of real instruments, mostly trombone and percussion, with electronically-generated sounds that are often made to imitate either the percussion or trombone sounds. It's a piece that's built in many, many layers, which start simple and get increasingly complex. It was a technical nightmare to do in our studio, but that was part of the challenge. The structure is very simple, but the technique is very complicated.

With this composition, I intended to present a series of layers of sound that would give the listener what I think of as x-ray hearing. And the listener would be able to pick out certain layers at certain places and hopefully be interested in that process of finding different things that exist inside its very thick layers.

B. WENTZ: Electronic music in the United States, for the most part, sprung out of universities like Columbia. Is the music still considered rigorously academic?

PRIL SMILEY: It really depends on whom you ask, and where they live, and whether they're composers or listeners. Our composers here at Columbia have had works produced in Los Angeles and in San Francisco. The University of Michigan and in Texas have very active programs.

And when our pieces get put on at those programs, it's not labeled as academic. We're told that they're simply good pieces, and that's why they call the center here asking us for new compositions. It's because the basic quality of what we do seems to hold through time.

But some of the composers here write music that's very different from one another. Mine is about as totally opposite from Davidovsky as you can get. I spent fifteen very intense years working in theater and film, especially at the Vivian Beaumont Theater in New York and other theaters, including Shakespeare Theaters, doing all electronic music. And so I'm influenced from a theater background in terms of the way I write. Davidovsky's music is more often called "academic." But people mean different things when they say that. They also mean their image of Davidovsky, maybe, and that has nothing to do with his music.

B. WENTZ: Do you think it's difficult for the listener to understand electronic music?

PRIL SMILEY: Not most listeners. I don't know about going out here on 125th Street and taking the average person by the hand and bringing them into our studio and asking how he feels about hearing electronic music, but certainly, most people that walk in the door here, especially if they had to pay to get through the door to hear a contemporary music concert, they don't have any trouble listening to electronic music.

And again, I find the bottom word is just *quality*. I've done lecture demonstrations of electronic music all around the country, sometimes in remote areas where people are not even exposed much to classical music, let alone contemporary music. And I find that if a piece is good, a listener will be curious and usually open-minded enough to hear the quality. They may not understand the vocabulary or what it's all about, but they enjoy the experience, especially older people and children.

Elliott Sharp
Artist

New York City was a place where we all went to
each other's gigs and see each other at shows,
movies, gallery openings, and the few hang-out
places: the Kiev, Veselka, Binibon, Baltyk, and
the Sixth Street Indian restaurants all in the
East Village, Dave's Luncheonette, or Magoos in
Tribeca. The main music clubs were Tier 3, Mudd
Club, Hurrah, Squat Theater, CBGB, Danceteria,
A7, Pyramid Club, Darinka, 8BC, Soundscape, A's,
Limbo Lounge (the original on Ninth Street),
Studio Henry (later renamed Mort's), The Ritz,
Armageddon, and Maxwell's in Hoboken. I was the
bass player for Michael Musto's Motown band
The Must, and with that group, we played a lot
of bigger, showier places such as Peppermint
Lounge, Bonds, The Bank, The 80's.

In 1981, I produced a compilation for my zOaR
label titled *Peripheral Vision: Bands of Loisaida*
which presented pieces from Mofungo, The
Ordinaires, The Scene Is Now, Crazy Hearts, The
State, Hi Sheriffs Of Blue, V-Effect, and my band
I/S/M. We had a marathon release party for the
album at Mort's, a basement beneath the Exotic
Aquatics pet store on Morton & Bleecker, with
sets from all of the bands. It was packed beyond
belief with the audience flooding out onto the
street and back into the club for hours and hours.
Incredible fun and great sets from everyone.

Mort Subotnick, Composer - 1995   ©Jack Mitchell

FIGURE 9.1 MORTON SUBOTNICK
SOURCE: JACK MITCHELL

9
MORTON SUBOTNICK
August 1983

Morton Subotnick is probably best known in New York City for his revolutionary composition *Silver Apples of the Moon*. The 1967 album of electronic music was commissioned by Nonesuch Records after Subotnick played the piece at the opening of the East Village nightclub Electric Circus—a show that was attended by Tom Wolfe and members of the Kennedy family. The album subsequently became an underground hit. Subotnick—who composed the piece using an analog synthesizer he had developed with Donald Buchla—quickly released two follow-up albums, cementing his place at the vanguard of electronic music.

Before coming to New York City, Subotnick had founded the San Francisco Tape Music Center with Ramon Sender, one of the first electronic music studios. Here, he first hit upon the idea of creating an "electronic music box," or modular synthesizer. His experiments with computers and modified sounds proved hugely influential in the city's nightclub scene. So, when Subotnick finally accepted an invitation to play at Soho's Knitting Factory in 1987, the show quickly sold out, with fans lining up around the block.

Subotnick also composed works for symphonies, chamber orchestras, and multimedia productions. In 1984, he was commissioned to write a performance piece with director Lee Breuer and visual artists Irving Petlin for the Olympics Arts Festival in Los Angeles. The result was *The Double Life of Amphibians*, a "staged tone poem" that combined visuals with singers interacting with instrumentalists and computers.

B. WENTZ: What was the response by your peers to working with tape when you started in the fifties?

MORTON SUBOTNICK: It was a new medium. I started working with tape around 1958, which was fairly early on in the development of electronic music. The first studio for electronic music, the Cologne Studio [Studio for Electronic Music of the West German Radio], had started around 1952. At the time, I was a graduate student in San Francisco, and I met Herbert Blau, the director of the Actors Workshop. He asked me to write music for their production of *King Lear*. Tape music had just come on the scene at the time. The Columbia-Princeton Center had just gotten going. And I thought tape music would work great as a theatrical medium. My idea was to make a piece of music by manipulating tape recordings of the sounds in the play, like the closing of doors and the voice of the guy who was going to play Lear, so that all the sounds were somehow emotionally and psychologically integrated into the experience of the play. The idea was closer to the French school of musique concrete. The crew liked it, I got an advance, and with that, I went out to buy a tape recorder!

B. WENTZ: Not long after, you started a tape studio at the San Francisco Conservatory of Music with Ramon Sender, Terry Riley, and a couple of other composers. That eventually became the San Francisco Tape Music Center. Is that when you met Don Buchla?

MORTON SUBOTNICK: Don came on the scene around '61 or '62. Ramon and I had envisioned a black box that would be a composer's palette. I called it the Electronic Music Easel, which would be like a small, inexpensive palette that a composer could work with a tape recorder and make music in one's own studio at home and not have to go to a big musical center.

I had read the Navy manual on electricity and electronics, and Ramon had done some work, and we had a vocabulary. We had sort of theoretically designed a couple of different potential systems. One was based on the way the Hammond organ worked at the time, which was a light-sensitive sound system where a disc rotates and it creates different light patterns, which will create a different sound. But we couldn't build anything. We didn't know enough.

We put an ad in the *San Francisco Chronicle* searching for an engineer who could build our device. And Buchla came by, and we showed him what we wanted. Three days later, he came in with this contraption: a paper disc attached to a little rotary motor mounted on a board, a couple of batteries, a flashlight, and a little loudspeaker. It did exactly what we imagined it could do. But Don said that wasn't the best way to do it, and so he began to outline what would eventually turn into his synthesizer system.

B. WENTZ: Were you still interested in orchestration at that time?

MORTON SUBOTNICK: I mean, up through that time, there was no possibility of doing anything else but instrumental music, so I was mostly writing orchestral music. I didn't think of electronics as replacing the music I was writing. I thought of it as part of the theater. The first electronic pieces I did were all for the theater or for dance. At the time, I was the composer for Anna Halprin's dance company, and we staged two major productions that were done with taped music and live processing of audience sounds, things like that.

B. WENTZ: When did you begin exploring the concept of the composer interacting with machines?

MORTON SUBOTNICK: It was really after I met Buchla that I began to imagine a situation in which a composer would be able to sit in one's own studio and paint a sound. That intrigued me so much. It took Buchla two years to develop and produce his first box, the Buchla 100. It cost only five hundred dollars, which we got from the Rockefeller Foundation. That was incredibly inexpensive.

I got so enamored with the Buchla 100 that I began to think of it as pure music. I had the studio. I had the instrument. And so I decided I wouldn't write any more instrumental music for a few years, just do everything directly from my fingers to the loudspeakers, so to speak.

B. WENTZ: Around this time, you moved to New York City to become an artist-in-residence at NYU and had a Buchla 100 installed in your apartment on Bleecker Street. That was where you composed *Silver Apples of the Moon*, the first piece of electronic music commissioned by a record company. Were you surprised when the record became an underground hit?

MORTON SUBOTNICK: Truthfully, I was not satisfied with what I had done. *Silver Apples* has become a classic of some sort, and even the one that came after it, *The Wild Bull*, is close to a classic piece, but there was something missing. I didn't intend to compose more than a couple of pieces of electronic music, but I somehow felt incomplete with it, and so I kept at it. The first piece that I really felt was almost there was *Until Spring*, which came out in 1975. It sold the fewest number of records, but in many ways, it's the best in terms of what I was trying to do. And then *A Sky of Cloudless Sulfur*, a much lighter piece that I did three years later. By then, I felt like I had finished something, and it took ten years to get to that point.

B. WENTZ: Your work since then has increasingly involved the use of ghost electronics, which you described as "sculpting with sound in time and space." Can you explain this a bit more? As I understand it, the tape sends a high signal frequency, inaudible to the audience, to the electronics, which then acts on the instruments—hence, it is an interaction of electronics with instruments?

MORTON SUBOTNICK: It was the early development of what eventually became the ghost pieces that brought *Until Spring* that final feeling, the gestalt, to a close. In '74, I finally perfected with Buchla the electronic music easel I had envisioned back in San Francisco. We devised a way of using pressure-sensitive keys, which the Buchla provides, to etch nothing but energy, or intensity—intensity from my voice and intensity from the fingers—to make a piece out of energy shapes. And then those get recorded like on a piano player. Except instead of recording pitches and durations, it's recording this swooping energy field as it goes. That was the technique which developed the ghost pieces.

So I would do my grunts and groans onto tape and then that would control the amplification, the shifting of the frequencies, and the position, the location, the panning of the instrumental sound that was on the stage. The original image I had was of a Hollywood movie, where the composer is a pianist and he's sitting writing his last symphony, which is sort of in the style of Rachmaninoff, and the house is burning down around him.

B. WENTZ: Your ghost pieces involve live performers accompanied by electronics. The 1981 piece "Ascent into Air," took that dynamic even further, with a chamber ensemble playing along with computer-generated sound.

MORTON SUBOTNICK: "Ascent into Air" was really the beginning of the use of the computer for me in live performance. The computer is responding to the instrument. I wasn't actually performing the computer; I was only putting in memory and advancing the computer from place to place to let it know where the conductor was. But it was always responding to the two cellos and doing what it was preprogrammed to do. When the cello does X, it does this. When the cello does Y, it does that.

The ghost electronics will eventually incorporate that kind of logic in them: They'll take the sound of an instrument, and when an instrument does Y, it will take the sound X and send it back in a different way. It will be completely dependent on the instrumental.

B. WENTZ: What aspect of music do you like or focus on more? Duration? Pitch? Timing? Harmony?

MORTON SUBOTNICK: Music is a preverbal language because we never can pinpoint what it means. It's one of the things that has kept music from being important in our society, but it's also one of the things that keeps it so important in our personal lives: It *means* so much, but we never can quite define what its meaning is.

So I think of these gestures of mine as the phrasing. The gesture is the main meaning. The reading, the feeling, the moment just before you have utterance of the word, and then music, to me, is the articulation or orchestration of the preverbal message.

B. WENTZ: Could you tell us about the piece you'll be premiering at the coming Summer Olympics, *Music for the Double Life of Amphibians*?

MORTON SUBOTNICK: I'm just getting ready to direct the liner notes for the record, which has "Ascent Into Air" as part one and "A Fluttering of Wings" as the third and final part. So I'm just starting to think about the whole thing.

At one level, it's a quasi-theatre piece in three big parts. I haven't named the second part yet, it's only half finished, but it deals with beasts and men. The latter half of the second part is for my wife, Joan La Barbara. It's a solo voice and electronics that overlaps into "A Fluttering of Wings."

The first half of the second part is a theatrical piece that deals with visceral human-animal conflict, probably. It goes between ecstasy and violence, somewhere in that range of experience. And Lee Breuer is interested in directing it, so it looks like we'll get the thing off the ground.

B. WENTZ: You seem to have a fascination with the idea of metamorphosis.

MORTON SUBOTNICK: I think what I've been doing for some time now, starting formally with *Butterflies*, but informally with *The Wild Bull*, is to use biological models. I am always interested in biologically dynamic models, if there is such a phrase, starting with the metamorphosis of the butterfly.

And using that as a way to generate a piece of music. But it's become much more now. The butterfly idea is still at the heart of the whole thing. But it's become much more embedded in my whole thinking, so that this metamorphic quality has to do with static, no movement, which builds up an energy, which bursts forth into this big struggle of some sort, and finally evolves into its beatific self at the end.

I see everything at that level. Take the lifespan of a human being. First, there's the infant, who grows up through middle childhood. And that suddenly springs forth into the adolescent struggle, that period of awkwardness, that physicalness where all the juices are all mixed up, and it's just crazy. Then gradually we sort of pull out into a kind of another static state through a part of adulthood in which everything begins to settle. And gradually through the end of one's life, hopefully, everything kind of coalesces in that beatific quality. It's an idealization.

DJ Smash
Artist, DJ, producer

It was a pivotal time in the 1980s. The disco
years ushered more people wanting to go to
clubs. Going out to clubs Danceteria, the Ritz,
and Peppermint Lounge was frequent. Timmy
Regisford and Justin Strauss became my DJ idols.
Monday night at the Ritz had a video night . . .
dance, new wave videos . . . a lot of stuff from
the UK: the Clash, Pretenders, Stray Cats, the
Cure . . . they had a great sound system with
DJ Delphine Blue. They played all UK and French
videos that you could not see on MTV. I was
astounded that this music wasn't on the radio.
My early influences for making music and DJing
came out of going to those clubs. Hearing new
sounds that I couldn't hear on the radio or see
on TV.

I'd then go on Tuesdays to Bleecker Bobs and
buy the 45s, and they were the only one that had
the imports. Dancing, learning and listening,
and meeting different types of people.

At that time, the club scene was interracial;
it didn't matter where you were from, as long as
you knew how to dance and dress.

A lot of things overlapped, people were trying
to cross pollinate and they were intentionally
going about it. . . . We would want to know what
the hip-hop cats were doing. What the electronic
guys were doing. What the punk guys were doing

and the new wave guys doing. Everybody was
trying to figure out how they could make their
scene more interesting, and they knew we had to
cross-pollinate. That was the best thing about
Manhattan: you may have come from a monoculture
like the Bronx or Brooklyn, but when you came to
Manhattan you couldn't keep that mentality, you
had to interact

FIGURE 10.1 JOAN TOWER

SOURCE: STEVE J. SHERMAN

10

JOAN TOWER

Unknown date, 1987

Female contemporary classical composers were rarely acknowledged in the 1980s, and Joan Tower is no exception. An avid composer and pianist, Tower has always been a highly vocal advocate of greater recognition for new music and women composers. There were no female mentors to look up to, nor were any mentioned in any books while growing up. Tower recalls that at one conference when educators were confronted with why this was, they had no answers . . . and couldn't come up with any names prior to the 1900s; That in itself, she says, "is discrimination."

But during our conversation, Tower quickly acknowledged her talented peers—Ellen Taafe Zwilich, Libby Larsen, Shulamit Ran, Meredith Monk, Laurie Anderson, Pauline Oliveros, and Thea Musgrave, to name a few.

What puts Tower in league with the female wunderkinds is her pivotal work, "Fanfare for the Uncommon Woman." This pioneering contemporary composition gives a nod to Aaron Copland's "Fanfare for the Common Man" yet is "dedicated to women who are adventurous and take risks." Her statement and bold naming of the piece became a historic feminist comment in music. This punchy, bold, and effervescent composition is so audibly bombastic it almost pokes fun at Copland's famed piece.

Tower's music is rooted in the serial tradition and garners much praise among her peers, colleagues, and critics. Orchestras around the world have commissioned Tower for works.

We sat down and spoke about her upbringing, the formation of the Da Capo Chamber Players, an ensemble created to promote new music and broaden its recognition, and her current teaching posts. Her effervescent no-holds-bar personality, tinged with a slightly New York accent, upholds her stance as a provocateur of contemporary music.

Born in upstate New York, Tower started taking piano lessons at age six. Her family moved to Bolivia, and her piano lessons fluctuated due to the change of teachers all the time. When the family moved back to the States, Tower enrolled at Bennington College and then moved to New York to attend Columbia University. There, she studied composition under Otto Luening, Jack Beeson, and Vladimir Ussachevsky, all part of the Columbia-Princeton Electronic Music Center. While getting her doctorate at Columbia, she gravitated toward the cerebral atonality of Milton Babbitt and Charles Wuorinen but began writing in her own voice, which stood out over time.

She married a jazz pianist, Hod O'Brien, who taught her a lot about jazz, although she had an innate love of percussion due to her early childhood living and hearing the rhythms in South America.

She won the Grawemeyer Award for *Silver Ladders* and had her composition *Sequoia* performed with great success all around the world. But most notably now, as an educator, Tower has paved the way for many future women composers.

B. WENTZ: As a child, you were a prodigy piano player. How did you end up composing?

JOAN TOWER: I started playing piano when I was six, and I had a wonderful piano teacher. At the time, we lived in Larchmont, just north of New York City. Then my father, who was a mineralogist, moved us to South America when I was nine, and we bounced around there until I was seventeen. So I had to change piano teachers every time we moved, and my technique got all screwed up. In a way, that was a blessing in disguise because if I had stayed with that teacher in New York, I probably would have become a concert pianist.

Then when I went to Bennington College for undergrad, I was asked for the first time to write a piece for a class. It had never occurred to me to compose before. I guess I had never been around any living composers. And I heard this piece that I wrote, and it was such a mind-blowing experience that I wrote another piece and another. It was such a different way into music than playing Beethoven or Mozart or whoever. It was very compelling. So the excitement I felt at the time got me going, and I haven't stopped since.

B. WENTZ: After Bennington, you came to Columbia to get a master's degree.

JOAN TOWER: Yes, because people said, now the next step is for you to get a master's and then a PhD because in order to teach, you should have those degrees.

So I dutifully went on to get my graduate degrees. It took me fourteen years because I was basically bored with the whole situation. I am not an academic type at all. It's taken me a while to even say that.

B. WENTZ: While you were at Columbia, you helped form the Da Capo Chamber Players, an ensemble dedicated to playing new music.

JOAN TOWER: I was very lucky. When I came to New York to study, I got a job at a music settlement house called the Greenwich House in the West Village. I taught piano and eventually also composition. I was very active there. My students gave recitals and I was forming groups. And I decided to start a series there focused on contemporary music. I raised the money for it, and did all the publicity for it, and made it into a viable series. It was a wonderfully exciting thing for me because that's what I really wanted to do. I wanted to play and I wanted to hear my music being played. There were so many performers I got to meet and play with because of that series, and over time, I developed a core group of friends who became the Da Capo Chamber Players. And Da Capo became a great education for me as a composer. Because here I was dealing with performers day in and day out. They were friends, and so it became a healthy kind of creative situation where I could say, How does this A flat sound in that register? Or, Can you flutter at this speed? And then I wrote pieces for each of them, which was very exciting because they really wanted to play these pieces and they would devote hundreds of hours to learning them.

It was all very natural. It wasn't like I was handing them a piece and saying, "Will you play this?" It was a genuine desire for me to write the best piece I could for this friend of mine and a genuine desire on their part to do a good job with it. The dual careers I've had as a pianist and a composer were very important to me because I was always on both sides of the coin of music.

B. WENTZ: Do you still do both today?

JOAN TOWER: No, I stopped performing about two years ago. I quit the Da Capo Players because they were getting too good for me. I had this whole other life going on with my compositions.

B. WENTZ: The Da Capo Players are a small ensemble. How did you transition to writing for orchestras?

JOAN TOWER: Over time, my pieces started getting picked up by other groups and other soloists, and then the American Composers Orchestra asked me to write an orchestra piece. And I said, "An orchestra piece?" That was very scary. I didn't feel comfortable writing for an orchestra at all. But the head of this organization, Francis Thorne, was determined to get a piece from me. So I wrote this piece called "Sequoia," and I was sure it was going to be a disaster. I remember sitting at Alice Tully Hall—the show was sold out because Keith Jarrett was performing a piano concerto by Alan Hovhaness, and Dennis Russell Davies was conducting that night as well—and I was a nervous wreck. I just thought my piece was going to fold.

B. WENTZ: And instead, it was a huge success.

JOAN TOWER: Well, the audience seemed to love it, and subsequently, it's been played by fourteen other orchestras, including the New York Philharmonic. And I'm still sitting here thinking, how did that all happen? How did what I thought was going to be a disaster turn into a piece that's played so much? I guess I wrote a better piece than I had imagined. This continues to happen with me, even though I've written a number of pieces since "Sequoia." I'm my own worst critic. I think this is too long, that's too short, that's too high, this is too simple. I'm still very hard on myself.

B. WENTZ: Your latest piece is a short work called "Fanfare for the Uncommon Woman." What inspired that?

JOAN TOWER: The Houston Symphony commissioned twelve fanfares to celebrate their sesquicentenary. And when I was asked to compose something for that series, I immediately thought of Aaron Copland's "Fanfare for the Common Man" because it's a really good piece. And I thought maybe I should make it a tribute to Copland. And so on this itinerary that I was sending around to my agent and some other people, I put the date of the performance, January 10th, the word *fanfare*, and then in parenthesis I wrote, "for the uncommon woman?" as a joke. And a very smart friend of mine, Fran Richards, who heads the classical division at ASCAP, said to me, "You know, you should really think about using that as a title." So I made it a kind of double tribute to women who take risks and who are adventurous and to Copland, who was one of my influences.

B. WENTZ: Did the audience like it?

JOAN TOWER: Oh yeah. A lot of these blue-haired ladies came up to me and said they were so excited that it was written for women. It's not a big serious piece. It's a three-minute fanfare for brass and percussion. The brass players loved it.

B. WENTZ: You've spent a lot of time advocating for women composers.

JOAN TOWER: I think the women's movement had a lot to do with raising the visibility of female composers. And more women composers are being played now, but it's still nowhere near enough. Take orchestral programming. In a subscription series, you may see five living composers in an entire year. And if you see one woman among those five, it's a miracle. Then look at chamber music. It's rare to see a woman on those series. Even contemporary music groups around New York, which play mainly living composers, you'll see them play maybe one female composer in a given year. So I think the situation still needs a lot of work.

B. WENTZ: Is this naivete on their part? Discrimination?

JOAN TOWER: I think it's both. It's this kind of attitude like, I don't know any women that are composers of value, do you? They're just not willing to go out and find interesting women composers. They're just not willing to make the effort. And that is a form of discrimination, I think.

B. WENTZ: Which of your female colleagues are getting more attention these days?

JOAN TOWER: Ellen Zwilich is definitely the most visible. She has a lot of firsts. She was the first woman composer to win the Pulitzer Prize. And she was the first woman to graduate from Julliard in composition. She's a very solid, good composer. I think it's wonderful that she's doing so well because she's a role model, you know?

And there are some younger composers coming up. Shulamit Ran, who's originally from Israel. Meredith Monk. Laurie Anderson. Elizabeth Swados, who did the musical *Runaways*. The Scottish composer Thea Musgrave. They're all very different types of composers, but I think all of them are pretty visible.

B. WENTZ: You also champion contemporary music in general by sitting on panels and the like.

JOAN TOWER: I'm basically a person among people, and the more juries and panels I'm on, the more I learn about the structure of the music world and how people think. And one thing I noticed early on is how dead composers get top priority over living composers. And that got me going. I said, "We can't just sit here and take this. We've got to fight for our rights, and we've gotta fight for our music." We've got to keep classical music alive and bubbling and creative. The same way the pop music world does. New music in the pop world gets pushed around a lot, but it's a healthy kind of fit. In the classical music world, new music is viewed as being kind of leper-like, especially among the more prestigious classical music societies in the United States.

B. WENTZ: And women composers are part of that issue.

JOAN TOWER: The whole issue of the living composer has to be addressed first because women fit inside that picture. Women composers also have an historical problem: There's very little history for us. You open any music history book, and if you find a woman composer mentioned from before the twentieth century, it's a miracle. Now that is starting to change because there's research that's finally being done. But when I was coming up, women composers were never mentioned in the history books I studied so carefully at Columbia University.

David Weinstein
Artist, curator, Roulette

My most enduring memory and treasured experience
was seeing Jerry Hunt perform; he fascinated me,
both for his technical innovations and also the
mystery of his ritualistic performances. Glenn
Branca and Rhys Chatham kind of scared me, but I
was drawn to their work. I was mostly surrounded
by the exploding downtown improvisation scene,
which centered around John Zorn, Fred Frith,
Derek Bailey. It took me time to unlearn my
compositional training and truly appreciate the
value of the work, not to mention participating
in it.

The Knitting Factory underscored the high/
low art schism; concert works in a club became
acceptable, and that was attractive. PS1 was a
major destination, both for music and installation
projects. In fact, many alternative spaces from
Franklin Furnace and Artist's Space, along with
the raw club scene like 8BC, Pyramid Club, even
CBGB's, were regular places to haunt for the
adventurous.

Recording sessions with John Zorn at the
Radio City recording studio (now dismembered),
where I participated for several albums (*Cobra,
Spillane, The Big Gundown*), was memorable because
Zorn was wrangling unconventional musicians
like Arto Lindsay, Anthony Coleman, Christian

Marclay, alongside jazz and classically-trained
virtuosos like Carol Emanuel, Bill Frisell, Zeena
Parkins. The studio was across the hall from
the Rockettes rehearsal room and, our band of
downtown misfits would commune with the dancers
in the hallway between takes, sharing coffee and
cigarettes.

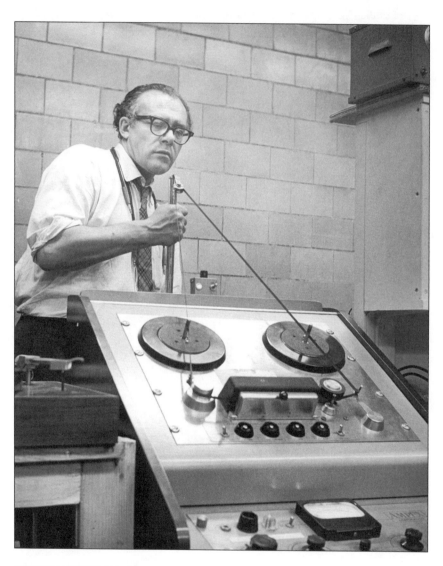

FIGURE 11.1 VLADIMIR USSACHEVSKY
SOURCE: COLUMBIA UNIVERSITY

11

VLADIMIR USSACHEVSKY

Unknown date, 1985

Born in Manchuria, deep in Inner Mongolia, composer academic Vladimir Ussachevsky grew up playing gypsy music in nightclubs and accompanying silent films. He emigrated in the early 1930s to California and earned a scholarship to Pomona College to study counterpoint and composition. During his postdoctoral studies, he was invited by New York–based composer Otto Luening to work under him at Columbia University in 1947, where his job was to take care of the classroom tape recorders. When a large Ampex 400 tape machine arrived at the department in 1951, Ussachevsky did what any curious student would do—fiddle with the machine. Along with fellow student Peter Mauzey, he created the first electronic music compositions, resulting in a concert at MacMillan Auditorium on May 5, 1952.

Over the next few years, Ussachevsky and Luening forged a bond and started inviting other composers to work with them. To expand their facility, they joined forces with Milton Babbitt and Roger Sessions at Princeton to create the Columbia-Princeton Electronic Music Center.

Located in Manhattanville, the center is housed on 125th Street in a gray industrial factory. When I met Ussachevsky, I got a tour and then sat down to speak with the big, burly Manchurian. What a thrill it was to be surrounded by the RCA synthesizer and all its knobs, tape loops, phasers, and oscillators.

Tall and overwhelming at first, Ussachevsky is passionate about what he does. At the time, he had just visited George Lucas's California studios. He was concerned about where electronic music was heading yet resigned to the supremacy of the computer. He said, "The computer is here not only to stay but to progress."

B. WENTZ: I read that you didn't hear Bach until you were nineteen years old, when you emigrated from the Soviet Union to California in the early 1930s. How did that impact you?

VLADIMIR USSACHEVSKY: I was very interested in him. I studied composition with a very famous organist, Clarence Mader of the First Presbyterian Church in Los Angeles, and he was a Bach specialist. He introduced me to a collection of short Bach compositions called *Inventions and Sinfonias*. And I thought these inventions were fascinating. Perhaps you can't imagine, but evidently, there are many parts of the world where nobody has ever heard of Bach!

B. WENTZ: I find that extraordinary.

VLADIMIR USSACHEVSKY: I lived in Manchuria, in far east Russia, and we didn't even have a phonograph player in the house. My mother taught me piano. I knew [Georges] Bizet. I knew Beethoven, I knew Mozart, and I knew Chopin. But it wasn't until I was sixteen that I heard a recording of an orchestral piece, "Danse Macabre, Op. 20" by Saint-Saens. I was really taken with it. And then Erik Satie's "Variations on a Theme." That was an incredible experience. My interests had been thoroughly Romantic, with the exception of Mozart. So when I heard Bach, it sounded quite different.

B. WENTZ: Your first major work was a choral piece in a neoromantic style, "Jubilee Cantana," and several years later, you opted to do postdoctoral work at Columbia with Otto Luening, which would take you in a radically different direction. The two of you created the Columbia-Princeton Electronic Music Center in the mid-fifties, with a studio on 125th Street. The last time we spoke, you mentioned that the place had been used for nuclear research?

VLADIMIR USSACHEVSKY: I think they were more focused on radar. At the time, the only space the university could provide us was on 125th Street, in a former milk factory. It was already occupied by Riverside Research, which was a very, very large research organization connected with Columbia, and which was doing some military work.

Dr. Cyril Harris, the acoustical engineer who designed Avery Fisher Hall, was at Columbia at the time, and so he designed the studio. He had to build walls and start from scratch, bring in electricity, and so on. And then we had to build special facilities on campus at McMillan Theater for our concerts.

B. WENTZ: When you were at the center with Luening, you were mainly focused on tape music, but by the late 1950s, RCA leased the center the most advanced synthesizer available at the time, the Mark II. Did anyone there compose pieces on it?

VLADIMIR USSACHEVSKY: Luciano Berio composed a couple of pieces with it. And Milton Babbitt's piece "Philomel" also involved the RCA sound synthesizer. There were some others as well.

B. WENTZ: At that time, were you in touch with the other electronic music studios, such as the San Francisco Tape Music Center on the West Coast?

VLADIMIR USSACHEVSKY: I knew Morton Subontick and had heard there was a tape studio in San Francisco, so I went to see it. And there, I encountered the first synthesizer produced by Buchla. I came into the studio and I saw a sequencer clicking away, producing patterns of sounds, and said, "That's the end of electronic music." It meant that we were now going into automation. In other words, it was the beginning of automation replacing the hand craftsmanship of tape music.

B. WENTZ: Years later, in 1968, you began using computers. How did you view them as musical tools, given that you're such a hands-on composer?

VLADIMIR USSACHEVSKY: I had two or three opportunities to work with computers around then. One of the systems I used at Columbia was the so-called groove system, which was essentially a computer driving a synthesizer created by one of our students at the center, Robert Moog. In that role, I consider computers very valid and very important, from the standpoint of a marriage of computer and analog studio. In other words, the computer is a controlling instrument and has many different functions, but the main thing is that with the memory having become so cheap, you can deposit concrete material in a computer, and if you have the skill and the proper software, you can manipulate that easier than rewinding and cutting tape.

The interesting thing about computers also is that it makes it possible to control the mixed media better than anything it's ever done before. So you can control video versus sound, control lights with it, and synchronize it with music, and so forth. But as a sound-generating device, it is undoubtedly the present instrument. And so some people prefer for it to control digital synthesizers, while others prefer to work within the computer itself on the programming to alter and produce sounds, such as Paul Lansky at Princeton, who is very, very good at it.

B. WENTZ: You mentioned mixed media and video. You've composed a number of scores for film and TV. One of them, a short film called *The Boy Who Saw Through*, stars a teenage Christopher Walken. Do you have any interest in doing more film work?

VLADIMIR USSACHEVSKY: Well, that was in the sixties. I did the music for a film adaptation of Satre's *No Exit* with actor Viveca Lindfors. That was probably the longest dramatic film with electronic music that had been produced at the time. It was an hour and a half. I also collaborated with Otto and two of our first students at Columbia, Pril Smiley and Alice Shields, on a television documentary called *The Incredible Voyage*. And I did a nine-minute short film based on my 1968 work, "Computer Piece No. 1."

B. WENTZ: Have you heard Boulez's piece, *Repons*, which was written for computer and electronics?

VLADIMIR USSACHEVSKY: Oh yes, I've heard it five times. I think that it is a piece which demonstrates the advantages of precision that you can achieve with computers. I heard it in its original version, which was only twenty minutes, in 1981. And then I heard it in its next version in Paris, which was forty minutes long. The rumor is that it's going to be eighty minutes!

B. WENTZ: You're working on a number of commissions right now, yes?

VLADIMIR USSACHEVSKY: Well, yes, but . . . let's return to the fact that the electronic valve instrument of Mr. [Nyle] Steiner was something I was more interested in because it is a very versatile instrument played in real-time and was controlled in real-time. So I have written and recorded a piece called "Divertimento" [released in 1983 on Gramavision]. And I was suddenly blessed with commissions, which are mainly interested in the same old thing that you mentioned at the beginning of this interview, that is, changing the sounds of conventional instruments and recording them with real instruments. So I have a piece for oboe and oboe-changed sound. I have a piece for brass and a quintet in brass-changed sounds. Then there's a brass quintet piece coming out on CRI Records, And I'm now commissioned to write a string quartet—which is a formidable assignment, And a piece for the one-hundredth anniversary for Pomona College.

B. WENTZ: Do you care to use computers yourself?

VLADIMIR USSACHEVSKY: Yes, I do. I will do it increasingly, except that everything now, of course, is done with mini-computers. I do not think I am going to get involved with a mainframe computer or with a specialized computer. I worked with those at Stanford, and I enjoyed it enormously, but I can't afford to become a real expert on that machine. It will take a year of my lifetime.

Vincent Chancey
Artist

I moved to New York right after graduating college with a degree in classical music. As a child I wanted to learn jazz, which was my love. After arriving in New York I only played classical music for the first few years. Then I began studying French horn with jazz horn virtuoso Julius Watkins. He taught me how to work with bands, but then I expanded on my own. I joined the Sun Ra Arkestra, whose level of creativity was a huge inspiration, and played with them until the early eighties, when I toured extensively with the Carla Bley. There are so many musicians' names buried in my memory. But some that I remember well from the eighties include Butch Morris, his brother Wilber Morris, the Frank Foster Big Band, Muhal Richard Abrams, Arto Linsey, Ahmed Abdullah, David Murray, and many others. If I wasn't in New York none of this would have been possible.

One of the places I really remember well was Joe Papp Theater. They were doing a lot of new music concerts at that time. I played there with Sun Ra, Carla Bley, Sam Rivers, Monty Waters, and Leroy Jenkins and more.

ORIGINAL KNITTING FACTORY AT 47 E. HOUSTON ST., 1986
SOURCE: PHOTO BY JOSH DORF

THE YIN-YANG MERGER WITH
JAMES LO, WES VIRGINIA, FAST
FORWARD, KUMIKO KIMOTO, AND
YUVAL GABAY AT PS 122, 1990
SOURCE: PHOTO BY MICHAEL
BELENKY. COURTESY OF FAST
FORWARD

GUY KLUSEVIK, ROULETTE, POSTER
SOURCE: COURTESY OF THE AUTHOR

THE MAGENTA LIGHTS BY MARIAN ZAZEELA, AN INSTALLATION AT THE 6 HARRISON STREET DREAM
HOUSE, NEW YORK CITY, WITH LA MONTE YOUNG PERFORMING *THE WELL-TUNED PIANO* ON THE DIA
CUSTOM BOESENDORFER IMPERIAL GRAND, 1981
SOURCE: PHOTO BY JOHN CLIETT. COURTESY OF MELA FOUNDATION

SEMANTICS (ELLIOTT SHARP, NED ROTHENBERG, SAMM BENNETT)
SOURCE: PHOTO BY HOPE MARTIN. COURTESY OF NED ROTHENBERG

FAST FORWARD
Ensemble ⟶

with
YUVAL GABAY
KUMIKO KIMOTO
JAMES LO
WES VIRGINIA

Tuesday January 27, 9pm $7
Paula Cooper Gallery
155 Wooster Street, NYC

FAST FORWARD ENSEMBLE AT PAULA COOPER GALLERY, 1990
SOURCE: COURTESY OF THE AUTHOR

89.9 FM

	MON	TUE	WED	THUR	FRI	SAT	SUN	
5am								
						JAZZ 'TIL DAWN		6am
	DAYBREAK EXPRESS — Jazz —					GUNJANA Music from India	L HEURE HAITIENNE	
8:20								8am
9am	BIRD FLIGHT—THE MUSIC OF CHARLIE PARKER						AMAZING GRACE —Gospel—	9am
	IN TOUCH — News & Public Affairs							
9:30								
	CEREAL MUSIC —Classical —					SOUNDS OF CHINA		10am
							MOONSHINE — Bluegrass —	
11:55								
noon	Newsbreak							noon
	OUT TO LUNCH Jazz					THE MIDDLE PASSAGE	COWBOY JOE'S RADIO RANCH	
								2pm
	AFTERNOON MUSIC —New Music/Classical—					LATIN MUSICIANS SHOW		4pm
						SOMETHING INSIDE OF ME — Blues —	JAZZ PROFILES	
5:50								
6pm	Newsbreak							6pm
	JAZZ ALTERNATIVES NY's Longest Running Jazz Radio Program					TRADITIONS IN SWING — Jazz —	CARIBBEAN MAGAZINE	8pm
								8:30
							COMPOSED ON THE TONGUE	
9pm								9pm
	LATE CITY — News Magazine —				Live from THE WEST END		STUDIO A	
9:30								9:30pm
10:00	LAUGH TRACK	HONKY TONKIN'	FIRING LION	THE AFRICAN SHOW	STREET SAMBA	OPERA NIGHT AT WKCR	American Musical Theater	
10:30			NUEVA CANCION Y DEMAS Central American Update					
11:00	NEW MUSIC SMORGASBORD	TUESDAY'S JUST AS BAD — BLUES —		CARIBBEAN RHYTHMS	THE MAMBO MACHINE			midnight
1am							IN ALL LANGUAGES — Music of the World —	
	TRANSFIGURED NIGHT — New Music							2am
						JAZZ 'TIL DAWN		
5am								
								6am

LOU REED AND JOHN CALE, BROOKLYN ACADEMY OF MUSIC, *SONGS FOR 'DRELLA: A FICTION*, 1989
SOURCE: PHOTO BY RISE. COURTESY BROOKLYN ACADEMY OF MUSIC

TOM CORA, ZEENA PARKINS, FRED FRITH, CBGB, 1985
SOURCE: PHOTO BY JAMIE LIVINGSTON. COURTESY OF ZEENA PARKINS

POWER TOOLS: BILL FRISELL, RONALD SHANNON JACKSON, MELVIN GIBBS, 1988
SOURCE: PHOTO BY STUART NICHOLSON

ERIC BOGOSIAN DRINKING IN AMERICA

P.S. 122 1ST. AV. + 9TH ST.   INFO: 477 5288
AUGUST 2,3,4 8 THRU 11 15 THRU 18 9 PM

ERIC BOGOSIAN, *DRINKING IN AMERICA*, FLYER, 1985
SOURCE: COURTESY OF THE AUTHOR

MEN IN DARK TIMES, ERIC BOGOSIAN, THE KITCHEN POSTER, 1982
SOURCE: COURTESY OF THE KITCHEN

WAYNE HOROVITZ AND THE PRESIDENT (HOROVITZ, ELLIOTT SHARP, DAVE TRONZO, DAVE HOFSTRA, DOUG WIESELMAN, BOBBY PREVITE)
SOURCE: PHOTO BY TONY CORDOZA

EAR MAGAZINE COVER, AUGUST/SEPTEMBER, 1986

SOURCE: COURTESY OF THE AUTHOR

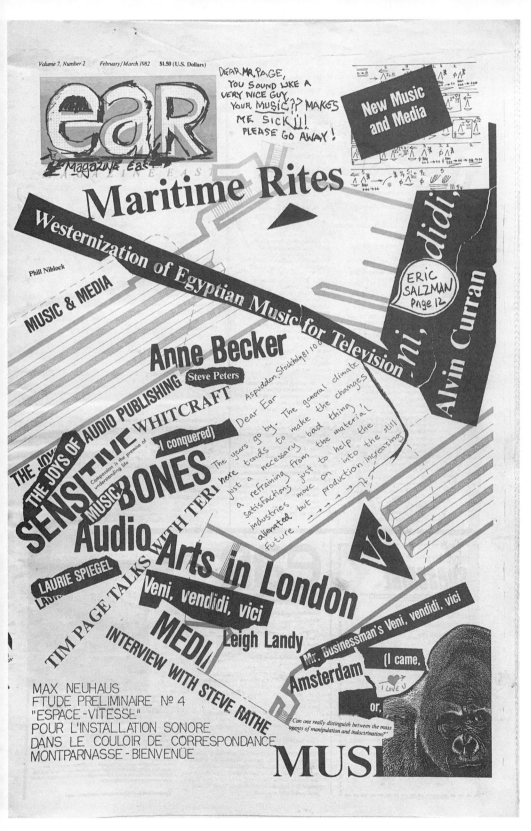

Volume 7, Number 2   February/March 1982 $1.50 (U.S. Dollars)

eaR
MAGAZINE EAST

DEAR MR. PAGE,
YOU SOUND LIKE A
VERY NICE GUY
YOUR MUSIC?? MAKES
ME SICK!!!
PLEASE GO AWAY!

New Music and Media

Maritime Rites

Westernization of Egyptian Music for Television

Phill Niblock

MUSIC & MEDIA

ERIC SALZMAN
Page 12

Alvin Curran

Anne Becker

Steve Peters

THE JOYS OF AUDIO PUBLISHING

WHITCRAFT

(I conquered)

Compassion is the premise of understanding life

SENSITIVE

MUSIC BONES

Audio Arts in London

LAURIE SPIEGEL

TIM PAGE TALKS WITH TERI

Veni, vendidi, vici

Leigh Landy

MEDI

INTERVIEW WITH STEVE RATHE

Mr. Businessman's Veni, vendidi, vici

Amsterdam

(I came,

I LOVE U

or,

Can one really distinguish between the mass agents of manipulation and indoctrination?"

MAX NEUHAUS
ETUDE PRELIMINAIRE № 4
"ESPACE-VITESSE"
POUR L'INSTALLATION SONORE
DANS LE COULOIR DE CORRESPONDANCE
MONTPARNASSE - BIENVENÜE

MUSI

Aspudden, Stockholm 81 00

Dear Ear

The years go by. The general climate
here just a necessary bad thing!
a refraining from the material
satisfactions just to help the still
industries move on into the
alienated but production increasing
future.

EAR MAGAZINE COVER, FEBRUARY/MARCH, 1982

SOURCE: COURTESY OF THE AUTHOR

Volume II, Number 3, November 1986

EΛR
MAGAZINE OF NEW MUSIC

$2.00 (US) Worldwide

OLU DARA

PHILIP
GLASS

BOSSI &
SALANT

VINCENT
CHANCEY

A. LEROY

GRETCHEN
LANGHELD

LINDA
BOUCHARD

TERI LYNNE
CARRINGTON

EAR MAGAZINE COVER, NOVEMBER, 1986
SOURCE: COURTESY OF THE AUTHOR

New Wilderness Foundation, Inc.
325 Spring Street, Room 208
New York, New York 10013
Volume 8, Number 5
March 1984
$2.00 (U.S. Dollars)

EAR MAGAZINE COVER, MARCH, 1984

SOURCE: COURTESY OF THE AUTHOR

MIKEL ROUSE: BROKEN CONSORT, THE KITCHEN, FLYER, 1985
SOURCE: COURTESY OF THE AUTHOR.

NEW YORK POSTCARD, 1984
SOURCE: COURTESY OF THE AUTHOR

SOUND FACTORY, 1990
SOURCE: PHOTO BY ALICE ARNOLD.

COMPOSER, DRUMMER WILLIAM HOOKER
SOURCE: UNKNOWN

TAPE RECORDER MUSIC

Otto Luening · Vladimir Ussachevsky

Sonic Contours · Fantasy in Space · Incantation
Invention · Low Speed · **Poem In Cycles And Bells**

Ronald Clyne

SOUND IN SPACE

CACOPHONIC

OTTO LUENING AND VLADIMIR USSACHEVSKY, *TAPE RECORDER MUSIC* ALBUM COVER
SOURCE: UNKNOWN

JOHN CAGE MEETS SUN RA IN CONEY ISLAND
SOURCE: COURTESY OF THE AUTHOR

RHYS CHATHAM AT ROULETTE FLYER, 1986
SOURCE: COURTESY OF THE AUTHOR

STEVE LACY, SAMM BENNETT, TOM CORA AT KNITTING FACTORY
SOURCE: UNKNOWN

PART III

THE COMPOSERS

Notable Contributors
of Contemporary
Musical Repertoire

FIGURE 12.1 ANTHONY DAVIS
SOURCE: STUART NICHOLSON

12

ANTHONY DAVIS

August 7, 1983

T he African American composer and pianist Anthony Davis has always
been a pleasure to run into in New York. He exudes an air of laid-back
chill. He is always congenial and approachable, yet heady and profound when talking about music. His compositions—often built around complicated, constantly changing atonal lines—have been embraced by both the jazz
and New Music communities. He has written numerous operas and released a
variety of recordings of his octet, Episteme.

Davis's father, one of the first Black English professors at Princeton, was a
jazz fan. So growing up in New Jersey, Davis started teaching himself jazz on the
piano. He studied formal classical piano at Yale, where he met jazz trumpeter Leo
Smith. After graduating, he came to New York City in the late 1970s to hone his
"free-jazz" skills and sought out Cecil Taylor to perform in the city.

He visited WKCR-FM to discuss the chamber music of Episteme, his
octet group made up of members from New York's free jazz scene, that was a
mix of improvised and composed music. Their self-titled album was released in
1981. Sitting in the interview chair, his afro seemed as high as the ceiling, and his
conviviality was infectious. During this time, the popular jazz label Gramavision
(who released La Monte Young's *Well-Tuned Piano*) took a liking to Davis and
began releasing his jazz ensemble recordings in 1983.

B. WENTZ: We just heard the song "Graef" off of your 1978 record *Of Blues and
Dreams*. That came out a year after you moved to New York City from New
Haven, Connecticut. By then, you were a well-known free-jazz pianist and had
begun experimenting with different types of improvisation. What's the improvisational structure of that piece?

ANTHONY DAVIS: The improvisational structure was pretty simple. You're free to use a different mode from the composition itself, but basically, it was an interactive piece where only three out of the four performers could play at a given time. So the emphasis was on forcing your way into the improvisation. Each player had to force his way in, and someone had to drop out. At the time, I was really into structures like that, in which you could never get into any sustained kind of uni-directional energy, which I didn't want. I wanted the thing to be more scattered, more fragmentary, where each improviser just contributes a small idea and then is forced out and made to change direction. That's what I was after in that piece.

B. WENTZ: Let's talk about your current group, Episteme. The octet came together performing at The Kitchen and includes that space's musical director George Lewis on trombone. We're going to play a piece that takes up most of the group's self-titled record and has several sections. It's called "Wayang IV"—a term associated with Gamelan music of Southeast Asia. You recorded versions of this previously?

ANTHONY DAVIS: We played an earlier version of the duet version, but this is sort of the more mature form in the sense that I worked on developing more themes. It really developed out of some of the improvisational ideas I had in the duet piece. And then the third section is more of a counterpoint to the theme from the first part.

B. WENTZ: So it sounds like a lot of themes from your older works are reworked or improvised on in the newer pieces?

ANTHONY DAVIS: Yeah, I like to bring my old clothes along. I really like taking music and developing it, figuring out new ways to play it, and hearing new compositional ideas coming out of the old ones. I guess it sort of justifies what I've done before and also links the newer work to the older stuff. But in the "Wayang" series, especially, there are lots of things I felt I wasn't ready to develop yet. And with the *Episteme* album, I was able to develop ideas I really wanted.

I never look at the recording as the final product. I look at it as simply one step in the process of creating a work. The creation of "Wayang IV" was a process of three or four years of working on these ideas and working with players to develop ensemble techniques to realize those ideas and play it.

And it's still developing in our performances. I think in maybe a more precise way than the mathematical relationships of all the different repeating parts. And things that I was subconsciously aware of when I did it in 1981, I'm more conscious of now. I learned a lot about music when writing "Wayang IV (Under the Double Moon)." I used that piece to develop a lot of my compositional ideas and to test a lot of things I was experimenting with. I was interested in creating a longer, more sustained form in which there's a sense of musical development within a composition rather than just a string of short melodic statements interjected with improvisation.

B. WENTZ: Are we going to hear more Episteme-style music—meaning a mix of improvised and written works, in the future, or are you moving into more scored, opera and symphonic works?

ANTHONY DAVIS: I'll be doing some concerts with that group. We'll be playing this fall at Brooklyn Academy of Music as a ten-piece, with Molissa Fenley choreographing dancers. And this summer, I'm going to do a piece for quadraphonic tape and sextet. I want to do a number of things. For example, the composer and multi-instrumentalist Earl Howard and I want to create more with the octet and sextet. But right now, I'm happy with the group we have, which includes Rick Rosie, Pheeroan akLaff, Warren Smith, Abdul Wadud, Dwight Andrews, Jay Hoggard, and Mark Helias.

Charlie Morrow
Sound artist, curator

My heroes are the artists I produced events and recordings with, such as Annea Lockwood, Pauline Oliveros, Alison Knowles, Don Cherry, Sun Ra, Asa Simma (Sami), Leonard and Mary Crowdog, Karin Bacon, Sten Hanson, Derek Bailey, Jerry Rothenberg, Jackson MacLow, the Four Horsemen,

I frequented the Ear Inn, Experimental Intermedia Foundation lofts, and private gatherings, yet on June 21, 1989, New Wilderness Summer Solstice did a performance with Sun Ra and Don Cherry where a parade of artists and all the horns of all the boats in New York Harbor came together. The rain hung back in the clouds and fog until the show was over, then let loose!

FIGURE 13.1 DAVID DIAMOND
SOURCE: JACK MITCHELL

13

DAVID DIAMOND

April 1985

avid Diamond is one of America's most prolific composers. He's written eleven symphonies, ten string quartets, fourteen piano sonatas, ballets, film scores, and more. He achieved prominence early in his career, in the 1940s, with classical music that was melodic and deeply lyrical. But just over a decade later, his meticulously crafted works were eclipsed by the ascent of atonal and serial music, and traditionalists like Diamond faded from vogue.

Diamond, for his part, believed his prospects dimmed because of anti-Semitism and discrimination against his open homosexuality. This prompted him to leave New York City in the 1950s for Italy, where he stayed until the mid-sixties. Diamond also acknowledges that his career problems were furthered by his difficult personality. Emotional and strong-willed, he was prone to causing scenes. When a conductor for the New York Philharmonic wouldn't let Diamond in the hall during a rehearsal, Diamond punched him in the nose.

In the 1980s, Diamond's old-school Romanticism began to experience something of a resurgence, thanks in part to the support of various conductors. He visited the studio to promote his latest major work, Symphony no. 9.

R WENTZ: Your work gained national attention almost from the beginning of your career, in the 1930s and early '40s. Was your music at that time considered dissonant and atonal compared to what other American composers were doing?

DAVID DIAMOND: It was, and it was one of the reasons I left the Eastman School of Music in Rochester, New York, when I was still a teenager. I was really pushed up against the wall, so to speak, by the school's director, Howard Hanson. He said, "David, you have such a big lyrical gift, why don't you concentrate on that?

Why do you write such dissonance all the time?" And, of course, it struck me as very silly, because, at the time, I wrote a symphony in one movement, and it just sounds like Cesar Franck with wrong notes to me. It is in general very tonal.

B. WENTZ: And so you left to study with Roger Sessions in New York City.

DAVID DIAMOND: I had seen two of Sessions's pieces at the school library, and I was fascinated by them. A symphony and the "Black Masker Suite." I took them apart and tried to play them through. I had heard he was a remarkable teacher, and so, one Sunday I opened the *New York Times* and saw an ad saying, New Music School and Dalcrow's Institute. Scholarships offered. Which is where Sessions was teaching at the time. So I wrote away at once and sent lots of music I had written. I was only nineteen, but I must have written about fifty orchestral pieces by that point. I was always composing, even when I was a little kid. I got a letter back offering me a scholarship. And my poor mother was in tears—she didn't want me to go, she always thought of me as being a violinist and that was her whole dream. So once I was over that trauma, I left for New York City and eventually ended up living at the YMHA. It was cold as all get out—you turned down the heat to save money during the Depression. But I'm glad I stayed there. The library was very good, and there was a nice man who ran the music department, so he allowed me to work in the studio at night. I was up at four each morning to mop the floor for a dollar a day, which was the school's way of giving me a little extra money.

I met Sessions a few days after I arrived in the city. His influence on me was extraordinary in every way. First of all, Sessions was what I would call an intellectual giant. Anyone who has read his books on music knows that this is a thinking man, a man who took music very seriously and the problems of being a composer very seriously. And I remember the sentence that I always heard as a kind of life motif almost, was, "Deliver the goods and you will be well on your way." And that struck me rather strangely because I didn't have the courage to say to him, but I thought, "Well, why aren't you writing more music?" All I knew were those two pieces I had seen at the library in Rochester, the symphony and the "Black Maskers" choral pieces, and he had a violin concerto that had not been published. So those pieces were what the entire, let's say, oeuvre of Sessions. Later on, it hit me that maybe he doesn't write a lot because he is so self-critical. He certainly demanded a lot of me. He would say, "Now David, I think you can do much better here. Harmonically it's not clear. I think you can smooth this out very much and have a clear and more transparent harmonic texture, and the reason that you don't have that transparency is due to the fact that your chromatics are not very carefully gauged and your modulatory system is a little bit defective. Let's get that fixed up." And we would do lots of exercises in modulation. It was hard working with him because the lessons sometimes would go on for two hours. But really the only thing that bothered me is that there wasn't much enthusiasm. That was why I accepted Nadia Boulanger's invitation a few years later to study with her at Fontainebleau in Paris. I thought it might be a good idea since Sessions showed so little enthusiasm for my work. But I found out years later that was simply his way. He wasn't very enthusiastic about other people.

B. WENTZ: Before you left for Paris, you composed the music for two dance performances, one of which involved Martha Graham.

DAVID DIAMOND: When I was just a kid in Rochester, there was a hall at the Eastman School I enjoyed going to where they showed German silent movies. One afternoon, I opened the door and I saw on the stage three women rehearsing some kind of dance and moving in strange ways. I didn't know what a Denishawn dancer was at all. I had only known ballet movements. The hall was very small, and as I looked at the stage, there was this very strange member of the three who seemed to be dancing with her mouth open all the time, while the others had their lips closed. She had a very striking face with very deep eyes. I learned later that the woman on the stage that afternoon was Martha Graham.

Years later, in 1935, I was living in a little apartment on Perry Street, thanks to a scholarship I had been given to continue my studies, and I was invited to go to one of Martha Graham's recitals. There was the lady I had seen in Rochester, and I was so absolutely knocked out by her performance. I knew her music director at that time, Lehman Engel. He couldn't do the music for a piece she was working on, and so Lehman mentioned me to her and she asked me to come to her studio on Fifth Avenue. I went upstairs—it was in this art deco building, a very unusual kind of place—and she was there all alone. She made me take off my shoes and asked me to sit on the floor, and then she did this extraordinary dance for me. I had never written for a dancer before. And Martha simply said, "Here is the dance," but I thought, "My god, how will I remember what she's doing?" So I thought the only way I could do this is to have her go through the dance again, and of course, she did it exactly the same way as she did the first time except she added little things that made it even more interesting for me. So without saying a word, I took out my music pad and I thought I would bar out the number of phrases that I would need to cover a certain amount of movements, stupidly thinking that this is the way it would work. And I knew that it would have to be very asymmetrical because nothing seemed to want to come out in four or in three. So what I did was count out the number of bars by phrases and then asked her to stop, and then once I had those barred out, I would say, "Would you mind going on?" And she would go on from there until I had about seven or eight sheets barred out. Once I had that, I went back to my apartment on Perry

Street and I composed it. I wrote it for trumpet and piano, and one percussion instrument, and she did it, I believe, in October 1935. It was called *Formal Dance*.

Martha never mentioned a word about paying me. I was so absolutely thrilled to work with this lady from Rochester that I so admired, I never thought of remuneration. But a year later, I got a note asking me to come to her studio, and Martha handed me an envelope with $25 in it. I was so happy. I remember I went to the Hotel Lafayette and I had mussels.

B. WENTZ: In the 1930s and forties, several of your works were inspired by other artists. You wrote a ballet based on an idea by E. E. Cummings, an elegy for the French composer Maurice Ravel, and your Third Quartet, which is one of your most personal works.

DAVID DIAMOND: I composed it in memory of my dear friend, Allela Cornell, a painter who died far too soon. I wanted to write a eulogistic work ending with a kind of elegy. I remember everything about writing the first three movements. The last movement is the elegy, and I must have worked on it for five hours straight. I was living at the time in a loft on Hudson Street, and I remember it was around dusk. I had left the shade down on the window, and it was quite dark, and the streetlights were just coming on outside. When I turned on a lamp, I realized I had finished the entire movement, which ends in a very strange, suspended way, a very, very high kind of level of sonority, and I had a funny feeling that Allela was back in the room observing me. People heard the string quartet performed at the most recent Julliard festival, and almost everyone at that concert spoke to me about that last movement and how they were moved by it. When I hear it, I get the feeling that I'm right back at the loft on Hudson, sitting at my piano that night with Allela nearby. That's the only way I know how to explain that piece because I don't think there are words to explain that kind of feeling.

B. WENTZ: You left New York City for Europe again in the 1950s.

DAVID DIAMOND: I received a senior Fulbright professorship to the University of Rome in 1951. I stayed on and returned home for a while in 1956 because my mother was very close to dying, and I wanted to be near her. This was at the height of the McCarthy hysteria. Years earlier, in 1934, I had joined New York City's Pierre Degeyter Club, which was considered a socialist group since I came from a good socialist family. When I was a little kid, we used to bring canned goods to the amalgamated clothing workers to send to Eugene Debs in prison. We had all hoped that one day he would be president of the United States. He was a brilliant man who was in no way what you would call a dangerous anarchist, but of course, it didn't take much in those days.

When I came back to New York, we needed money to pay for my mother's hospital bills. My friend Leonard Bernstein suggested I play violin in the pit at a production of *Candide* he was conducting, and I would earn money quite fast. One day while I was sitting in the pit, I saw a woman approaching with a piece of paper in her hand. It was a subpoena to appear before the House Un-American Activities Committee. So I was stuck there for a while, my passport was taken away, and it was highly unpleasant. When all that was over and I didn't give any names, I wanted nothing more to do with the United States until things made more sense. So I returned to Italy and stayed there until 1965.

B. WENTZ: Did you notice any difference in your writing after experiencing so much personal and political upheaval?

DAVID DIAMOND: A great difference. Everything took on greater weight. I got more and more interested in the music of Arnold Schoenberg, who I had met in Hollywood when I was working there in 1949. And I got to know Anton Webern's music and [Alban] Berg's music, so there was a natural expansion of the chromatic texture compared to what was in the early pieces.

B. WENTZ: You've mentioned a desire to reach a sort of perfection in your work. In what sense?

DAVID DIAMOND: Structurally. To make the form work so well that there isn't a weak bar in it. And I think if that can be achieved in a piece then that is as close as one can come to perfection. Ravel seemed to me to be the composer who most epitomized that type of technical perfection. I have never been able to find a loose bar in Ravel.

B. WENTZ: You've been teaching at Juilliard since 1973. How do you find time for your own composing?

DAVID DIAMOND: I write during periods of vacation. I find that as experienced as I am, I can still get very, very nervous about getting work done. I am petrified that I am not going to get the orchestration done for my Ninth Symphony, and yet I sit down with a calendar and begin to figure out if I do so many pages from the end of Juilliard's term to, let's say, the end of July, I should have the first movement done. And then if I do so many more pages, I'll have the second movement done. It isn't too large a movement, so I should have the score in Mr. Bernstein's hands by the end of August or September.

At the same time, I foolishly accepted the commission for a flute concerto that will premiere next year. So there's this summer's work. But I'm finding my inspiration working at the top level now. I've never before had this kind of burst of energy. If you hear anyone tell you that the older you get, the harder it gets to write music—Aaron Copland used to say that all the time—I don't think so. I think it isn't an impression of getting old or becoming technically deficient, I think it's simply that burst. It comes or it doesn't.

Craig Harris
Artist

I followed the entire scene at the time in New York and frequented Sweet Basil's. There was a genre of crosspollination and you could catch people in many different settings. There are too many fond memories to name; if you were there, you would understand the beauty of the unscripted.

FIGURE 14.1 JACOB DRUCKMAN
SOURCE: HISTORIC IMAGES

14
JACOB DRUCKMAN
May 1983

I am waiting in the old-school linoleum-floored WKCR station for the maestro of the New York Philharmonic. Who would *not* be nervous? Here I am, this young twenty-something college student waiting for the musical director of the New Music Series called Horizons at the New York Philharmonic! One needs to make sure the station looks good even though it is littered with debris and smells like sweat and dirty socks. The record library is stuffed with spin-ruffled records and marked up with Sharpie pens. Whatever students are at the station at the time have no clue who is walking through the door. No one ever knows; in this case, a revered conductor.

Druckman dons a warm, welcoming smile. He's familiar with academic student-infested buildings, as he taught at six different schools. But here at Columbia, he appreciates the promotion of his forward-thinking festival called Horizons at the New York Philharmonic. Born in Philadelphia, Druckman attended the Juilliard School in 1956. He then studied with Aaron Copland and Peter Mennin at Tanglewood and pursued graduate studies in Paris, ultimately becoming interested in electronic music.

He won a Pulitzer and became the composer-in-residence of the New York Philharmonic from 1982–1985, where he initiated the Horizon Series in the summer of 1983. This very forward-thinking new music series ran for two weeks in New York and featured contemporary music aimed at the series title: "Since 1968, A New Romanticism?" Funded by Meet the Composer, a nonprofit focused on supporting music commissions (at a dire time when funding for the arts was being taken away), the series presented music by Luciano Berio, John Adams, David Del Tredici, and others. *New Music Box* said, "Over two weeks in June 1983, the Horizons festival boldly seized this moment, with six concerts of orchestral music, numerous premieres, several symposia, and a glossy program book. It was a box office phenomenon, with hundreds of people lining up outside Avery Fisher Hall to buy tickets on opening night."[3]

B. WENTZ: We just heard "Aureole" by Jacob Druckman, performed by the St. Louis Symphony Orchestra, Leonard Slatkin conducting. And that was composed in . . . I guess you should tell me what year.

JACOB DRUCKMAN: 1979. It was commissioned by Leonard Bernstein and the New York Philharmonic. Also, they took the piece on a tour of Asia, and it was one of the rare occasions where they took the composer along. So I got to go to Japan and South Korea.

B. WENTZ: Wonderful! Perhaps you can mention the programming of this year's Horizon festival in comparison to last year's and the challenges you face with programming contemporary music in a very traditional environment.

JACOB DRUCKMAN: As huge as these festivals are, there's no possible way to present all the music I'd love to. So while I was searching for music last year, I was also finding all kinds of pieces that found their way into this year's festival. If you remember, last year, we started with a theme that was based on my very firm conviction that there has been, in recent years, I would put my finger somewhere in the mid- to late-sixties, a major change. From around the time of the First World War, we moved into a period that most of us agree was a time of neoclassicism. That lasted until the mid-sixties, at which point, we entered into something new, in which we are now living, and for want of a better name, calling it the New Romanticism. So last year the festival was aimed at the New Romanticism.

We felt that this year, we could step back a bit and include some other music as well., There are people whose music is much more closely allied with music of the previous half-century. I would think of [Iannis] Xenakis that way, I would think of Milton Babbitt that way, for example. Both wonderful composers and absolutely worthy of notice, and yet not actually participants in the New Romanticism.

Also, this year we're doing a kind of festival within the festival. Out of our eleven concerts, three of those concerts will be devoted to music having to do with computers in various ways. Some of the pieces, for example, the Xenakis piece, is a piece in which the computer was used to make actual compositional decisions. Most of the pieces have computer-generated tapes where the computer actually manufactured the sounds. One of those three concerts is with orchestra and computer-generated sound, and that will be performed by the American Composers Orchestra, a wonderful freelance group that is unlike any other orchestra in the world.

B. WENTZ: How did you pick these people? Did they approach you?

JACOB DRUCKMAN: During the early planning stages of this year's festival, I had been thinking about doing something with computers, and in the midst of it had a call from Roger Reynolds. Roger said that he and Charles Wuorinen had been talking about doing a computer festival and were trying to find funds to do it in New York. And it occurred to them it might be fun to join forces with us.

And so we have the computer festival within our festival. In addition to the American Composers Orchestra, there's a concert with the Group for Contemporary Music, which is chamber music with computers. There are a few pieces for computer with just tape and no live performers. We'll do a piece by Joji Yuasa, the wonderful Japanese composer, who's just now finishing a piece for tape and piano. And Charles Dodge has done a piece for Joan La Barbara for voice and computer, so that will appear on that program as well.

B. WENTZ: Right now, we'll move to a piece by Jacob Druckman entitled "Windows," composed in 1972, conducted by Arthur Weisberger.

And perhaps you'd like to mention a little bit about this piece. I see here it was done for the Italian conductor Bruno Maderna, but I don't understand this, when it says—did you use chance operations, or aleatory, during the composing process for this piece? It says "we're simply part of the adventure of Romanticism." Now for me, aleatory and Romanticism are extremely far apart. I mean, of course, one is a title of music and one is a way of composing, but aleatory, when I always find that someone composes using aleatory methods, it's usually never compared with Romantic composition. So what is the connection there?

JACOB DRUCKMAN: It's not so much a connection as it is a conflict. In fact, conflict is very much the subject matter of the piece. I suppose the expression is acting out the spirit of the times or at least the feelings of this revolution that we are now calling the New Romanticism.

What this piece does use, yes, aleatory techniques, very thick, kind of contemporary structures, and, however, these structures are constantly cracking, or there are fissures in the wall. The title "Windows" refers to this image I had of chinks in a wall or like a sky full of clouds through which one can see every once in a while a bit of blue sky. And what one hears in this piece in those chinks, is music that is not really quotations but the feeling of some music remembered, some music of another time.

I know later years, for instance, Krzysztof Penderecki was talking about changes in his own music, and he said that during the sixties and the fifties, he had been going after this plunging racing forward to the new music—not rediscovering, but finding, things that no one had ever heard before. And apparently, he said that he was being nagged by the thought of where was the music that he fell in love with, that made him become a composer. I mean, this new music didn't exist. What was it that made him fall in love with music to the point where that's all he could do?

And this piece was exactly the same kind of action on my part. It was as though I was sort of exorcising all those ghosts, all those memories of older music, and little fragments of music that sounded like music that I love so much and are buried so deep inside of me.

B. WENTZ: Let's move on to a piece of yours from a few years earlier, "Animus II," which delves into electronic music.

JACOB DRUCKMAN: This also is very related to this change into inter-Romanticism. I think all of the composers of my generation—I'm thinking of people like Stockhausen, like Berio, like George Rochberg—each of us, in a different way, was struck by this change. I know, talking to composers in later years, that we all probably had the same feeling, that this was something that was happening only to us, and felt very peculiar about it. The rest of the world was plunging forward to this will o' the wisp modernity and somehow each of us was—

B. WENTZ: What did you feel the rest of them were doing?

JACOB DRUCKMAN: Well, we didn't know what each other were doing. I mean, we do find out rather quickly. Once a work is done, it's usually only a couple of years or perhaps even less before everybody else knows about it. It doesn't take as long as it took Bach to learn what Vivaldi was doing. But even with the communication, it's still while you're writing a work, nobody else is hearing it and nobody else is privy to your inner thoughts.

This work was part of my early experiences in the electronic music studio, you know, right here at Columbia, down in the bowels of Dodge. And it was in that studio that I first began to be aware of the fact that many ideas that I had held to be sacrosanct were beginning to crumble, and things that I had held to be kind of immutable truths were really no longer workable. And the things I thought I was interested in were not really those things that were exciting me. And part of it was just the simple reality of working with an electronic music studio.

If you're writing a string quartet or an orchestra piece, and you're putting little black dots down on paper, you're susceptible to the delusion that those black dots really represent music. Black dots are an idea. You write a black dot on the second space in the treble clef and you say that's an A. But when you go into an electronic music studio, you try to make an A.

It's easy to tune an oscillator up to 440, but then if you're going to be aware of the fact that there's an attack and a decay, and all these things we talk about in very intellectual mechanical terms, and yet in the long run, what it comes out to be is the impact of that sound. It was in the electronic music studio that I got to appreciate the wonderful sounds of human beings and how wonderful humans are, and all of the mistakes and the frailties and the strengths and the nuance of human expression. Just trying to make it and trying to imitate it.

So what happened is, I went into the electronic music studio thinking what I was going to do is get into a music of great exactitude and great precision and rhythmic complexity, and very shortly realizing that was not what I wanted. I'd made it, and listened to it, and thought it was terrible. And then was thrown back to those human sounds.

And this piece, "Number Two," has an interesting history of failures. I decided that I wanted to do a piece that used percussion and a female voice. And I had a simple image of vocal sounds that emerged from percussive sounds. Like, for instance, if you hit an instrument and have it emerge from a percussive sound, a human sound.

I thought, "Here I am in the greatest electronic music studio in the world, and I can make anything happen with my voice." Then, of course, you quickly discover that a male voice tuned up an octave is not a female voice. It's more like a chipmunk in popular music. And I said, "Well, I'll get a female voice and manipulate that." I asked a young lady who was a pianist in one of my classes at Julliard at the time, and I could not make anything interesting out of it. Intellectually interesting, yes, but not musically interesting.

I remember one day being very discouraged walking back from here over to the Julliard, which was then at 122nd Street, and bumped into a young lady who has now become the famous Barbara Marten, the mezzo, and at that point was a student in my second-year theory class. And she's saying, "Good morning, Mr. Druckman," with the wonderful voice of hers, and I said, "Hey, you, come with me." And I took her over to the studio and she recorded, just kind of directed improvisation.

So I asked her to improvise things. Be a child, be frightened, be this, be that. And at one point, I said, "Be seductive." And Barbara launched into this most incredible eroticism of about ninety seconds or so, and when she stopped, there was silence. And she said, "I want to leave." I said, "You want me to find you a taxi?" She said, "No, no, no!" Barbara would not listen to that tape for about a year or two. It probably was quite a personal epiphany for her.

There are two sections in the piece in which the improvisation is used, is treated electronically, and changed very much. In some cases, very heavy distortion is put in. But to my ear, at least, those noises contain that same human cadence and the same direction and the same rhythm, and eventually the same emotional impact.

Ben Neill

Artist, former music director at the Kitchen

I moved to New York in 1983, and before I
arrived, I had written to Jon Hassell, whose
work as a composer and performer blending
trumpet and electronics had been very inspiring
to me, and developing my own approach to
creating the Mutantrumpet. I met Jon soon after
I got to NYC. He was living in a storefront on
North Moore St. in Tribeca, which is now the
back room of Walker's Restaurant. I can still
vividly recall the extreme thrill of meeting him
and seeing his setup. Jon was the first person
who gave me positive encouragement to pursue a
career as a composer/performer, and while he
wasn't interested in a formal teacher/student
relationship, he shared some great insights that
continue to inform my work right up to today.

Jon introduced me to La Monte Young, who
I began studying and performing with. My
relationship with La Monte has continued up
to the present time, I have performed his
music extensively, and learning about just
intonation and tuning ratios was fundamental to
my development as a composer. La Monte's radical
artistic identity was extremely influential
on my overall concept of what it meant to be a
creative artist.'

The downtown scene truly shaped my musical direction and creative life during the 'eighties when my approach to being a composer/performer was in its formative stages. I was very passionate about the idea of blending popular music and art music influences into new amalgams, and that approach was very much in the air at the time. Both the collaborative camaraderie and the performance outlets were absolutely crucial to my creative development. My interactions with Jon Hassell, La Monte Young, Petr Kotik, Rhys Chatham, David Behrman, Nick Collins, and David Wojnarowicz were all extremely influential on me. We all lived downtown and had many casual and social interactions which were intertwined with the professional ones. I feel extremely grateful to have been living and working in lower Manhattan during those years, and the experiences continue to inform what I do today.

FIGURE 15.1 LUKAS FOSS
SOURCE: JACK MITCHELL

15

LUKAS FOSS

May 1, 1987

omfortably situated in his Upper West Side apartment in Manhattan, composer and conductor Lukas Foss spoke frankly about his life and the progression of his compositional style, from classical to pieces using chance operations and even some incorporating folk elements. We were periodically interrupted by phone calls and airplanes flying above while the amicable, erudite pianist explained how his father moved his family from Germany to the United States to start a new life, changing their family name from Fuchs to Foss. He proudly recounted the trek and acknowledged his father's foresight to relocate at the beginning of World War II.

A self-termed modernist who became close friends with Aaron Copeland, Foss was a child prodigy who attended the Curtis Institute in Philadelphia at fifteen and was even published by G. Schirmer at that same age. At Curtis, he became lifelong friends with Leonard Bernstein and later studied with Russian conductor Serge Koussevitzky and German composer and violinist Paul Hindemith. Although his music was more neoclassical, when UCLA's music department sought to replace atonal Viennese composer Aaron Schonberg, Foss was hired to rein in Schonberg's eccentric style. But, during his ten-year stint in Los Angeles, he stated, "I tried to free my students of the tyranny of the printed note." He wanted them to take chances, improvise, and open up to be true to their form.

In 1963, when he returned to the East Coast to fill the conductor position of the Buffalo Philharmonic, he was given the freedom to program groundbreaking works and promote twentieth-century music. During his seven-year period in Buffalo, Foss also started a student concert series at the Albright-Knox Art Gallery. During this time, he also wrote one of his most iconic works, *Baroque Variations*, an orchestral piece that floats in and out of a sort of "dream state." The piece references Bach, Scarlatti, and Handel and ends with a clanging cacophony. His composing style tested the limits of chance operations, introduced by John Cage and sometimes called aleatoricism, which allows the performer to make ephemeral decisions in the piece. Later, Foss even embraced minimalism and electronics. But Foss was not a critic of new music. He appreciated all styles and voraciously absorbed and excited audiences about new music.

B. WENTZ: You were born in Germany, then your family lived in Paris before moving to the United States in 1937. You enrolled in Philadelphia's Curtis Institute. Did your family move so you could study music here? You were considered a child prodigy.

LUKAS FOSS: I'd been composing music since the age of seven, but no, I suppose politics had something to do with it. I was fifteen years old, and Paris seemed too close to trouble—namely, to Germany. And so my parents decided to move to America. A move that I have never regretted. I am very grateful to my father for having predicted trouble at a time when many people didn't predict it.

B. WENTZ: What composers did you admire growing up?

LUKAS FOSS: You mean living composers?

B. WENTZ: Yes.

LUKAS FOSS: I had a long love affair with the classics, and the only composer that I liked at that time among the so-called moderns was the one who soon afterwards became my teacher, Paul Hindemith. But then, later on, I discovered Stravinsky and became a close friend of Stravinsky. And then I discovered Copeland and became a friend of his. And Charles Ives, whom I never met, but I'm very fond of, and so forth. That all happened later.

B. WENTZ: In the 1950s, you were teaching at UCLA, where you also founded the Improvisational Chamber Ensemble in 1957.

LUKAS FOSS: I didn't teach improvisation, but it started as a pedagogical project. I was trying to help my composition students through improvisation. But I didn't teach improvisation. We learned that together. We made it up together. It was really born out of an envy of jazz jam sessions. And I wanted to free my students from the tyranny of the printed note. And so I got on this kick, you might say, and it changed me, probably more than my students. It became very fashionable, and then there were all these improvisation ensembles, and then I dropped it. It taught me what I needed, and so I moved on.

I had a long love affair with the classics. It's called neoclassicism. And then, I became an avant-garde composer through this project at UCLA. Doors opened, and I drastically changed. So UCLA was about that transition period. And now, you might say I'm in a period in which I reconcile my earlier preoccupations with my avant-gardism, closing the arch.

B. WENTZ: And then you returned to the East Coast, where you became music director and conductor of the Buffalo Philharmonic Orchestra and founded the Center for Creative and Performing Arts at the University of Buffalo. You also started a series of new music concerts in the Albright-Knox Art Gallery around 1964. Was this started due to interest among the students?

LUKAS FOSS: Well, that was also a sort of first-time thing. We started these projects with a Rockefeller grant. My idea was that the young performer fresh out of school, instead of immediately going to some job, might do well to spend a year or two studying and performing new music and might find that that is really where he would like to spend the rest of his life. And so this center made history and lasted for fifteen years.

Now I don't think it exists anymore. But it was a very interesting, lively center that brought many Europeans and Americans to the cause of new music. But now Buffalo has also long since passed because I am now the conducting music director of two orchestras—the Milwaukee Symphony and the Brooklyn Philharmonic.

Both are very wonderful orchestras. Brooklyn is unusual in the sense that it is really not a year-round orchestra. It's more like a concert series. It's the best New York chamber musicians and soloists who play in that orchestra. In other words, the people who don't want to play in an orchestra are playing with me in Brooklyn. Milwaukee, on the other hand, is a full-time, fifty-week orchestra and quite marvelous. We're bringing Milwaukee to Carnegie Hall this spring. Then New York can decide just how good Milwaukee is.

B. WENTZ: Could you talk about the music program you're putting on in Milwaukee this summer?

LUKAS FOSS: That's another pet project of mine. Every year, we have a festival in Milwaukee, and every other year I wanted it to be a kind of one-man show for one composer, presenting him with a multimedia festival, as we did last year with Copeland, doing a ballet and a film and an opera and a symphony, and chamber music and song, piano pieces, and bringing the composer. It was actually a very touching event. It was the last thing that Aaron Copeland participated in. And so it was very beautiful to have him there.

So I thought, what on earth can I do now that would be of equal or greater impact than the last festival? So, I had this idea—How about an investigation of American sacred music? That is something that no symphony orchestra has tackled—it may have been tackled by a church, but we're thinking in terms of interfaith—Christian, Jewish, even Oriental, as long as it's written by, or conceived by, American composers.

So we're going to have some thirty American composers of various denominations and bring some of them to Milwaukee for the occasion. Bringing their music certainly. I think [David] Del Tredici, [John] Corligiano, and [Gian Carlo] Menotti will be there, and we will have premiers of Del Tredici and Corigliano, and we will present an opera of Minotti's called *The Egg*, and lots of other composers. And it will be very exciting.—very exciting.

B. WENTZ: Last year, as part of the New Horizons Festival in New York, you presented *Baroque Variations for Orchestra*. What do you think of the series, and why did you choose to perform a New Romantic piece that was composed nearly twenty years ago in 1967?

LUKAS FOSS: I didn't choose it!

B. WENTZ: Oh, you didn't?

LUKAS FOSS: No. They had a committee headed by Jacob Druckman, who chose *Baroque Variations*. I was astonished because who would have thought of the *Baroque Variations*, which is based on things by Bach, Handel, and Scarlatti? And so the last thing I thought was that they would choose that piece as an example of contemporary Romanticism, but I can see the point. It is romantic to go back to these three composers, use their notes in order to create a personal nightmare that has really nothing to do with them. I consider myself something of a misfit, and that makes me romantic. That's not the standard definition for Romanticism. If you call romantic going back to a traditional romantic style, that to me is nostalgia; that's not Romanticism. So it all depends. And we had panels at that point about whether there is a New Romanticism.

B. WENTZ: What do you think about that, especially as a conductor?

LUKAS FOSS: I would say, "No." There is not a New Romanticism, but that the idea of composing itself is a very romantic one, in a world where we don't know how long we will survive. To sit in your private chamber and compose beautiful new music is in itself such a romantic preoccupation that, of course, the composer is romantic, but I don't see a return to Romanticism at this very moment. It all depends on what you call *romantic*.

B. WENTZ: The composer Virgil Thomson once called you one of the "far-out" American composers, along with Milton Babbitt and Otto Luening. I think he was talking in the sense of your use of electronics. Do you consider electronics another instrument?

LUKAS FOSS: Well, I have sometimes used electronics, but in a rather primitive way, and often called upon my electronic colleagues to help me. Because the last thing that anybody could call me is an electronic composer. I have always favored the live performer over a form of music-making that does away with the performer. But there is, of course, such a thing as live electronics. That is, combining live music with electronics and electronic music has had an enormous impact on new music.

B. WENTZ: How did you decide to use electronics?

LUKAS FOSS: I'd written a piece, for instance, called "MAP," or "Musicians At Play," in which I originally had electronic tapes that I put together with the help of my friend Joel Chadabe, an electronic composer [and founder of the Electronic Music Foundation]. And then I discarded the tapes in favor of another procedure. He used electronic wizardry in a very primitive way in some of my works, namely as a kind of tape delay. That means that somebody will perform live, and it will be heard three seconds later or ten seconds later coming out of loudspeakers. Things like that have intrigued me, so I have not stayed away altogether from the electronic climate. But I don't think Virgil Thomson ever called me an electronic music composer.

B. WENTZ: No, but he called you "far out."

LUKAS FOSS: There are many other ways in which my music is far out.

B. WENTZ: How so?

LUKAS FOSS: Well, when you enter a certain no man's land of atonality, and you use various chance procedures, and you write music that has a certain crazy quality to it, then it's often called far out.

B. WENTZ: What do you think of Cage's works of chance procedures?

LUKAS FOSS: He's a very lovely influence on American music. . . . A very important influence, and a very wonderful mind, and he's been my friend for the last forty years.

B. WENTZ: Yes, It was very interesting to combine your *Baroque Variations* with Cage's prepared orchestra on *Concerto For Prepared Piano & Orchestra / Baroque Variations*. Was that your idea to put the two together?

LUKAS FOSS: It probably was.

B. WENTZ: That's the Nonesuch record from 1968.

LUKAS FOSS: Yes, the Nonesuch record. Yeah, now there, for instance, the question, which is more far out? *Baroque Variations* certainly is far out in the sense that the idea of a splendiferous destructiveness is probably the violence of it, you know? But I don't think it is.

B. WENTZ: I don't see how people could say it's violent and destructive.

LUKAS FOSS: They thought I was doing terrible things to my friend, Mr. Bach.

B. WENTZ. It seems a lot of modern composers nowadays go back to old pieces and they do variations on them.

LUKAS FOSS: Still, it's very different from the new classic procedure, which was to literally try to use it as a model and emulate the example. These are more like nightmares, so it's really quite—everybody uses it, I suppose, in a different way. We use it in different ways and with different connotations.

B. WENTZ: Speaking of which, the piece "Night Music," which is on your new Gramavision record, seems eerie, like a nightmare.

LUKAS FOSS: That's right, it's that combination that I now do, you know, of sort of tonal and then far-out and wild. There's that moment in it where the orchestra seems to be playing inaudibly, and then you have a choral audibly but in the distance. And the agitated music in the foreground, which is written into the score, is activity felt but not heard. It produces a strange feeling of crisis. People think, "What's gone wrong? Is it the recording?" You can't quite figure it out. Are you supposed to hear something you don't hear? Because you're very much aware of this activity. So that was fun.

B. WENTZ: There was an electronic compilation release on Gramavision around the same time, which was a mix of pieces by Ussachevsky, Cage, and Charles Ives called *At the Tomb of Charles Ives / Divertimento 1980–1981 / Party Pieces*. Was "Party Pieces" recorded before?

LUKAS FOSS: No. No one considered releasing "Party Pieces" before. Now that's a weird one because there is a piece where its four composers—Lou Harrison, John Cage, Virgil Thomson, and Henry Cowell—all wrote together these pieces. Sometimes one would write a bar, the other would write the next bar, and nobody put down who wrote what bar. But it's completely mixed up like a joint effort, like four people completely merging their effort into one. And they took it rather lightly. It was like a game, and therefore, it's called "Party Pieces." And I had the idea that it's about time that should be recorded. Why not?

B. WENTZ: When did you find out about the score?

LUKAS FOSS: I don't remember anymore. But you know, people send me something every day. I'm like a clearing house for new music, and it's almost too much. I mean, I have to tend to my own garden. I can't possibly keep up with it. But every day scores and cassettes arrive.

B. WENTZ: To go back a bit. There's a CRI record which has a recording of a string quartet and "Music for Six," recorded in the mid-1970s. Those pieces seem minimal in the sense that they're repetitive, but in the liner notes to the record, you said you don't think of them as minimal.

LUKAS FOSS: In the notes, I think I explained to what extent they're minimal. See, I don't like using one technique. I mean, I think it's naive to think that one technique will be like the magic key that opens up your music for you. I mean, what if Bach thought all you needed to do was write fugues? If you're primitive and you make yourself at home in just one little area, that could be very lovely, like [Conlon] Nancarrow does all his life long by playing the piano. That's wonderful!

But normally, your curiosity will lead you from one route to another, and you need many techniques. Even the twelve-tone system is not enough. It's just one of many, many possibilities and methods. I use minimal techniques. I use aleatoric techniques, twelve-tone techniques, you name it. Sometimes I use one and then I discard it like a scaffold that's no longer needed. So I have my own approach to techniques. And people who sit on a technique and form a school around it, well, that's polemic, and that's often very naive.

B. WENTZ: You've gone through so many phases in your music—improvisation, Romantic, contemporary. So what phase would you say you're in now?

LUKAS FOSS: Every composition, for me, is a solution to a new problem. I don't like to repeat myself. That doesn't mean that it's okay for someone else to repeat themselves, but not for me. I'd like to solve another problem with each composition. So it's always an adventure.

B. WENTZ: You also conduct and play piano. When did you perform last?

LUKAS FOSS: I performed last weekend in Milano. And I conducted from the piano. A piece by the German composer Paul Hindemith, "Four Temperaments," which is quite enough of a job just to play the piano part, let alone conduct it at the same time. So I keep up the piano but mainly in order to play Bach and Mozart. Hindemith, and Bernstein occasionally, or Foss, but mostly it's Bach and Mozart.

I don't give recitals, but I am very much a full-time conductor. So since I'm a full-time composer and full-time conductor, I have two lives. The trouble is, when you have two lives, you don't live. But once you've gotten to the point with conducting that I have, it's difficult to give up.

B. WENTZ: How long have you been conducting?

LUKAS FOSS: Well, I took lessons at the age of fifteen at the Curtis Institute with the great Fritz Reiner, and became assistant to Serge Koussevitzky. So it's been all my life.

B. WENTZ: Do you prefer to conduct new music or the classics?

LUKAS FOSS: When it comes to conducting, I'm like a fish in the world in of the classics because, after all, I've known a [Luciano] Berio symphony from memory all my life, whereas when I have to conduct the latest piece by Lukas Foss, I may have just written it, and so I don't know it yet. So my eyes are glued to the music lest I get lost in the score.

So the classical stuff, I do from memory, and I actually would say that when I conduct, I prefer doing the classics and the Romantic repertory because man has a double need. And that is, the need is, sure, to live in the present and explore the future but also to come back home, which means to have one big foot in the past. To make love to the past. That's really why I conduct. And to put a new search-light on that, to make it fresh.

B. WENTZ: Are you more aware of the audience response as a conductor or a composer?

LUKAS FOSS: Audience response is important to the conductor and not to the composer. As a composer, I don't care about the response, and as a conductor I do.

The performer is communicating too. The composer is communicating to an abstract though. It's a completely different form of communication. And you go deep into yourself and you come out with something that, whether people take to it and whether the critics like it or not, there's very little reality.

Robert Dick
Artist

I was transfixed by Evan Parker's solo music
back in the eighties. Steve Lacy's music was
very important to me in that period, too.
I was very involved with New Winds—the trio
of Ned Rothenberg, J. D. Parran, and myself—
as we opened up new musical territory using
the extended techniques and sonorities we were
constantly inventing.

   I went to a great many concerts at the
original Knitting Factory on Houston Street.
Very funky. Very relaxed.

   Living in NYC made playing in some amazing
groups possible: New Winds, duos with James
Emery and Steve Gorn, participating in John
Zorn's game pieces, Tambastics, and more. The
music was the consequence of the people making
it—and the particular and extraordinary mix of
personalities and talents stimulated my musical
growth in unique and very intense ways that
wouldn't have happened elsewhere.

FIGURE 16.1 PHILIP GLASS
SOURCE: ANN RONAN

16

PHILIP GLASS

February 5, 1981

In the 1980s, no other contemporary composer created more buzz among audiences and in the press than Philip Glass. His repetitive, minimalist style made classical music hip to younger audiences and mesmerized stalwart listeners. His music took its cues from the sustained tones of La Monte Young and Terry Riley's *A Rainbow in Curved Air* (1969) and echoed New York colleague Steve Reich's famed tape loop pieces. But Glass's subtle, shift-shaping chord progressions were entirely his own.

Glass grew up in Baltimore, where he poured over his father's record collection as if it were a canonical text. His formal schooling came at the Juilliard School, and he studied in Paris with Nadia Boulanger and Darius Milhaud. Around that time, Glass visited India and met Ravi Shankar and the Dalai Lama, whose expertise broadened his philosophical and sonic palette.

After returning to New York, he began performing small ensemble works in art galleries and for various avant-garde theater productions, including one he cofounded called Mabou Mines in Nova Scotia. Glass was attracted to the trance-like qualities found in Indonesian gamelan music and the soothing sitar of Indian music. His composing style began to bring in voices and electric keyboards. His 1971 composition *Music in Twelve Parts* was a pivotal four-hour piece that culminated in soprano voice under a twelve-tone theme and launched his definitive composition style for years to come. An upcoming performance of that composition at Town Hall was the impetus for what would be my first artist interview at WKCR. Even for a nineteen-year-old novice, Glass was an easy composer to chat with, with his quick wit, fast Martin Scorsese-like speech, tousled hair, and sad-eyed charm.

B. WENTZ: How would you describe your music?

PHILIP GLASS: That's always a problem. The ways that composers define themselves are broken down now, and that's a really good thing. It used to be called avant-garde music. Nobody calls it that anymore. Then we called it new music, but that could mean anything. So I think of it as concert music as opposed to, say, popular music. I was trained as a concert musician at Juilliard. I studied with Nadia Boulanger. I had a lot of academic training, so I came out of a world of notated, written-down music.

But in a certain way, my music is what you would call abstract music in the sense that it's music about music. Now, there are certain things about my music that have generated a lot of interest and a large audience: It's high-energy, and there's a strong rhythmic profile. So it's very accessible to people who come out of listening to rock music. We play in both concert halls and in clubs, but I don't think anyone mistakes us for a rock act. So I think of it as concert music that is very parallel to the popular music of our time.

B. WENTZ: You have a series of performances coming up at Town Hall here in New York. One of them is a five-hour concert of the experimental opera *Einstein on the Beach*, which you conceived with director Robert Wilson in 1976. It's a landmark work. Why not put on the whole opera, with singers and actors?

PHILIP GLASS: It's just not practical to put the whole thing together again. That's a little frustrating, but it's also frustrating not to be able to hear the music at all, either. So I'm doing an unstaged concert version of *Einstein*. All the music is there, and I think the theatrical content of the music is still there. The full trilogy did about thirty performances in 1976: Twenty-eight were in Europe and two were at the Metropolitan Opera House in New York. At the time, it was considered too renegade or maverick to find much of an audience. Now I'm talking with some European opera houses that are seriously thinking about producing *Einstein* again. That way, we would not be financially responsible for the production, which was the real killer with that piece. The thing about *Einstein* was that it really tied me and the ensemble up for a couple of years—playing it, rehearsing it, staging it, performing it, and then recovering from it. Basically, operas should only be put on by opera houses; they're just too expensive. It's like making a movie or something.

B. WENTZ: Is your work generally more popular in Europe?

PHILIP GLASS: Every major theater piece I've done has opened in Europe and then come to America for only one or two performances. Now with *Satyagraha*, my latest opera, which is partly based on the early life of Mahatma Gandhi, that opened in Holland and it will be here at the Art Park this summer and next year at the Brooklyn Academy of Music. There has been more interest in that opera because I wrote it for an orchestra and a chorus. *Einstein*, in the context of the world of opera, was considered a very weird piece. [The opera does not have a plot, and it was written for an ensemble.] In the context of the music world that I live in, it was not considered that weird of a piece. It was just another step in the work that I was doing.

B. WENTZ: What can people expect from this new one compared to *Einstein*?

PHILIP GLASS: I think they better give up any expectations. It doesn't sound like the son of *Einstein*. The music of *Satyagraha* really is, I would say, unrecognizable, except I don't think anyone could hear it without knowing that I wrote it. And the language of the opera is a language that I chose for its sound value: Sanskrit, which is a beautiful vocal language. Most of the Indian music you hear, when it's sung, you're hearing Sanskrit. When I was looking for a text for the opera, I picked up the *Bhagavad Gita*, which is a Hindu scripture that Gandhi based a lot of his thinking on. And I decided to use that text—which is written in Sanskrit—as a commentary on the action that we see on stage so that the singers are actually singing in a language that we don't understand. For me, when I hear opera, I find that the literal content of the language is always a problem. Even when operas are in English, I find I understand maybe 40 percent of what they're saying, and I can never hear the music because I'm trying desperately to hear the other 60 percent that I can't understand, so I get torn between literary comprehension and musical comprehension. It's not a very pleasant experience. So in my own operas, I just separate the content of the language into the sound and the meaning. The sound is what we hear. The meaning is often, like, in a book that came with the opera, just like in a regular libretto that you get when you go to an opera house, you quickly read the synopsis before the lights go down for the first act.

B. WENTZ: You recently produced an album by the New York post-punk band Polyrock. How does that fit into the scheme of what you've been doing?

PHILIP GLASS: I was interested in doing it because I had never done a pop record before. I've had a lot of friends in pop music, and I've always liked pop music. I'm more inclined to go out and hear a new wave band like Polyrock or an old new wave band like Talking Heads than go to Carnegie Hall and hear the League of International Composers or whatever the heck they are. I don't listen to that very much.

I got the idea of producing a pop record from Brian Eno. We were talking, and he told me how he really liked producing records, and he thought it might be fun for me to do it. I didn't think about it too much until RCA came to me and asked if I was interested in producing a rock band. I said, "Well, if I like the music, I might: We ultimately decided on the New York band Polyrock. I like them a lot. They play new wave, they're young guys, they have a lot of energy. It turned out that they knew my music and had been to hear my concerts—which isn't surprising. We're all in New York, and a lot of young people come and hear my music.

The only problem I had was that it took a really long time to make that record. It was a good month of work, which for me is a lot of time. I enjoyed doing it, but I have a lot of things I want to do on my own. So I'm not really looking to produce more rock records.

B. WENTZ: Eno's *Ambient 1* album shares some traits with the soundtrack you did for the documentary *North Star* about the sculptor Mark di Suvero. For the film, you composed short pieces that include repetitive melodies. I was wondering if that album got more airplay than your other work.

PHILIP GLASS: I wrote short pieces to go with sections of the film that were montages of di Suvero's sculpture, so the names of the pieces are named after the sculpture. I looked at pictures of the sculpture, and I wrote music in the way that you would write music for a dancer. But instead of looking at a dance or thinking about movement, I thought about the sculpture. So they were like musical portraits. They happen to be short pieces because that's how the movie went.

Virgin Records was very keen to do that soundtrack—I'm sure they were thinking that these were shorter pieces and therefore easier to put on the radio and easier to sell. Whereas more difficult pieces of mine, like *Music in Twelve Parts*—which is nearly three hours long—have been much harder to get recorded. The *North Star* record, which was done in 1975, sold more copies than any other record of mine until the *Einstein* record came out in 1978. And the pieces on that soundtrack were really just little sketches. Not that they weren't important, but it's not the same thing as a major work. I think it's good to find the kind of audience that will maybe listen to *North Star*, and then maybe later on they will listen to *Einstein* or *Music in Twelve Parts* or some of the other things that are heavier and longer and more complex. It's a good opener for a lot of people.

B. WENTZ: Will you do more music for film or other multimedia?

PHILIP GLASS: I'm involved in several things right now. I'm doing the music for a beautifully shot documentary called *Koyaanisqatsi*, about the decay of cities and the contradictions of technology in the modern world. Kind of heavy sociopolitical stuff, which I vaguely understand, but I liked very much what they were doing. There are no words in that film at all. It's just images and music.

I'm also working on a third opera now, and I have a kind of chamber opera that I did last year that will be done in New York sometime in the spring. It's called *The Panther*. It's a piece I wrote for six voices, violin, and viola. It's like a chamber opera for voices and a few instruments. So that's kind of like a small opera.

B. WENTZ: How would you describe the direction of music in general right now?

PHILIP GLASS: It's very hard for me to say because I'm less of a listener than other people at this point. I remember talking to the composer Moondog years ago. He lived at my house for about a year in 1970, and I got to know him pretty well. He was telling me about these pieces he did as a young man that would last all night and that changed rhythms and that went on and on and on. I said, "Moondog, that sounds great, what happened to those pieces?" He said, "Well, there I was leading the pack, and I turned around and no one was following!" So the thing is, I know what direction I'm going in. I'm not sure whether other people are with me or not.

Don Byron
Artist

The Knitting Factory was my home. I considered it to be very much like the Third Stream at NEC [New England Conservatory]. I enjoyed hearing world music, downtown bands, improvised music. There was nothing I thought about doing that I couldn't present there.

During this period, I worked with the four guitar players—Vernon [Reid], Brandon [Ross], [Bill] Frisell, and [Marc] Ribot—pretty much simultaneously, while playing in the Ellington band, Reggie Workman, Craig Harris, and Mario Bauzá. So many interesting artists, all in one place. I followed Robert Schumann, Joe Henderson, and Luis Perico Ortiz. At that time, I could work different gigs pretty much anonymously.

FIGURE 17.1 STEVE REICH
SOURCE: JACK VARTOOGIAN

17

STEVE REICH

October 17, 1984

Steve Reich is a New York-based composer renowned for his gorgeous, trance-like ensemble and tape compositions that build on arpeggios, looping, and real-time instrument phasing. One of his most formidable pieces, and a cornerstone in the history of tape music, is his 1966 composition "Come Out," which uses the voice of Daniel Hamm, one of the Harlem Six, a group of young Black kids who were put on trial for the stabbing death of a clothing store owner. The recording begins with a four-second snippet that loops Hamm's voice until it's just grunts. The process and fluidity of the composition perfectly exemplify Reich's understanding of emotional build, effectively accomplished in his earlier piece "It's Gonna Rain," in which the phrase, spoken by a Pentecostal preacher in 1964 at a rally in San Francisco's Union Square, was recorded by Reich and looped over and over again until just intonations of words can be heard.

Reich was born in New York City but grew up in California. He attended Cornell University and studied composition at the Juilliard School and then returned to California to get his master's in music composition at Mills College. There, he interned with French composer Darius Milhaud and Italian sound-collagist Luciano Berio. When Reich visited the newly formed San Francisco Tape Music Center, he met numerous like-minded theorists, such as accordionist Pauline Oliveros, Morton Subotnick, and one of the early founders of the minimalist style, Terry Riley. Riley invited Reich to play on his masterwork, *In C*, whose "rhythmic pulse" would become the basis of much of Reich's music.

Reich's other influences include modal jazz, and Balinese gamelan and African rhythms would shape one of his pivotal works, 1970's "Drumming," where the layering of rhythm and percussion instruments is at the forefront.

I met Reich at his apartment in downtown Manhattan. Tall and handsome, Reich speaks very fast and is very direct—except when speaking about his former colleague, fellow minimalist composer Philip Glass. He evaded my questions about their infamous falling out and how they haven't spoken since.

B. WENTZ: Let's start with your journey from the East Coast to the West Coast and back again.

STEVE REICH: I went to Cornell from 1953 to 1957, and then I studied composition with Hall Overton for a year before I went to Juilliard. I'm a New Yorker by birth. I went to San Francisco to get out of New York. I had been out West as a child because my parents were separated and my mother spent a lot of time in Los Angeles. She was a singer and a lyricist. She wrote the song "Love is a Simple Thing" and sang it on Broadway.

In any event, I ended up enrolling at Mills College to get a master's degree. While I was there, some interesting people passed through. There were my teachers, the French composer Darius Milhaud and the Italian composer Luciano Berio, and Phil Lesh, the bass player for the Grateful Dead, audited a lot of classes and we became very friendly. Lesh, at the time, was a very talented composer; he wrote these Stockhausen-esque pieces at his desk. Then one day, he showed up with a group called the Warlocks, which subsequently became the Grateful Dead.

It was the period in San Francisco after the beatnik thing was over and before the hippies arrived, so there was actually a lot of artistic work going on. For instance, Ramon Sender and Morton Subotnick had just formed the San Francisco Tape Music Center, which I became involved with.

B. WENTZ: So electronic music was just coming out at the time.

STEVE REICH: It was just beginning. The Tape Music Center was involved in presenting what was called electronic music or musique concrete, which is made out of real sounds. I was working in musique concrete at the time. One of the first pieces I did after graduating from Mills was called "Livelihood," which was made of sounds I recorded in a taxi cab that I drove. Around the same time, Terry Riley came back to San Francisco from Europe, and at the center, we put together the first performances of *In C*. I helped him put the ensemble together for that performance and played in it myself. That had an enormous influence on me.

B. WENTZ: One of your earlier pieces during that time was your tape loop piece "It's Gonna Rain."

STEVE REICH: I did that in January 1965. I had recorded a Black preacher in San Francisco's Union Square preaching about the Flood. I had two tape recorders with tape loops of him saying, "It's gonna rain." Both loops were the same length, and I ran them on two machines at the same speed. I tried to line them up, but I noticed that if I didn't touch them, the different motor speeds caused a change of phase to happen and the voices would separate. They would go from being in unison, to completely out of phase, and then back into unison. It was its own musical structure.

B. WENTZ: You used the idea of "phasing" in a number of pieces after you returned to New York in 1966.

STEVE REICH: I did two more tape pieces in New York, "Come Out" and "Melodica." There was a period of feeling like a mad scientist. I felt like, "Yes, this is really fascinating, this gradual change of phase, but can it be done with instruments?" Because if it couldn't, then it's not really music. I went to the piano and recorded myself playing a repeating pattern, played it back on a tape loop, and started playing the piano again myself. What I wanted to do at the piano was to move very slowly from being in unison with the tape loop, to being one beat ahead of it, then hold, then very gradually move two beats ahead of it, and so on until I was back in sync with the loop. And I found, to my surprise, that while I couldn't do it as perfectly as I did using tape recorders, I could do it, and it was interesting.

The next step was to get rid of the loop entirely. So one night, my former Juilliard classmate Arthur Murphy and I went out to Fairleigh Dickinson University, in New Jersey, on the eve of the very first concert we ever gave because we didn't know where else we could find two pianos. And we wanted to know if phasing could be done by two people, playing simultaneously, without any tape. And we did it! That was very exciting.

Out of that came a series of pieces using phasing techniques with just instruments—"Piano Phase," "Violin Phase," and "Phase Patterns," which featured four electric organs. And then I said, "OK, enough of this," and there were no phase pieces after that.

B. WENTZ: Around the time you were doing phase pieces with live instruments, you began collaborating with Philip Glass. How did the two of you connect?

STEVE REICH: In March of '67, I put on a four-piano version of "Piano Phase" at the Park Place Gallery in Soho. At that concert, we also presented the tape pieces "It's Gonna Rain" and "Come Out." That concert got an enormous amount of attention. It was reviewed in the *Village Voice*, and people like Robert Rauschenberg came. That really put me on the map.

Philip and I met at that concert. We had met before when we were both at Julliard, but we weren't close. Anyhow, Philip said he'd like me to hear some things he was working on because, judging from what he heard that night at Park Place, he thought I might find them interesting. He showed me a string quartet, which is certainly not what you know him for now. But he was beginning to get into repetition, and I suggested that he ought to go further and systematize it. He tried a number of things, and then, around 1968, he did a piece called "One Plus One," and that was really the beginning of his work. The next piece that followed was dedicated to me. It was called "Two Pages (for Steve Reich)," which subsequently became "Two Pages."

B. WENTZ: That piece was retitled after the two of you famously had a falling out. What happened?

STEVE REICH: At the time, around '68, I said to him, "Look, I think what you're doing is very interesting, let's get an ensemble together, I'm glad to play in it." When he gave his concert in 1969 at the Whitney, the musicians were him, me, Arthur Murphy, John Gibson, James Tenney, and he had brought Richard Landry.

And it stayed that way through 1970 when it became clear that something was happening and we were getting some work. Then there was a little ugly scene, the ensemble divided, and some tensions began.

B. WENTZ: Around that time, you visited Ghana to study with drummer Gideon Alorworye. What sparked your interest in African music?

STEVE REICH: I was a drummer when I was fourteen, and at Cornell, I made a living playing in bands. I swept that under the rug when I went to Juilliard because, at the time, being a drummer wasn't really the thing to be. So I went back to learning keyboards. It wasn't until 1969 that I made peace with the fact that I loved drumming and I had rudimentary keyboard technique, so in some of the later phase pieces, I began drumming on the keyboard.

I went to Ghana in 1970, but my interest in African music really began at Mills when I learned about a book called *Studies in African Music* by the British scholar A. M. Jones. He had spent decades in Rhodesia and later worked with a Ghanaian master drummer in London and created a technique to produce the first full scores of African music. I had heard African music, I knew that it swung, that it was exciting, and it was very rhythmic, but I had no idea what those musicians were doing. Those scores made it possible to look at African music as a structure. They showed these repeating patterns, put together mostly in what we would call 12/8 time or divisions of 12/8, so that the downbeats didn't coincide. That was quite a bit of fresh information for me in terms of a compositional method.

I went to Ghana to study those structures first-hand by playing them. What I learned there encouraged me to go in the direction I wanted to go in, which was to make acoustic music in a period when electronics were very strong and to make percussion the dominant voice in the music. It was like a big pat on the back, with someone saying, "Yes, this stuff can be incredibly complex in texture and sound, and you're not a lunatic."

B. WENTZ: When you returned to New York, you wrote "Drumming," a percussion-driven piece that seemed to mark a transition out of phase music.

STEVE REICH: What happened was this: I became involved, very early on, with a very radical kind of rhythmic procedure, which generated the pieces "Violin Phase," "Piano Phase," and "Phase Patterns." And during that period of time, let's say roughly from about 1965 to 1971, which is when I wrote "Drumming," everything else was made subservient to hearing that rhythmic process.

Starting in '71, certainly by '73, I began to reconsider both the harmonic development and the orchestrational development that had been shoved aside because now the rhythmic procedures were like gut-level automatic. They were going to happen one way or another. They didn't need my riveted attention. It would be boring and repetitious in the worst sense of the word for me to just grind out another phase piece. So I began to look at the neglected areas of the Western tradition's gifts to their musicians, which is the enrichment of the harmony and the enrichment of the orchestration, and I've been focused on that ever since.

B. WENTZ: In 1974, you wrote *Music for 18 Musicians*, one of the first in a series of pieces for larger ensembles that use "pulses," or modules of acoustic sound. It also incorporates elements of Balinese Gamelan music.

STEVE REICH: I studied Balinese music at the Center for World Music in Berkeley and in Seattle. This was in '73 and '74. I studied and taught my own music when I was out there those summers. I would give concerts, and the people who came were musicians like Lakshminarayana Shankar, the Indian violinist who became a friend of mine, and the Indian percussionist Ramnad Raghavan gave me an analysis of my music. So that was the first time I could present my music in a context where non-Western musicians could hear it. That was very positive.

B. WENTZ: You have a concert coming up this fall at the Brooklyn Academy of Music of a large piece called *The Desert Music*, which you premiered early this year in Cologne, Germany. How did that work come about?

STEVE REICH: The musical director of West German radio, Wolfgang Becker, approached me at a performance there a few years ago about putting on a large orchestral choral piece. I said I would think about it, and then back in New York,

I had a conversation with Harvey Lichtenstein from BAM, who thought it was a great idea. So first, I wrote a small piece called "Vermont Counterpoint," which helped me bring some things to "Desert Music." Then I had the idea of using the poetry of William Carlos Williams for the choral text. I discovered his work when I was seventeen, and there was something about it that really got to me. When I went through his books again, I found I was really drawn to his later work, especially the book called *Desert Music*. The parts I used from it were laid out in a way that became the structure of the piece: Fast, moderate, slow, moderate, slow, moderate, fast. And then I went to the piano and composed the harmonies for the first movement, second movement, and third movement, which then recurred in other parts of the piece. Finally, I composed all of it. It took about a year and a half to put together, including the purely orchestral stuff.

B. WENTZ: Your work is generally defined as minimalism. How do you feel about that term?

STEVE REICH: The term is already an historical fact, so whether I like it or not is beside the point. It came probably from the British musician and critic Michael Nyman in about 1970, and what he and other people were originally referring to were the similarities between a scattered style of music made by a group of composers and the work created by artists like Frank Stella and Donald Judd. So minimalism means me, Philip Glass, Terry Riley, La Monte Young, and other people who will surface in the future.

If you want to get serious about it and say, "Well, does it describe your music?" I would say, "If you want to describe some of the early pieces—'Piano Phase,' 'Violin Phase,' maybe 'Clapping Music'—as minimal, then yes." There's only one chord, there are multiples of the same instrument, the harmony and the orchestration are constrained to the rhythm. But starting with "Drumming" and "Music for Mallet Instruments, Voices and Organ," and certainly with *Music for 18 Musicians*, the term is no longer descriptive because there's too much going on. But I see its purpose, and it could have been worse. If it had been called something like trance music, I would have been much more upset.

Samm Bennett
Artist

Among the many folks that were on what's called
"the downtown scene," the most intriguing ones
with were the people I played with—guitarist/
violinist Hahn Rowe, Yuval Gabay (from Israel),
and Kumiko Kimoto (from Japan). We soon felt
the need for more harmonic/melodic personality
in the music, and Hahn was a great fit. Hahn
was, in my opinion, one of the freshest and most
intuitively creative musicians on the scene
at that time. I've always been in awe of his
musicality.

The very early days of the East Village
avant-music and performance scene shine in
my memory. Basically 1983 through '86 or so.
Things just seemed so fresh and so open: the
possibilities seemed infinite.

PART IV

THE ICONOCLASTS

Eccentric
Thought-Provoking
Performers

FIGURE 18.1 KELVYN BELL
SOURCE: BRUCE JOHNSON

18

KELVYN BELL

March 10, 1987

The Black Rock Coalition (BRC) is a New York City group of African American musicians whose members proved to the music industry that rock music was not just white. Although the Washington DC hardcore band Bad Brains and LA-based Fishbone had come into the indie scene in the late 1970s and played CBGBs often in the early '80s, it wasn't until Living Colour, a member of the BRC, signed with Warner Bros. in 1988 that the press and listeners took note. BRC members have always been an amalgam of artists who play in one another's bands. They include Meshell Ndegeocello, Ronny Drayton, Vernon Reid, Greg Tate, Jean-Paul Bourelly, Jared Nickerson, Melvin Gibbs, Will Calhoun, Nona Hendrix, DJ Logic, Burnt Sugar, The Family Stand, and Sandra St. Victor. They all moved fluidly from one band to another. Kelvyn Bell was one such member whose funk band Kelvynator rocked the house night after night.

Originally from St. Louis, the laid-back guitarist Bell garnered his chops working with renowned saxophonist Oliver Lake. Bell met members of the Art Ensemble of Chicago (Hamiet Bluiett, Lester and Joseph Bowie) through a musician collective in St. Louis. He played with them extensively. Upon moving to New York City, Bell joined Joseph Bowie's band Defunkt, which fused jazz with improvisation and funk. He also got swooped up by saxophonist Arthur Blythe whom he played with for years.

In 1984, Bell started his own avant-garde funk group called Kelvynator. The band's core members—Alfredo Alias, Eric Person, and Bruce Johnson—were all fluid members who played with other New York bands. But together, the band's grooves and funky rhythm section got audiences dancing, which landed Bell gigs with James Brown's saxophonist Maceo Parker, Fred Wesley, Pee Wee

Ellis, and many more. He actively served on the executive committee for the BRC, getting involved in conducting and performing at many of their orchestra and benefit events. Here, Bell and I had time to talk about his present involvement and upbringing.

B. WENTZ: You've been connected with the Black Rock Coalition, a nonprofit organization that promotes Black musicians. Who are the active members these days, and what is it doing?

KELVYN BELL: Those are good questions. I haven't been actively involved with the organization. I'm more of an associate member, someone who supports the organization wholeheartedly in spirit. Some of the actual members are Vernon Reid, a group called JJ Jumpers, Melvyn Gibbs and his band Eye & I, and singer D. K. Dyson. The organization is basically trying to address the racism that exists in the music industry, which has been a big problem for a long time. Like, it's very easy for white artists to cross over into the Black market and make money there. But it's very difficult for a Black artist to cross over into the white market, even though those that have done so have done very well. Look at Michael Jackson or Lionel Richie. When you see how well they've done crossing over, you would think that the industry would be more interested in promoting Black cross-over groups, but it seems the opposite is true. It seems Black artists are held back until they can't be stopped anymore, like a force of nature.

So Vernon has taken it upon himself to address this issue directly. And I'm very proud of him for doing that.

B. WENTZ: You grew up in St Louis, Missouri. What kind of music were you exposed to there?

KELVYN BELL: I came up in a strong tradition of musicality. St. Louis is known for its blues and its jazz roots. People like Miles Davis, the trumpeter Clark Terry, the jazz guitarist Grant Green—they all come from there. In more modern times, there was Lester Bowie and his brother Joseph, you know, going into the more avant-garde music stream.

So growing up, I was exposed to all of these great musicians, going to clubs and seeing all different kinds of music. And you have to play those different kinds of music to survive as a musician, so I learned a lot.

B. WENTZ: What made you move to New York?

KELVYN BELL: I came to New York because I had done as much as I could in St. Louis, and I wanted to further my career. I wanted to make more money. I wanted to travel and see the world. So I came to New York at the advice of Joseph

Bowie and landed a gig playing with him and drummer Charles Bobo Shaw in the Human Arts Ensemble. I toured Europe with them in 1978. So that was my first trip to New York and my first trip to Europe. The whole situation was very inspiring.

B. WENTZ: You're generally known for your electric guitar playing. Could you talk a bit about how you use the electronic guitar in ensembles? When I've seen you play with other musicians, you've mostly played acoustic.

KELVYN BELL: Well, I play what is called an electric acoustic guitar, which is an acoustic guitar that has a pickup on it, which makes it electric. As far as my approach goes, I don't deal with the guitar as a guitar. I deal with it as a means of expression, you know? Like, I don't try to imitate other guitarists. I'm not trying to play guitar like Jimi Hendrix or someone else did. I'm basically trying to express just what's inside of me through the use of a guitar.

So the technique that I've developed in playing the instrument and the type of ideas I try to come up with, I don't think those are necessarily related to a guitar—except for the fact that I'm playing them on a guitar. Most of the time, I'm thinking of other things, other types of sounds. Sounds of nature, sounds of the city, sounds of my feelings, you know, things that are going on around me.

In terms of mixing that with other acoustic instruments, one example would be playing with saxophonist Arthur Blythe's group. That group was made up of tuba, cello, alto saxophone, and drums, and I play guitar. And that being such a unique set of instrumentations, my approach worked well in that group because I wasn't thinking in terms of like, well, I'm a guitarist, I have to do what a guitar would do. I thought more like, the music needs this, or it needs that, or I can place this or that there. That's how I would approach it. Because one thing, the cello is very similar to the guitar. We're in the same range, so in that group, I always had to try and do something different than Abdul Wadud, who is not an orthodox cellist.

B. WENTZ: You're playing now with the avant-funk group you formed in 1984, Kelvynator. What are you trying to do musically with that group?

KELVYN BELL: With Kelvynator, I'm developing world-class dance music that's a mixture of funk music, jazz, Brazilian and African music. I'm using a lot of the things that I developed playing with people like Arthur Blythe and Defunkt, and now bringing it to a much wider audience. Taking ideas from avant-garde music, and from avant-garde jazz in particular, and applying it to dance music. In the process, I hope to get people to understand some of the concepts, some of the sounds, some of the ideas that we're dealing with in this music.

B. WENTZ: Can you give me an example?

KELVYN BELL: Basically, it's the aspect of intuitive communication that's going on musically. Look at Black music historically. The blues was very emotional. When bebop came along, it got somewhat intellectual. Moving into avant-garde music, the focus shifted beyond the intellect and centered more on the intuitive aspect of the music. The interplay of communication between musicians. The ability to take certain abstract sounds and put meaning to them and communicate in a common language from one instrument to another.

So, what I'm doing with Kelvynator is bringing this element of intuitive communication to dance music so that people can have something that they can dance to but that they can also listen to and get a little more from than your average dance music. And by mixing in other styles of music from different parts of the world, I think it makes it more like world-class music.

B. WENTZ: What do you learn from working with Arthur Blythe that you're using in your group today?

KELVYN BELL: That's a very big question. When I first started to work with Arthur, I'd already worked with Charles Bobo Shaw, which had allowed me to develop a foundation in avant-garde music. So with Arthur, I was able to refine those ideas. Arthur gave me plenty of space to do as I please.

B. WENTZ: You mean improvisation?

KELVYN BELL: Yes. As a soloist and also as part of an ensemble. I was able to play many different textures behind Arthur, things that would blend with the tuba and the cello and the drums. There was an infinite number of colors that I could deal with. And Arthur, great musician that he is, he was able to handle all of that, like he wasn't intimidated by any of the things that I would come up with. In fact, he helped me make them more musical, which, in turn, helped me define what I was doing. Ultimately, I refined those ideas and sounds to the point that I felt I could take what I've learned and apply it to dance music.

B. WENTZ: Your current drummer in Kelvynator, Richie Harrison, also was a member of Defunkt, a hard-edged funk-fusion group started by Joseph Bowie that you played with in the early eighties.

KELVYN BELL: Defunkt was my first opportunity to take some of these avant-garde ideas and put them into a pop market, working rock clubs across the United States and Europe. It gave me the opportunity to see how different sounds affected a younger audience, a more energetic dance audience. And it gave me a chance to see exactly what worked, you know?

It was a great experience for all of us. Joe had suggested, "Hey, let's play some funk." So I said, "I'm going to play funk, but you know, I'm not going to come down and play this standard ice cream music that you hear on the radio. I'm going to play the most creative thing I can think of in a funky nature." So I did that. And it was very well received. Before I knew it, we were in Europe and we had an album out. I was amazed at the speed of success with that band. It was somewhat overwhelming.

And so that gave me the idea for Kelvynator. The thing that's different between Kelvynator and Defunkt is that I'm trying to include more types of music. Joe was basically dealing with jazz and funk, whereas I'm trying to incorporate Brazilian and African sounds, as well as Middle Eastern sounds. There's a song on the album called "Another Time in Space" that draws heavily upon Middle Eastern tonalities.

B. WENTZ: Are you working on anything else right now besides Kelvynator?

KELVYN BELL: Kelvynator is my center of attention. But I've been doing some projects with other people. I've been working with Steve Coleman, who's a very fine alto saxophonist. I've done two albums with him. I also just did another record by a fine guitarist by the name of Jean-Paul Bourelly. I think he's a very important guitarist in this whole new music movement.

B. WENTZ: There seem to be a lot of Black musicians right now who are moving out of jazz and trying different styles of music, like hard rock or Tropicália.

KELVYN BELL: What's happening is that right now, musicians around the world are in total communication with one another. I mean, something can happen in China, and we can know about it within twelve hours. Something can happen in Nicaragua, something can happen in Japan, something can happen in Honduras, or something can happen in Paris, and we can know about it almost immediately. The world is more connected than ever before. So artists are responding to that naturally. They're trying to create music now that incorporates more things than just their own cultural base. You see a lot of different cultures coming out of Black music now.

I think it's basically a need to communicate with the world and to recognize that we all have to live together on this planet. We have to deal with each other, and I think musicians especially are bringing people together. Plus, it's just a lot of fun to play Indian music, Brazilian music, or African music. There's just a need to break out of the same old pop formulas or same old jazz formulas. I mean, after playing every type of bebop song, it's like enough, let's move on to something else. Not to say that it's not a great art form. But I think Art Blakey once said, "Music is like a river. You have to let it flow and keep it going."

Brandon Ross
Artist

In NYC, I followed Leroy Jenkins, Oliver Lake, Ornette Coleman & Prime Time, Lawrence D. "Butch" Morris, and frequented Sweet Basil, Sounds Of Brazil, Lower East Side, Neither Nor, Knitting Factory.

ANY night at the Knitting Factory in the late eighties was a memorable night!

FIGURE 19.1 JEAN-PAUL BOURELLY
SOURCE: LONA FOOTE

JEAN-PAUL BOURELLY

January 27, 1988

Jean-Paul Bourelly has always been a pleasure to watch onstage. He champions a groove that any listener can connect to and enjoy because it borrows from many influences. Born and raised in Chicago by Haitian parents, Bourelly has always embraced other cultures' music, especially that of the African Diaspora that his parents turned him on to. He first learned music on the piano and guitar, but once he heard Jimi Hendrix, he ran out to buy an electric guitar and got hooked.

He moved to New York City in the late seventies and began playing with Roy Haynes, Olu Dara, Elvin Jones, Pharoah Sanders, McCoy Tyner, Elliott Sharp, and Cassandra Wilson. He formed the group Jean-Paul Bourelly and the BluWave Bandits, releasing *Jungle Cowboy* in 1987, with funky, groove-based songs such as "Trying to Get Over" and "No Time to Share." Although released on the JMT label and distributed by Polygram, *Jungle Cowboy* fell within the cracks of jazz, funk, and pop music during a time when genre categorization was imperative—at least for the record store bins.

In the eighties, Bourelly played the Knitting Factory when it first opened in 1987 on Houston Street, Pyramid Club, and places all around New York. At that time, the vibe was to play one show, head over to another, and possibly "sit-in" on a jazz gig. And Bourelly fit in everywhere.

B. WENTZ: Let's start with where your name comes from.

JEAN-PAUL BOURELLY: My family comes from Haiti. And I was raised in Chicago. So musically, I had a lot of influences. There's the Haitian music influences, and within that, you have the popular music called kompa dirèk, like merengue, and they commercialize it and do a lot of stuff with it.

Then my grandmother was into a lot of religious music. People here call it voodoo or whatever, but she was into Yoruba, which is West African folk music that also is popular in the Caribbean. And then, growing up in Chicago, you can't help but learn jazz because it's a great jazz town, and it's a great blues town and a great funk town.

As a kid, I did opera. My mother signed me and my older brother up. When I was like ten years old, I was doing opera, big opera, at the Lyric Opera House. We would go out there as extras. They cut my hair off and straightened it, and we made two dollars a night. I was doing *Cavalleria rusticana*, that's the Italian opera, and *The Barber of Seville*. Then in the day, they were teaching me gambling at school.

B. WENTZ: You can hear some of the music you grew up with in the music of your current group, BluWave Bandits.

JEAN-PAUL BOURELLY: The principle behind the music that I'm trying to do now is like, because the blues is so heavy, the feeling there is underneath all of the tunes, all the compositions, but we try to expand it and go off in different directions. Be it Afro-Cuban, be it pop, be it jazz, whatever. We combine them all and aesthetically make them one.

It's like surrealistic paintings. How a guy could put a bowl of cereal in one part of the picture and a dragon in another part of the picture, and maybe a cassette tape recorder looking like it's blasting some music, and some snakes down in the other corner. Even though those images are seemingly unrelated, a guy who really has an artistic eye and a certain aesthetic can put it together so you see all these things as being related. And everything on this earth is related. Boy, I'm getting spiritual. I don't want to do that.

But everything is related, you know? And that's where music is going, whether the purists like it or not. And I love y'all. So if y'all don't like me, I still love you. It doesn't matter.

But the people who are coming up now listen to all these different kinds of music. That's what we grew up with. Like, as I kid, I would hear one station go from playing James Brown to playing a Donny Hathaway song. For me, those are two totally different things. But you could hear them on the same station. And if you were blessed enough to be exposed to jazz in the sixties like I was, it was mind-blowing. Miles Davis went through four different styles over the course of seven years, and that was before he released *Bitches Brew*. So if you were exposed to these things growing up, it was a lot to take in. And as the people of my generation have blossomed into whatever it is they're doing, it just stands to reason that they're going to take in all these different influences and do something with them. If you don't, you would be cheating yourself, you know?

I come from a jazz background. That's how I came to New York when I was nineteen years old. I was playing guitar with a lot of jazz people. I played with Elvin Jones and McCoy Tyner and Chico Hamilton and some others. And so when people ask me, "Why don't you play the jazz thing?" I'm like, "If you can't see the connection between John Coltrane and Sly Stone . . ." See, jazz is basically an art form. But R&B can be an art form, too. And if you can get with that, then you can understand what I'm trying to say tonight.

B. WENTZ: Now, on our show tonight, you're playing whatever music you like.

JEAN-PAUL BOURELLY: Just music for people. The first piece is by Howlin' Wolf, called "Backdoor Man." I don't know what he meant by that, but it's a beautiful piece. The next one is one of my favorite pieces, also by Albert King, called "Crosscut Saw." He's the king of the electric freaked-out blues guitar. And then after that, we're going to play some Sylvester Stewart, or Sly Stone, from Oakland, California.

[Four songs play.]

B. WENTZ: Can you tell us about what we just heard?

JEAN-PAUL BOURELLY: These musicians we just heard are artists. They're taking music to a high art level. That's my opinion. And to hell with everybody else.

Now we're gonna listen to a group of brothers from Havana, Cuba. Los Papines. This composition is unique because it's all vocals. In other compositions, they're playing congas and timbales and everything else. I'm sure it will perk your ears up. [Song plays.]

B. WENTZ: We're back with Jean-Paul Bourelly. He is playing at the Knitting Factory tomorrow night. Two gigs at 9 and 11 p.m. And the Knitting Factory is at 47 East Houston Street, here in Manhattan. We're gonna play music from his new record *Jungle Cowboy* a little bit later. But right now, what are we going to hear?

JEAN-PAUL BOURELLY: This is Hector Zazou. He's French Algerian. Oh, you have the record right here!

B. WENTZ: Yeah. The station was playing him earlier tonight. It's great!

JEAN-PAUL BOURELLY: Ah, so we're on the same wavelength.

B. WENTZ: Apparently. Is this something from Mister Manager?

JEAN-PAUL BOURELLY: It is! I was going to play something from an album he did with the Congolese singer Bony Bikaye called Mr. Manager. But we don't have to play that.

B. WENTZ: We can play something if you'd like. I don't know if it's the same piece we played earlier.

JEAN-PAUL BOURELLY: The piece I wanted to play is "Nostalgie." Let's just play it. What we're trying to do here is just desegregate the music. You see what I'm saying? The Supreme Court has desegregated people, supposedly. Music should be the same way. Because there are so many different types of music in the world.

I remember when I first heard Charlie Parker on the radio. I was around seven or eight years old. And I heard this guy playing saxophone, and he sounded like some kind of martian. It sounded like martian music. And a cat was playing drums, and I said, "What is this?" I had never heard anything like it. Because I usually stayed in the middle of the dial, where the Beatles were playing.

But that night, I said, "Let me go way over here." And I heard this stuff, and I said, "Wow." And it started opening me up, like how much music is out here that we don't know about and that we're not conditioned to. And if people were more conditioned to understanding music, understanding art, maybe they wouldn't be out here killing each other, hating each other. Everybody's negative, you know what I'm saying?

They could stop racism right now. Everybody needs to understand that. They can stop all the ignorant stuff right now. Give the kids some art. Let them understand music and art and they'll grow up more open to people, you know? Just more open to life.

B. WENTZ: So let's open them up to some music.

JEAN-PAUL BOURELLY: Let's open them up to some music. The music we're going to play now is from Hector Zazou. He's a bad cat. Let's check it out.

[Music plays.]

B. WENTZ: What did we just hear?

JEAN-PAUL BOURELLY: Asha Bhosle. She's a very popular singer in India, along with her sister [Lata Mangeshkar]. That was just a tune just to show how everybody borrows. Even though the piece has a very Indian texture to it, if you hear the rhythms of it, it's very African. If you listen to some music from Pakistan, you can hear a heavy African influence as well. So music is here for everyone, and we're all dipping into the same pool and taking out what we want.

B. WENTZ: Does anybody call your music derivative in a bad way? That can happen if they hear a lot of other influences in it.

JEAN-PAUL BOURELLY: If you're sensitive, certain things will bother you, but nothing like that has ever stopped me from doing what I feel I'm supposed to do. I've changed musically. In my little short life, I've changed maybe three or four times. I'm talking about drastic changes, from playing certain styles of music to researching and trying completely different things. And with every change, you get some people and you lose some people. Certain people are open to change, and other people, you just have to leave them where you picked them up.

And after a while, you do build up a kind of callousness on you. When I first started seeing things written about me, it kind of got into my stomach, even though most of the things were good. It still got into my stomach because, you know, you spend all this time, and you write this tune, and your heart is bleeding. And then some critic comes along and says, "Oh yeah, that was a combination of so-and-so, so-and-so and so-and-so." You can get into really caring about that stuff, but that's a losing battle. People are always going to comment. And actually, you want them to comment. It's when they stop talking that you need to worry.

B. WENTZ: Should we play something from the new record?

JEAN-PAUL BOURELLY: This is unreleased music from my group, the BluWave Bandits. This first composition doesn't have a title yet, but it has something to do with some kind of passionate feeling. I don't know if it's sexual or if it's some kind of spiritual feeling. And I guess the next three or four pieces we'll play will be my original compositions. So here's the BluWave concept coming right at you.

B. WENTZ: I need the tape.

JEAN-PAUL BOURELLY: You need the tape. Oh man, I was segueing really nice.

B. WENTZ: I know you were.

[Three songs play.]

JEAN-PAUL BOURELLY: That was an original composition by yours truly, Jean-Paul Bourelly and the BluWave Bandits. It was called "Groove With Me." And it was about a woman I wanted to groove with. The tune before that was another original composition called "Baby I Wanna Buy You a Brand New Diamond Ring." That's pretty sophisticated stuff. And the one before that was the title track "Jungle Cowboy" from our new record, *Jungle Cowboy*. The first one was a song of mine that was previously untitled but, but I just named it "The Song of Passion" and whatever else.

Also I'm reminding everybody that we're going to be at the Knitting Factory tomorrow night. BluWave Bandits, and we're gonna be doing it to death, playing from the heart, you understand? So we want to see everybody down at the Knitting Factory. Wear all your hip stuff, whatever you got, multicolors, whatever color, come in with some art on. If you want a feather going through your head and some other stuff coming out your shoe, that's cool. Because if it looks good and you feel it, then you've got to wear it. Okay, I'm going to stop talking.

Ned Rothenberg
Artist

My local ringleader, John Zorn, with his
game pieces involved many of the most gifted
improvisers in a way in which we could all
meet and show our characters. Playing in his
piece "Track and Field," I had a chance to
play with Zeena Parkins, Bill Frisell, Arto
Lindsay, George Lewis, Polly Bradfield, Eugene
Chadbourne, Ikue Mori, Vernon Reid, and Wayne
Horvitz. Some of these folks are my friends and
collaborators to this day.

Roulette started in 1981 and remains central
to this day. Concerts at The Kitchen on Broome
Street were often important. That's where I got
a chance to play with Julius Eastman and Pooh
Kaye.

The Semantics' first gig was at the Cooper
Hewitt Museum, but we also played at CBGB's
and the Knitting Factory—three VERY different
venues. This kind of musical melting pot was
a hallmark of that time and, in many ways, is
still my modus operandi.

FIGURE 20.1 GLENN BRANCA
SOURCE: DEBORAH FEINGOLD

20

GLENN BRANCA

April 1985

T he avant-garde, no-wave composer Glenn Branca attracted listeners who enjoyed his very loud wall of sound created by his visceral
electric guitar riffs and the resulting overtones they made. His
unique blend of single-note progressions, which grew from his work with
theater pieces and later transformed into symphonies, all started in the late
1970s when he came to New York from Boston. Growing up in Harrisburg,
Pennsylvania, Glenn Branca began playing guitar at an early age, later studying theater in Boston at Emerson College. He headed for New York City and
became ensconced in the downtown scene in the late 1970s. Upon meeting
like-minded colleagues, he formed the rock band Theoretical Girls with Jeffrey
Lohn. He later joined guitarist Rhys Chatham's noise group, which laid the
groundwork for Branca's ear-blistering style. Volume became his instrument,
and his forward-thinking work with sound and guitar rubbed off on members of Sonic Youth (Thurston Moore, Lee Ranaldo), Swans (Michael Gira,
Dan Braun), and Ned Sublette, who all played with Branca before their respec-
tive bands were even formed.

Branca's earliest recordings, *Lesson No. 1* for electric guitar (1980)
and *The Ascension* (1981), with cover art by visual artist Robert Longo,
both demonstrate the powerful sound that multiple guitars, mallet guitars,
keyboards, and drums can have when tracks run up to thirteen minutes long.
This compositional idea transformed Branca's ability to score and record
long-form symphonies, which later premiered at the Brooklyn Academy of
Music and other established performing arts venues.

At the time of this interview, Branca had firmly crossed the boundary
between uptown and downtown music scenes, and Joseph Papp's Public Theater

had just commissioned him to produce a major theater piece, a nonnarrative work based on the harmonic series, for spring 1986. He was concerned about the way his music was portrayed. He did not want to be misunderstood but respected as a fine composer. Although he carried himself in a swashbuckling, disheveled way, New Yorkers loved him. Rhys Chatham and La Monte Young were fans. John Cage, the man who brought attention to "silence," appreciated his sensibility toward loud sound. Ironically, his influence on other musicians still remains to this day—Helmet, Flying Saucer Attack, Carsick Cars.

B. WENTZ: You studied acting and directing at Emerson College before forming your own theater group in Boston. Did you study music as well?

GLENN BRANCA: I was always flipping back and forth between music and theater, but I never thought I would become a musician, certainly not a composer. Since junior high school, I had always had tape recorders that my parents bought me for Christmas. Before cassette machines, there were these small reel-to-reel recorders. I produced a lot of tape collage pieces by taking, for example, a recording of my grandmother's birthday party, mixing it with acoustic guitar playing, and mixing that with a text.

B. WENTZ: In 1973, you started the Bastard Theater in Boston with John Rehberger, doing productions in a nonnarrative style, like Richard Foreman. I understand you would look for things on the street, such as bells, gongs, and other metal objects, to incorporate into theater pieces. This continued when you moved to New York in 1976 and started doing pieces with guitarist and composer Jeffery Lohn.

GLENN BRANCA: Yes. [Conceptual artist] Dan Graham was doing a performance at Franklin Furnace in Tribeca and invited me and Jeffrey to play as part of the show. We spent three weeks frantically writing music and finding musicians to perform the work, and I never returned to theater again.

B. WENTZ: So that was the beginning of the band Theoretical Girls?

GLENN BRANCA: Yeah. Jeffrey and I would come up with ideas that were so far out there you could hardly imagine it possible. But that was what the audience wanted. The rougher, the better; the more outside, the better. It got big so fast it was beyond belief.

B. WENTZ: You played together until 1981. What happened then?

GLENN BRANCA: The sets, the props, and the use of tape became so unwieldy that it finally got to a point where the band could not work anymore.

There were ideas I had in my mind but could never imagine realizing. "Lesson No. 1" and Symphony no. 1 are the first two recordings of these realizations—conceptual works with dramatic development incorporating seven to twelve musicians and creating a string orchestra performing on guitar and flat mallet guitar, which is a guitar played like a percussion instrument.

I also use octave tuning [making the open sound of each string and the sound of the twelfth fret (octave) the same], double octave tuning, and unison tuning, with every movement of the symphony incorporating a different instrumentation.

B. WENTZ: Last year, you debuted Symphony no. 5—"Describing Planes of an Expanding Hypersphere," which is a very atmospheric, beautiful building up of layered guitar piece, very different from your more jarring, clanging pieces that you've done previously. What prompted the change in direction?

GLENN BRANCA: I'm trying to achieve a sound of great depth, a transparent kind of depth. I'm not going for an impenetrable wall of white noise, which occasionally happens because of lacking technical facilities. The mallet guitars used in Symphony no. 2 made it possible to have hundreds of strings that were open [like on a piano] instead of having a hundred guitars. It's not a matter of having more guitars to create that atmospheric sound but of having more compositional control over the material and to achieve the sound that I want all at the same time.

It's also a matter of having a different attitude towards the guitar. There was a point after I started changing the tuning of the guitar and putting different strings on the guitar that I started to think of the guitar as a piece of wood with a microphone on it. In theater pieces, I was dealing with contact microphones and amplified sound. So it came natural for me to start seeing the guitar not so much as an instrument but as a microphone.

I am always going to work with volume, but I don't always work with extremely loud sounds—for instance, the first movement of Symphony no. 5, which starts out very soft, builds and, therefore, volume becomes an important aspect of the music; it becomes one of the instruments. When something gets louder, the sound changes, the timbre changes, the relationship of the harmonics changes, and the room becomes a large sounding box. As volume increases and decreases, the actual tone changes, almost a quarter tone. It's like the Doppler effect. The volume acts like a magnifying glass. You aren't even looking at the same thing. It becomes something totally different.

B. WENTZ: You have recorded and partnered with Josh Baer's Neutral Records and with John Giorno on his Giorno Poetry Systems label. Do you feel you could jump to a major label?

GLENN BRANCA: There is a point that independent labels can reach and one they cannot, will not, and will not be allowed to reach. If the commercial world is really only trying to appeal to a commercial sensibility or listeners who are interested in commercial work, how are they even going to know that another audience exists? In five to six years, I think there is going to be a very real, relevant, serious music scene in this country. But it is going to take a long time to develop because it has no support from the commercial world whatsoever.

B. WENTZ: But you've got committed audiences, you tour, and are being presented by the Brooklyn Academy of Music?

GLENN BRANCA: Noncommercial music is hard to get out there. I'm always losing money I don't have, which puts me in debt to somebody. The more deeply I go into debt, the more difficult it is to make the next step. On average, I lose $10,000 a year. That is the situation I have been in. People automatically assume that you are on the same level as Boy George if you play on the same stage he does. I got up there by clawing and scraping and beating my head against the wall. Usually, when I walk onstage, I don't have a cent in my pocket or in my bank account, and I don't know where I'm going to get the money to pay the musicians. It is a *very* real problem. It is not a matter of complaining, but it is irritating to me when people think the number of times your picture is in the paper is equivalent to the amount of money you have in the bank.

B. WENTZ: Are you happy with your music?

GLENN BRANCA: No! I have never been satisfied with any piece. It's just the way I am. The reason the music has developed the way it has is because it is based on a dissatisfaction with the way it sounds. It is always a matter of trying to get it the way I want it to sound. I like a piece better from a distance than I do at the time. If I waited until I had a piece of music I was happy with, I would never have performed once in the past seven years. There is an element that happens in a concert situation which has nothing to do with what I plan when I am writing a piece. Performance is a different thing; there are moments that I am happy, but as far as the composition and the sound is concerned, I have a long, long way to go.

Paul Shapiro
Artist

The early 1980s was a very flavorful time. In
the East Village there were many spaces that
had been vacant or were little used. Basements,
storefronts, small lofts could be rented for
not too much money. That led to many performance
spaces that were often run by artists themselves.
At the time a lot of people formed bands to play
in these spots. Many of them were new on their
instruments. But the sounds and the energy spoke
to the times and had a strong influence on me.

Around 1980 A7 opened on the corner of Avenue A
and Seventh Street in the East Village. He had a
stage, a sound system, a drum kit, and a couple
of amps. That meant that you could have lots of
bands every night. One band would finish and
jump off the stage and another would climb up.
There would be five or six bands a night or more.
Everybody got to do their thing, and we all got
to hear what each other were doing. It was great.
And I'll always remember the incredibly loud
feedback that came with the price of admission.

FIGURE 21.1 FRED FRITH
SOURCE: LONA FOOTE

21

FRED FRITH

April 13, 1983

WKCR-FM is notorious for its extended multiple-hour music celebrations of various artists. Past radio festivals include Sun Ra, John
Cage, La Monte Young, Miles Davis, Charles Mingus, and Max
Roach. They even do annual birthday celebrations of Duke Ellington, Coleman
Hawkins, Roy Eldridge, Louis Armstrong, Charlie Parker, and Lester Young. Yet,
one of my favorites was the Fred Frith festival called Frith and Friends, which I
produced in 1983. This sixteen-hour celebration of past and current collaborators with multi-instrumentalist, songwriter, and composer Fred Frith included
interviews with Bill Laswell (Massacre, Curlew), John Zorn (Naked City), Bob
Ostertag (*Voice of America*), David Moss (Dense Band), and Tom Cora (Skeleton Crew, Curlew), who he had worked with over the years. Looking back on
this and knowing Frith today, the list of collaborators has grown exponentially!
His expansive range of work includes scores for ballet and film, teaching improvisation, and he holds the title of Professor Emeritus of Music at Mills College
(1999–2018).

At the time of the festival, the British-born artist lived in the Lower East
Side of Manhattan and became a pivotal member of the experimental music
scene with contemporaries Elliott Sharp, John Zorn, Christian Marclay, Shelly
Hirsch, Ned Sublette, and numerous others. He has collaborated with The Residents, producer Brian Eno, and West Coast guitarist Henry Kaiser. His style
of working with prepared guitar, where the guitar lies flat with objects either
inserted between the strings or thrown or tossed at the strings to produce sound,
has always captured audiences.

He's always had a low-key demeanor and wit, with a bit of acerbic British chagrin and a sense of humor. He arrived in the States after having been a

founding member of the British experimental rock group Henry Cow, together with Chris Cutler, Tim Hodgkinson, Lindsay Cooper, and John Greaves. Later, he was a founding member of the group Art Bears with Dagmar Krause and Chris Cutler. Fred's unabashed underground stardom and expertise improvisation skills made him a go-to instrumentalist when international artists came to town, such as Peter Brötzmann, Evan Parker, Ikue Mori, and Evelyn Glennie.

Frith has always pushed the envelope and has been keenly interested in bucking the system. He has a commanding understanding of music theory and is a strong believer that improvisation is copyrightable. He taught himself guitar at an early age and was a huge fan of The Shadows. By age fifteen, he was into the blues and an admirer of Alexis Korner, who he still talks about. His musical language expanded once he delved into the musical philosophy of John Cage and Frank Zappa, developing his own theories and dictums of musical theory around improvisation.

His prolific life in music has allowed him to be in rock bands, collaborate with numerous like-minded musicians (Derek Bailey, Lol Coxhill, Mike Patton, Jad Fair), teach and score over thirty-six films, my favorite being the soundtrack to Andy Goldsworthy 2001 documentary *Rivers and Tides*. Frith also has produced many albums by other musicians, including Curlew, the Muffins, Etron Fou Leloublan, and Orthotonics. He was awarded the 2008 Demetrio Stratos Prize for his achievements in experimental music.

I've always admired Frith's work, and producing this celebratory, all-friends-included festival was an amazing experience that I am so grateful to have been able to see fulfilled.

B. WENTZ: I read that you don't like being labeled a guitarist, but it seems that's your primary instrument.

FRED FRITH: The reason I resent being constantly referred to as a guitarist is because that term represents only a very small part of my activity, especially now.

My second solo album, *Gravity*, which was released a few years ago, was promoted by the label as a guitar record. But I play a lot of other instruments on that record as well. Violin. Kazoo. A lot of percussion. I was exploring dance music from different cultures and mixing a lot of stuff together. For me, what's important is the songs and the pieces of music, not the means that are used to get them across. I mean, obviously, I like playing the guitar, but I do other things, too. In Skeleton Crew, the group I formed with Tom Cora here in New York, I play other instruments more often than I play guitar. I play bass. I play homemade stuff. I do some singing. I play guitar on maybe two or three numbers.

B. WENTZ: As a teenager, you played in folk and blues clubs before forming your own band, the experimental outfit Henry Cow. How did the group come together?

FRED FRITH: I met Tim Hodgkinson at a blues club in May 1968 when we were both students at Cambridge University. Then we hooked up with bassist John Greaves. We started out as a kind of loose blues band, and it evolved from that. We only really began taking ourselves seriously after we met drummer Chris Cutler. We responded to an ad he had placed in the *Melody Maker* because it was so bizarre. At the time, I was about to work on a doctorate in composition, and Tim was going to do graduate studies in anthropology. Instead, we dropped all that and moved to London to work full-time with the group.

B. WENTZ: Henry Cow was an avant-garde group that incorporated jazz, folk, and tape loops, among other elements. What were your influences?

FRED FRITH: In terms of rock music, we had two very important influences early on: the British psychedelic group Soft Machine and Frank Zappa's The Mothers of Invention. Those groups mapped out for us approaches to playing that we wanted to pursue.

There are certain trace elements of those two bands that you can hear in our very early music, mostly in the prerecorded music. So in 1969, we were probably sounding incredibly like the Soft Machine, certainly from our use of complex time signatures and the drone sound of Tim's organ.

The thing is, a lot of my early influences were discernibly an attempt to gain respectability on my part. A lot of the composers who were having an effect on me were not from the world of rock music, which is what I'd always loved. But another part of me wanted to achieve some kind of respectability, in a bourgeois sense. So I was constantly looking to twentieth-century composers and trying to bring those influences into what I was doing in a rock band.

Looking back, a lot of the music I wrote at that time sounds kind of absurd. On the early Henry Cow records, my compositions like "Yellow Half-Moon" and "Ruins" and stuff like that, which are probably the more substantially composed kinds of pieces we did, sound very dated and silly to me now. I had a kind of superficial grasp of how to write that kind of stuff, and I could do it in a fairly superficial way, but it all sounds like it's on the surface. Whenever good qualities come through in my music, it's underneath rather than on top. And that usually has to do with rhythm, not with the string quartet kind of stuff.

B. WENTZ: Do you still follow twentieth-century composers?

FRED FRITH: Of course. I wouldn't put down the people who are actually doing it properly. I guess the biggest influences on Henry Cow in the early days from contemporary classical music were the French composer Olivier Messiaen and, in my case, [Luciano] Berio, and a bit later Karlheinz Stockhausen. This was all in the '69 period. That's when we were really looking at those people. And you can hear a lot of Messiaen in the way that I composed in blocks. And you can hear very superficial drawings from Stockhausen in the way we use certain kinds of sound effects and contact microphones in our improvisation. I think we were more influenced for a while in our improvising by composers because we weren't drawn to the kind of improvised music that was going on at that time whose practitioners had mostly come from jazz.

B. WENTZ: Did you know about John Cage at that time?

FRED FRITH: Yeah, I read Cage in '67.

B. WENTZ: What did you think about his approach toward sound and composing using chance operations?

FRED FRITH: I was really impressed—it changed my way of thinking about music, particularly my attitude toward sound. It got me thinking about what a piece of music was and what it could be. Looking back, I think I'm lazy in certain respects. Because despite the strong effect his writing had on me back then, I didn't actually seek out Cage's music. Most of the records that I bought in those days were rock records. I accumulated other records when people would give them to me, but I never actually went out and looked for them, which I think says something.

B. WENTZ: You must have studied classical music growing up?

FRED FRITH: I played violin as a child. I had a very good advisor, my godfather, who was a self-taught musician. He told me that it would be a terrible mistake to become a professional musician because it would cease to be any fun. And that the only real driving force behind music is that you should enjoy it.

As it turned out, I disregarded his advice and became a professional musician. But it still means a lot to me that the primary purpose behind my music should be that I'm getting something out of it and transmitting at least a little joy. If I started thinking about music as making a living, it would probably rapidly go downhill for me.

Melvin Gibbs
Artist

I grew up in Brooklyn in what later became known as one of the classic areas of New York in terms of the beginnings of hip-hop. I was playing different kinds of music, and I fell into playing with a bunch of avant-garde jazz guys, in particular, the guys out of St. Louis who were living at La MaMa's at that time—[Charles] Bobo Shaw and Joe Bowie—and later Butch Morris, Frank Low, [Ronald] Shannon [Jackson], and Lester [Bowie]. That was my niche.

AIDS and crack hit around '84, and everything changed. And a bunch of those scenes fell apart, and a bunch of new scenes came up.

A bunch of my friends were the main graffiti guys in New York, and when I was hanging with them during that time, I met this kid who told me his name was SAMO. I saw him a couple years later he was [Jean-Michel] Basquiat.

I used to visit the African Record Center, the exclusive distributor of Fela's music in America, in Brooklyn on Nostrum Avenue. And Coxsone Dodd's place out in the 'hood if you were a reggae head.

FIGURE 22.1 WAYNE HORVITZ
SOURCE: TONY CORDOZA

22

WAYNE HORVITZ

Unknown date, 1987

I n the 1980s, the keyboardist Wayne Horvitz was a fixture on New York City's Lower East Side, a nexus for genre-shifting musicians who would play with improvisers one night and electronic wizards the next. Horvitz could be found performing in the neighborhood with his own ensembles as well as with John Zorn's rebel-rousing outfit Naked City, saxophonist Elliott Sharp, or conductor Butch Morris.

Horvitz studied music at the University of California Santa Cruz before migrating to New York City, where he bonded with improv-minded musicians, performing on some thirty albums and composing works for theater, dance, and film. One of his own ensembles, The President, gained a following among the college-radio set, thanks in part to the launch in 1984 of the new music label Nonesuch, which also released recordings by Zorn, Philip Glass, and Kronos Quartet.

The President focused on repetitive themes that cycle, with no solo instrumentation, and was a radical departure from Horvitz's work with Zorn or Sharp. Congenial and energetic, Horvitz welcomed me to his apartment and chatted excitedly about his many, many projects, talking at length about his latest album.

B. WENTZ: You have been an active player with a range of improvisers and composers, and now you have a new group, The President. So what direction are you moving into these days?

WAYNE HOROVITZ: I guess I'm moving in about five directions at once, for better or for worse. I do two kinds of things. I play keyboards with people like

Butch Morris and John Zorn, and lots of improvisers, and I do my own work at home in an 8-track studio. I do it track by track and it's very composed, and because of that, I've been really interested lately in writing music on paper again, which is why I've started this ensemble with the singer Robin Holcomb called the New York Composers Orchestra. It's a traditional jazz ensemble, but it's not traditional jazz music. So I'm doing that, and then I also play some jazz piano with people like John Zorn and Bobby Previte's quintet. If I wasn't playing piano, I'd be really upset. I'm doing a lot of electronic stuff lately, and I'm really interested in it, but I also get sick of it in a way too. I still have to go out and play acoustic music.

B. WENTZ: What sort of work do you do with electronics? Do you like to work with electronics in real-time or with prerecorded tape?

WAYNE HOROVITZ: Well, I like to improvise. I use a [Yamaha] DX7 keyboard, which a lot of people think is a pretty cold instrument. And they're right, but I like it as an improvising keyboard because if you know how to use it, it can be pretty expressive. At the same time, I'd be very frustrated if that's all I did. I really like to work at home with tape decks as well because then I can get something I can work over and over again. So it's sort of schizophrenic, but I like to do both.

B. WENTZ: The ensembles you're playing with now—are most of them improvised?

WAYNE HOROVITZ: Nobody's ensembles are really improvised anymore. I played with Christian Marclay and drummer David Linton the other night, and I realized it was the first time I'd actually really done a completely improvised gig in a long time. Everybody that I used to play those sorts of gigs with, they all do something a little more structured now. Zorn's been doing his game pieces for a long time, and those have an element of improvisation; and his new pieces that use more genre material, like the Godard/Mickey Spillane album and the reworked covers of Ennio Morricone pieces. I play keyboards in this band, Curlew, and there are tunes that have themes and structures. The composer and saxophonist Steve Lacy once said that he used improvising as a way to experiment and find out what he wanted to use in his compositions. I think a lot of musicians wouldn't agree with that statement, but, in fact, they have indeed gone and done just that. They were doing completely improvised music three or four or ten years ago, and now they're not.

B. WENTZ: The jazz you hear in New York clubs now sounds more composed and not quite as chaotic as it used to.

WAYNE HOROVITZ: I think it's an improvement, personally. When I first came to New York in the mid-seventies, I met a lot of people who were politically adamant about improvising. I was never that way. I played in jazz ensembles and rock ensembles, and improvising was a part of those groups. For me, one of the things that's too bad is that rock groups don't improvise like they used to.

One of my heroes growing up with sixties rock music was the guy in the Byrds who was influenced by John Coltrane, and you could hear that, for instance, in the recurring guitar solo on "Eight Miles High." People did solos back then. Rock music now is either extremely low-budget, or it's completely pop and carefully executed. There's no room to breathe in it.

B. WENTZ: How'd you hook up with a lot of the people you've been playing with?

WAYNE HOROVITZ: Mostly just from moving to New York. I went to school in Santa Cruz, California, and I actually met some of the people I work with now. Quite a few, in fact. The people I hooked up with when I came to New York—particularly Eugene Chadbourne and John Zorn and a bit later Butch Morris—were people that knew people I knew from Santa Cruz.

B. WENTZ: Were you trained as a classical musician before you got into jazz at UC Santa Cruz?

WAYNE HOROVITZ: I wasn't trained at all. I had done the usual stint of piano lessons as a kid, but I'm talking a very small amount. When I got to college, I could barely read music. I still don't read music that well. I read jazz charts. Chord changes and the like. Zorn, by contrast, is much more classically trained than I am and a better-trained jazz musician, too.

B. WENTZ: I have here the pink record you put out a couple years ago, *Dinner at Eight.* Is this mainly a solo record?

WAYNE HOROVITZ: It's the McDonald's record, as I like to refer to it. There are other people on it—Elliott Sharp, Chris Brown, Joey Peters, and Doug Wieselman—but they're only on a few cuts each. It's basically a solo record.

B. WENTZ: And most of that was done in the studio?

WAYNE HOROVITZ: Yeah, I was living in San Francisco at the time, and it was done in my house on an 8-track studio. Mostly I used a Yamaha DX7 and a drum machine, and that's it. . . . I wanted to see what I could do if I just sat down and spent a week and made a tape. I didn't have a record deal or anything at the time. And then this label was interested in it. So it worked out really well.

B. WENTZ: So, in what direction does your latest album called *The President* go? Is this more of a group effort?

WAYNE HOROVITZ: It uses my band—which is called The President—but the record turned out more like the first record because I couldn't afford to take them into a studio and do it live. So although I think the music is great, it's done track by track in an 8-track studio. We couldn't record live drums or anything. So I think that it doesn't really have the feel of how the band sounds live. What I would like to do next is take the band, which now is really an ensemble, and go into the studio and make a live record with them.

B. WENTZ: So, who's in the ensemble now?

WAYNE HOROVITZ: Elliott Sharp, Doug Weiselman, Bill Frisell, Bobby Previte and Dave Hofstra. It's actually a band that I've had together for a long time but with slightly different people. The guitar lineup is new, and I'm really excited about it. Obviously, Bill and Elliott are both great guitar players.

B. WENTZ: What's the concept behind the band?

WAYNE HOROVITZ: Well, It's an instrumental band, it's song-oriented. The rhythms are sort of R&B, almost New Orleans–style rhythms. Allen Toussaint and The Meters are a real influence on the band but also a lot of Indonesian music and, melodically, a lot of the great things the Art Ensemble of Chicago used to play, like those marches they did at the end of their concerts that Roscoe [Mitchell] used to write. So it's sort of idiosyncratic that way, but the grooves are a lot like New Orleans grooves. It's not like a modern rock feel in that sense.

B. WENTZ: The pieces on the record don't seem like songs, they seem more like themes taken from improvisations.

WAYNE HOROVITZ: That's half true. About half the pieces are more like songs, and the other half aren't like songs. One of the things I did was I put down sync tracks on tape, which is tempo information that any computer instrument can read. So some of the pieces, I literally just put down a tempo, and then I put down maybe one kind of track from a drum machine, but I wouldn't necessarily use that track later. In some cases, I had someone come in and play it live, like Elliott Sharp, and improvise soon thereafter. Or Chris Brown, who also did a lot of that.

And then, other pieces were much more structured. I mean, I wrote them on the piano and executed them on tape. But it is probably the most rhythmic record I've ever done. And I have to say, drum machines are great. I work with some really great drummers, but drum machines allow me to just work at my own whim. And drum machines don't sound anything like drums. I mean, you're kidding yourself if you think they do.

B. WENTZ: What do you have coming out next?

WAYNE HOROVITZ: I'm going to make another solo record. But I'd like my band to perform a lot. I have this trio with Butch Morris and Bobby Previte, and we have a record coming out. Actually, it was supposed to have been out. It's on the Sound Aspects label, a small German label. And I have The President. So the trio and The President are the two groups I'd like to pursue. One is really structured, like a rock band, and can play in those kinds of clubs, and the other is much more open, and there's more improvising. So those two outfits take care of things I like to do a lot. And John Zorn and I did a collection of Sonny Clark covers. It's like a bebop record. I'd love to tour with that because it's great to go out and play some jazz.

B. WENTZ: Last year [1986], you formed with Robin Holcomb the New York Composers Orchestra, a big band to play works you commission from composers.

WAYNE HOROVITZ: One of the reasons that Robin and I put the orchestra together was because we felt that there were so many brass and reed players who improvised well, and they weren't being used because so many people were putting ensembles together that had three keyboards, and two drummers, and one electric violin, and one cello. And while those ensembles are great and they make great music, you weren't getting to hear that nice thing you get when you hear some players play something and the ensemble is tight, and the unisons are tight, or the harmonies are tight. And I wanted to hear that again.

It's great, but it's tough too. A Lot of these players haven't played in ensembles that much. If they were twenty years older and came up in a different era, they would have, but nowadays, everyone's looking for a very individual sound, and although they may be great at that, they aren't necessarily great ensemble players, but they're getting good fast.

B. WENTZ: We just heard a track from your latest solo album, *This New Generation*. It's called "Please Take That Train From my Door." What instruments do you use on it?

WAYNE HOROVITZ: There's actually a tuba, saxophone, and keyboards, and that's it, except for the drum machine. And I play the harmonica.

B. WENTZ: Are those live musicians?

WAYNE HOROVITZ: The tuba and saxophone were done live. The rest of it is overdubbed. It's just sort of a typical piece of mine. It's repetitive in some ways, and it cycles a lot, but there's a melody, and that's something. And, unlike most of this record, there's no soloing on it.

One of the things I really like about Indonesian music, as opposed to other kinds of repetitive music that are currently popular, is that inside that music, there's always an expressive element, like the flute player or the violin player. And that means a lot to me. The thing about that music is that it can be hypnotic, or you can listen to this guy playing who's extremely expressive. So you had this individuality and all the musicians together. And that's something I try for.

When I have people solo in my band, sometimes it's not really to listen to their solo so much, as that the piece builds and builds, and then when the solo comes in, it changes the texture of the composition. And I try to use soloists who aren't concerned enough with their ego that they're willing to solo that way. So sometimes, I'll ask Elliott Sharp, who has an extremely idiosyncratic style of playing, but I'll say to him, "I really want you to play the blues at this point." And he loves to do it, and he's great at it. Because the composition calls for that. Which is different than keeping it commercial or something because that's not what it's about. It's just about what I hear.

Cyro Baptista
Artist

I came to the United States in 1980, straight
from JFK to Woodstock Creative Music Studio
where I stayed for two months. At the end of my
stay, I was heading back to Brazil with sixty
dollars in my pocket; I decided to stay another
day, and I'm still here, in New York City,
43 years later.

New York was a cauldron of misfits from all
over the planet. I started playing on the street,
which was a very common at the time. I met the
most incredible musicians. I eventually landed
a gig with Astrud Gilberto, so I started to
lead dual lives by playing fancy jazz clubs,
Studio 54, CBGBs and the Mudd Club and then
playing a kind of improvised, avant-garde rock
street music. Also, I began playing with John
Zorn, who I would work with for the next forty
years. He encouraged me to play my own music,
eventually adding me to his Tzadik label roster.
Yet I would have never survived without all the
help and inspiration that Nana Vasconcelos gave
me during that decade.

SOUL COUGHING (MARK DEGLI ANTONI, YUVAL GABAY, MIKE DOUGHTY, SEBASTIAN STEINBERG), 1990
SOURCE: PHOTO BY JEREMY WOLFF

the knitting factory
presents
the premiere performance of a new band

NAKEDCITY

John **ZORN** alto sax

Bill **FRISELL** guitar

Wayne **HORVITZ** keys

Fred **FRITH** bass

Joey **BARON** drums

Wed, May 18 thru Sat. May 21
Concerts at 9pm and 11pm

Naked City will be performing 8 completely different sets of
music over the course of the 4 night engagement   With NO
REPEATS so come early + come every night! Repertory will
include original compositions--music by Ennio Morricone,
John Barry, Bernard Herrmann, Jerry Goldsmith--hardcore
and surf music deconstructions--blues tributes to Larry Dav
Albert Collins, Albert King--new versions of Zorn's "Spillan
"Two Lane Highway"--solo, duo, + trio improvisations and mo
PLACE: Knitting Factory Annex 49 E. Houston
(next to and east of the K.F.) call 219-3055

NAKED CITY PROGRAM AT THE KNITTING FACTORY, 1989
SOURCE: COURTESY OF THE AUTHOR

COMPOSER PHILL NIBLOCK WITH PHOTOGRAPHER LONA FOOTE AT EXPERIMENTAL INTERMEDIA
FOUNDATION, 1984
SOURCE: COURTESY OF THE ESTATE OF LONA FOOTE

ALUMINUM NIGHTS POSTER, THE KITCHEN, 1981

SOURCE: COURTESY OF THE AUTHOR

ORCHESTRA

BROOKLYN ACADEMY OF MUSIC
30 Lafayette Ave., Bklyn., NY 11217   718-636-4100

LOC.

8 C

SEC.   ROW   SEAT
           K   103   JOHN ZORN/MORRICONE

871031 PE 47 "ONCE UPON A TIME..."
                    CAREY PLAYHOUSE

8610291633

PRICE
       $.00   FRI OCTOBER 31, 1986 8:00 P

No refunds or exchanges

JOHN ZORN, BROOKLYN ACADEMY OF MUSIC TICKET STUB, 1986
SOURCE: COURTESY OF THE AUTHOR

SPECIAL MIDNIGHT CONCERT
WORLD PREMIERE OF JOHN ZORN'S
HU DIE

RUBY CHANG   narration
original texts by Arto Lindsay
translated into the Chinese by Ruby Chang
Thursday April 23 Midnight
THE KNITTING FACTORY
47 E. Houston   219 3055

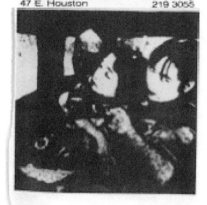

JOHN ZORN'S HU DIE PREMIERE, KNITTING FACTORY, 1987
SOURCE: COURTESY OF THE AUTHOR

STEPHANIE AND IRVING STONE FESTIVAL OF IMPROVISATION—JIM STALEY, BILL FRISELL, DAVID
WEINSTEIN, TOM CORA, IKUE MORI, LINDSAY COOPER, FRED FRITH, JOHN ZORN AT ROULETTE, 1985
SOURCE: COURTESY OF THE ESTATE OF LONA FOOTE

JOHN ZORN AT THE KITCHEN, 1980
SOURCE: PHOTO BY © PAULA COURT

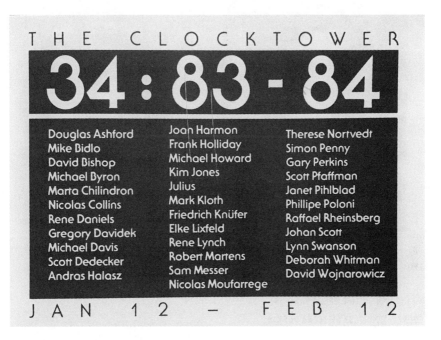

THE CLOCKTOWER

34 : 83 - 84

Douglas Ashford	Joan Harmon	Therese Nortvedt
Mike Bidlo	Frank Holliday	Simon Penny
David Bishop	Michael Howard	Gary Perkins
Michael Byron	Kim Jones	Scott Pfaffman
Marta Chilindron	Julius	Janet Pihlblad
Nicolas Collins	Mark Kloth	Phillipe Poloni
Rene Daniels	Friedrich Knüfer	Raffael Rheinsberg
Gregory Davidek	Elke Lixfeld	Johan Scott
Michael Davis	Rene Lynch	Lynn Swanson
Scott Dedecker	Robert Martens	Deborah Whitman
Andras Halasz	Sam Messer	David Wojnarowicz
	Nicolas Moufarrege	

JAN 12 — FEB 12

THE CLOCKTOWER EXHIBITION SHOW, FLYER
SOURCE: COURTESY OF THE AUTHOR

COMPOSER, CLARINETIST DON BYRON
SOURCE: PHOTO BY CORI WELLS BRAUN. COURTESY OF DON BYRON

OWT (DAVID LINTON, ZEENA PARKINS)
SOURCE: COURTESY OF ZEENA PARKINS

DAVID MOSS AND STEVE PAXTON AT DANCE THEATER WORKSHOP, 1980
SOURCE: PHOTO BY STEPHEN PETEGORSKY. COURTESY OF DAVID MOSS

OBSOLETELY

yves musard fast forward

at the PYRAMID

sun. oct 9   midnight

YVES MUSTARD, FAST FORWARD, OBSOLESTELY, PYRAMID CLUB, 1985
SOURCE: COURTESY OF THE AUTHOR

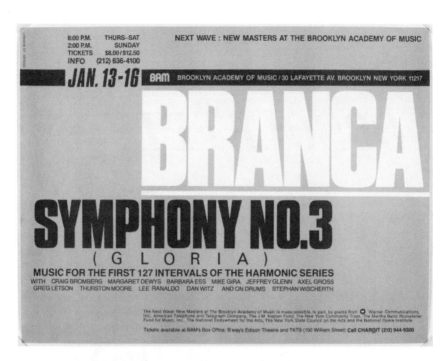

GLENN BRANCA, SYMPHONY NO. 3, BROOKLYN ACADEMY OF MUSIC, 1983
SOURCE: COURTESY BAM HAMM ARCHIVES

GLENN BRANCA CONDUCTING SYMPHONY NO. 3 AT BROOKLYN ACADEMY OF MUSIC, 1983
SOURCE: PHOTO BY TOM CARAVAGLIA. COURTESY BAM HAMM ARCHIVES

GLENN BRANCA CONDUCTING SYMPHONY NO. 3 AT BROOKLYN ACADEMY OF MUSIC, 1983
SOURCE: PHOTO BY TOM CARAVAGLIA. COURTESY BAM HAMM ARCHIVES

NED SUBLETTE & GLENN BRANCA AT BOND'S INTERNATIONAL CASINO AS PART OF THE KITCHEN'S
ALUMINUM NIGHTS SERIES, 1981
SOURCE: PHOTO BY PAULA COURT

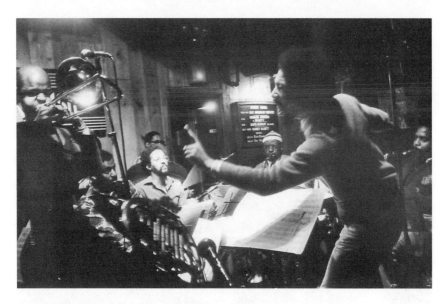

BUTCH MORRIS WITH CRAIG HARRIS ON TROMBONE AT SWEET BASIL

SOURCE: COURTESY OF THE ESTATE OF LONA FOOTE

**THURSDAYS
AT THE
KNITTING FACTORY**

**New and
Improvised Music**

March 19th:	Fred Frith Butch Morris	Solos
March 26th:	Lesli Dalaba Wayne Horvitz	Solos & Duos
April 2nd:	David Weinstein Shelley Hirsch	Solos & Duos
April 9th:	Tim Berne Hank Roberts	Duo
April 16th:	Marty Ehrlich Anthony Cox	Duo
April 23rd:	Bill Frisell & Doug Wieselman play the music of Robin Holcomb plus David Garland	Solo
April 30th:	Guy Klucevsek Bill Horvitz	Solos
May 7th:	Zeena Parkins Jim Staley	Solos

All concerts begin at 9:00 pm $4.00

THE KNITTING FACTORY
47 E. Houston Street (near Mulberry)
For more information call: (212) 219-3055

This poster was made and booked by
Wayne Horvitz in March of 1987.

THURSDAYS AT THE KNITTING FACTORY, POSTER, 1987

SOURCE: COURTESY OF THE AUTHOR

HARVEY LICHTENSTEIN   HENRY GELDZAHLER

KENT AND HEDY KLINEMAN

cordially invite you to
the closing night party for

BILL T. JONES/ARNIE ZANE & COMPANY
World Premiere
SECRET PASTURES

Choreography by Bill T. Jones & Arnie Zane
Music composed by Peter Gordon
Set design by Keith Haring
Costume design by Willi Smith
Lighting design by Stan Pressner
Music performed by Love Of Life Orchestra

BROOKLYN ACADEMY OF MUSIC
NEXT WAVE FESTIVAL

Sunday, November 18, 1984
6:30 – 8:30 p.m.
1175 Park Avenue (93rd St.)

R.S.V.P. by November 14, 1984
Carol Willis (718) 636-4138

BILL T. JONES/ARNIE ZANE & COMPANY, PARTY INVITATION, 1984
SOURCE: COURTESY OF THE AUTHOR

BILL T. JONES WITH ARNIE ZANE

SOURCE: PHOTO BY PEGGY JARRELL KAPLAN. COURTESY OF BAM HAMM ARCHIVES

POST COITUM OMNE ANIMAL TRISTE

A DANCE BY

ISABELLE MARTEAU

WITH

ERIC BARSNESS AND **CAROL CLEMENTS**

INSTALLATION_____

KIM CHESELKA

MUSIC_____

DAVID BEHRMAN   **JILL KROESEN**

FREDERIC CHOPIN   **CHRISTIAN MARCLAY**

FAST FORWARD   **CAROL PARKINSON**

LIGHTING

STAN PRESSNER

APRIL 18–20, FRI. THRU SUN. AT 9PM
P S 1 2 2, 1 5 0 F I R S T A V E, N Y C
TICKETS: $6 OR TDF + $1 RES: 477 5288

ISABELLE MARTEAU, POST COITUM OMNE ANIMAL TRISTE, PS 122
SOURCE: COURTESY OF THE AUTHOR

RYKODISC and THE BLACK ROCK COALITION
invite you to an apocalyptic party and performance.

Behold all 10 bands from the upcoming compilation
album: THE HISTORY OF OUR FUTURE

Good Guys
Blue • Print
Bluesland
Shock Council
JJ Jumpers
dadahdoodahda
Jupiter
Royal Pain
PBR Street Gang
Blackasaurus Mex

PLUS SPECIAL GUEST MC's AND DJ's!

Wimpy? NOT. Intense? Please!

Monday July 15th
Wetlands Preserve
161 Hudson St., NYC
Starting around 7pm

FREE WITH YOUR NMS BADGE
For more info, call
RYKODISC 508/744-7678 or
SET TO RUN 212/687-0522

THE BLACK ROCK COALITION, THE HISTORY OF OUR FUTURE, INVITATION
SOURCE: COURTESY OF THE AUTHOR

THE BLACK ROCK COALITION, POSTER
SOURCE: COURTESY OF THE AUTHOR

NO IMAGE" WITH GRAHAM HAYNES, BRUNO D'ALMEIDA, LANCE BRYANT AT VILLAGE GATE, 1988

OURCE: UNKNOWN

Wilberforce Quartet

WILBERFORCE QUARTET, FLYER
SOURCE: COURTESY OF THE AUTHOR

SHELLEY HIRSCH AND DAVID WEINSTEIN REHEARSING, 1988
SOURCE: UNKNOWN

Pandit Pran Nath

India's Master Vocalist

Raga Cycle

with

LaMonte Young Marian Zazeela - Tamburas & Voices
Ray Spiegel - Tabla

Spring 1986

Morning Ragas - Sunday, May 25, 11:00 AM
Afternoon Ragas - Sunday, June 8, 3:00 PM
Night Ragas - Saturday, June 21, 9:00 PM

presented by
M E L A

at Dia Art Foundation Performance Space   155 Mercer Street   New York NY 10012
Admission $8.00, Students $4.00, Seniors/Handicapped $3.00, TDF +, Limited Seating
On Gramavision Records & Tapes   For Information 212-925-8270

© Marian Zazeela 1986

FAST FORWARD WITH TAKEHISA KOSUGI
SOURCE: COURTESY OF THE ESTATE OF LONA FOOTE

THE LOUNGE LIZARDS, KNITTING FACTORY FLYER
SOURCE: COURTESY OF THE AUTHOR

PART V

THE VOCALISTS

Experimenters with
Voice and Words

FIGURE 23.1 LAURIE ANDERSON (WITH JOHN CAGE)
SOURCE: MARION ETTLINGER

23

LAURIE ANDERSON

February 1983

The first thing you notice about Laurie Anderson is her voice. Straightforward and matter-of-fact, folksy and familiar, it is the voice of Middle America, earnestly asking what is happening to America.

Like many people, I first encountered Anderson's voice in the song "O Superman." Recorded in 1981, it features haunting snippets of plain-spoken electro poetry influenced by the recent hostage crisis in Iran. The song was as addictive as it was poignant, with Anderson's heavily-processed voice saying "Ha" on a seemingly endless loop, layered over bird sounds and synths to create a hypnotic, almost childlike beat. Fellow artist B. George released the single on his small independent label, and it became an unlikely hit in the UK—and a favorite of the staff at WKCR.

Anderson grew up outside of Chicago and might have pursued a career as a concert violinist, but her curiosity brought her to New York, where she studied sculpture at Columbia University. In the 1970s, she began to make a name for herself with her experimental violin pieces and could be seen busking at the city's subway stations, wearing ice skates attached to frozen blocks of ice while playing her violin. When the ice melted, her performance ended.

I met Anderson just as she was moving into a new loft space on Canal Street. Perhaps welcoming a distraction from unpacking boxes, she was warm and chatty, sitting crossed-legged on a temporary, fold-up chair. She was working on an upcoming project called *United States*, which she would stage as a vast, two-night, eight-hour show at the Brooklyn Academy of Music.

B. WENTZ: Before turning to music full time, you earned a graduate degree in sculpture here at Columbia.

LAURIE ANDERSON: I had a studio on 125th Street and was making stuff with polyurethane and polyvinyl. I got really sick doing it because of the fumes. It's really toxic stuff. Lose a lot of brain cells that way. You have to wear a mask, gloves, and an asbestos suit, have exhaust fans going, and even if you are really careful, the fumes still get to you. So I stopped using that and started making things out of paper, crunching up the day's newspapers and making it into a kind of brick papier maché—projects like that. I hated art school. I was asked to leave three times. Kicked out, reinstated. It was a really checkered career. I couldn't stand it!

B. WENTZ: You grew up in the suburbs west of Chicago, where you studied both visual art and violin. Did you stop playing while you focused on science in college and art in grad school?

LAURIE ANDERSON: Yes, I started playing the violin when I was five years old. Then when I was sixteen, I quit entirely. That's one of the few things in life that I am really proud of—just being able to stop cold turkey—because I realized I was becoming a kind of technocrat, just learning to play accurately and very fast. It didn't leave much room for anything other than practicing all day. There were other things I wanted to learn, so I stopped. Totally.

When I returned to the violin years later, I modified a lot of violins and used them as a kind of ventriloquist dummy or other kind of voice. I built one with a speaker inside and played it by itself. One has a battery-powered turntable on it, so I cut records for that. The needle of the record player is mounted on the middle of the violin bow and is lowered like a tonearm on a turntable.

B. WENTZ: What does that sound like? Do you move it back and forth like a bow?

LAURIE ANDERSON: It sounds pretty bad. Like barking seals. It's very unpleasant. I also modified violins so they worked like tape instruments. I mounted a tape head on the bridge of the violin, and on the bow, instead of horsehair, there's a strip of recorded audiotape, so you play that back and forth over the head. That allows you to create sounds that are backwards as well as forwards.

B. WENTZ: What sort of music could you play like that? Is this the violin you invented?

LAURIE ANDERSON: Bongos, saxophone, piano—whatever was recorded on the tape that I used as a bow. Generally, only a few phrases of those instruments. But by moving the bow, you can establish whole other kinds of rhythms. It's just like editing tape—going back and forth until you find that sound. And I engineer a lot of my own tapes, so moving from that editing motion to the motion of playing a violin is not a great jump.

B. WENTZ: It's difficult to say what genre of music you make. You can't say, "I make pop music" or "I make avant-garde music." What do you call it?

LAURIE ANDERSON: I think performance art. I thought that term was very clumsy when I first heard it. But it has the advantage of being very nonspecific. Nobody has a clear idea what that is. The closest definition of performance art is to say it's a hybrid of a lot of things: images, language, gesture, sound, not quite theater, and not quite other things. Each time somebody does something within that general area and calls it *performance art*, it redefines the term in interesting ways. So I like it because it's loose.

B. WENTZ: In performance, you use these tapes and then add your own voice as well?

LAURIE ANDERSON: Right. For violin, some are just tape sequences. The tapes I make for performances tend to be very dry. In other words, I don't add reverb, and I don't mix them in ways that are complicated at all—they are very simple rhythm tracks in which to make combinations. Making a record that exists only on audio tape is a very different process than performing. It's a different way of thinking. Because without the pictures and the spatial aspects of the performance, you make different decisions about the music.

B. WENTZ: Were you influenced by electronic music composers like Milton Babbitt, who also worked with atonal rhythms but on synthesizers? Or Harry Partch or George Crumb?

LAURIE ANDERSON: I don't like music made by machines that much. I prefer some kind of real signal to a filter. But at the same time, I try to have a balance between something made with a machine—magnetic tape—and something made by a human—a violin.

Electronics has filters—I don't have the same feeling about it as electronics straight from the machine. A filter will act like a window, which shifts all the way up and looks at those harmonics and exaggerates them and brings them into the limited range of human hearing, so there are things you can guess at that are suddenly within your range, and that function of electronics is wonderful.

B. WENTZ: I was amazed to see "O Superman" released on vinyl after hearing it performed at The Kitchen in Soho. It reached number two on the UK charts. Do you see this sort of popularity as a step forward?

LAURIE ANDERSON: It's hard to say. In the last two or three years, I've noticed a change in the audiences that come to see my work. They tend to be a very mixed group. There are some kids now, which I like a lot.

In terms of performance art being presented in a more pop way, I think it's a mistake to try to nudge it into pop culture if it doesn't have any kind of place. On the other hand, it has always been my fantasy that American artists could think of doing something like that because the avant-garde has been very snob-bish. The whole history of it is generally a kind of ghetto of museums and art galleries and publications and a downtown scene, whether it's clubs or venues or things like that. A certain attitude that involved a certain snobbism. Artists haven't wanted anything to do with pop culture because it's typically made for a ten-year-old brain, and most artists aren't interested in working on that level. Why do it? Particularly here in the United States. Take pop music. It's just a very tight system that is regulated by what the average listener wants to hear or what the average listener will be willing to put up with hearing. It's not a DJ reaching into a bin and saying, "Well, here's a record I'd like to play for you," unless it's like a college station. And it's not that way in Europe. European radio is much more open. Particularly in Germany and England, people are freer to experiment in terms of what goes on the air. That makes a big difference.

I've gotten letters from DJs from big pop stations here in New York that said, "I just want to let you know, I did play your record and I received this photo-copied letter from the station manager that says, 'There is no playing of unautho-rized material, i.e "O Superman." ' " It's very strange. Unless it's on the playlist, it is not on the air. So you can produce whatever you want, but unless it falls into a certain category, only a limited number of people will hear it.

B. WENTZ: Has the response to your music been greater in Europe than in the United States?

LAURIE ANDERSON: About half the work I do is in Europe, and that's been the case for about six years now, since 1976. It's much easier to work there. Europe-ans care about things in a different kind of way. The audiences tend to be more general than here. You could never picture an American audience made up of as many different kinds of people as you see in Europe. The New York crowd does not mix. In Europe, you can see the Peking Opera and Robert Wilson on the same night.

B. WENTZ: Your music seems to be very conceptual, in an American kind of way, with the things you say and the phrases you use. Avant-garde music tends to be conceptual too. But you use phrases that appear in everyday language—very direct and very American.

LAURIE ANDERSON: Most of my phrases come from eavesdropping. I travel a lot, so I meet a lot of different kinds of people. My main goal is to use ordinary material so you can feel somebody is really talking to you, and not through any kind of music filter or lyric filter. One reason why I don't typically use ABAB in verse-chorus arrangements is because real speech doesn't fit very well into those structures. I like to create a stable, rhythmic ground that doesn't move. It moves in a very limited way, over a very static ground and over which the language travels at its own speed. So you feel all the hesitations and riffs that you do when you talk. Talking is like improvisation, really, and those rhythms interest me much more than any kind of musical phrasing. So it is spoken language that dictates the shape of the music.

B. WENTZ: In the seventies, you wrote art criticism for magazines. Do you still do any writing? I saw your book *Hotel*, which seemed to be excerpts from dream-like states.

LAURIE ANDERSON: I have published a few texts from performances, and I have written things that are more or less notes for performances. I used to write the work first and then incorporate it into the performance, but I found it very static. So I tried to figure things out just by talking through them and then see how that felt. I worked on them by speaking through them.

B. WENTZ: What are you working on now?

LAURIE ANDERSON: The piece that I am working on now is called *United States*. It's the result of being in Europe a lot. You sit around and have dinner with people who are going, "How could you have elected that guy president?" And you go, "Well, uh . . ." You have to come up with an answer, and I try to make up some good answers, but I realize that I have to think about it a little bit more. The final version will be produced next fall at the Brooklyn Academy of Music. I wanted to play with some of the parts since I've been working on them since 1979.

B. WENTZ: Some of us have seen parts of that piece at The Kitchen. I recall some visuals—big maps and lights. Will those be included in the BAM performance? Or will that strictly be a piece of music?

LAURIE ANDERSON: A combination of both. And I hope that it doesn't seem to be more of one than the other. I try to work sort of simultaneously on things, so for me, the danger is in being illustrational. You write a song and then you realize, wouldn't some pictures be nice? It's very tempting to just sort of illustrate the song rather than let the pictures have a whole other meaning that will add to the song rather than just sort of repeat it in the visual world. For me, that means working a lot slower because I go back and forth a lot between how the song looks and how it sounds. I've been working on *United States* for three years, and I had hoped that this would be the final version of the work, but I'm finding that I'm really more interested in adding parts to it than in sort of going back and perfecting things I've already done. So I'm frantically writing some new things for it now. I guess the best way to describe it is songs and stories with pictures. The whole thing is an attempt to describe a country, really.

B. WENTZ: What will you use on stage?

LAURIE ANDERSON: There will be a great big screen, 30 x 40 feet, because, to me, it's very important that the image is very bright and visible from every place in the hall. So there's a whole barrage of projectors: one that turns around and one that goes up and down, and a film projector and several slide projectors that have other kinds of motions to them. It's a way of making a still picture move in ways other than you would normally do with film so that it has a kind of slower movement. If I take longer with a song, I'm not locked into the length of a film that accompanies it. So the technicians can, in a way, do a kind of collaboration with me in terms of the timing of it because it's all done live and not in a studio and then put on film.

B. WENTZ: Will there be any electronics involved? Or actors?

LAURIE ANDERSON: I'd like to sort of feature the electronics rather than hide them, so they all sort of sit in a mound in the middle of the stage. And I do a lot of the turning of the dials myself, which is good because sometimes you can feel a little bit like a puppet if suddenly the whole electronic situation changes. So I like to have a certain amount of control of that. And there will be, I guess, ten people who will be in it, as well as me. There will be two saxophone players, a percussionist, and a bagpipe player. And a soprano, a keyboard player, and some people who talk, and some people who walk.

B. WENTZ: How would you define avant-garde or /new music today?

LAURIE ANDERSON: The nice thing about the word *avant-garde* is that it is constantly updating itself, and so is new music. For me, in a totally personal way, what I like the most is music that makes me feel most awake. I don't care whether it's new or not. An old Captain Beefheart album sounds newer to me than something I heard in a club last night.

Christian Marclay
Artist

Everyone was supportive of one another. Especially in the East Village, where you could live very cheaply, and the rents were low. It felt like a small village. Artists ran into each other in the street. I remember going to see shows in Soho and the East Village, concerts by DNA, [Elliott] Sharp, [John] Zorn, Butch [Morris], and Shelley [Hirsch]. Information circulated through Xeroxed posters and word of mouth, there was a kind of fluid mixing between music, dance, performance, sculpture, and painting, which seemed like very normal.

We were inventing ourselves. I don't think I would have performed music had I not discovered punk in NYC. It gave me freedom. I picked up a turntable instead of a guitar, and records were cheap. Working with [John] Zorn, I learned how to improvise in a group context. It seems that every month there were new revelations and strong experiences that have lasted until now.

FIGURE 24.1 JOAN LA BARBARA
SOURCE: BETTY FREEMAN

24

JOAN LA BARBARA

November 1, 1983

Joan La Barbara's voice is her instrument, and magnetic tape is the tool she uses to manipulate it. Her vast work includes solo recordings of her compositions, recordings by composer colleagues who incorporate her voice, and others who commission works specifically for her. She released her first recording, *Voice Is the Original Instrument*, on her label, Wizard, in 1976. The following year saw the release of her follow-up, *Tapesongs*, the cover of which shows a seemingly naked La Barbara draped in oodles of quarter-inch recording tape. It reflects the changing of the time, an almost symbolic precursor to the future of music, as the manipulation of tape and electronics drove sonic experimentation in the late 1970s and early 1980s.

We got together in 1983 when she and her husband, electronic music composer Morton Subotnick, were readying for an upcoming New Music America festival performance. Her friendly, open demeanor and grounded, thoughtful way of explaining her experimental style come naturally. Yet hearing the amazing malleability of her voice and what comes out of her body makes her sound like a creature from another planet. She incorporates circular breathing and what she calls "extended techniques," almost like what one would hear from native Inuit or central African sing-song or call-response form. Her multiphonic tricks have made her popular with avant-garde composers, including John Cage, Alvin Lucier, and Steve Reich.

La Barbara played piano as a child but took to the voice because, as she told me, it was easier and less stressful. She studied at the Tanglewood Music Center and honed her craft working with colleagues like composers Robert Ashley, Morton Feldman, and Philip Glass. Yet it was John Cage who was her true mentor, a relationship she cherished. Cage specifically scored

"Song Books" for La Barbara's voice in 1976, followed by "Winter Music" and "Atlas Eclipticalis." Her extended vocal technique takes her voice and sends it through a tape recorder to be manipulated via speed and pitch. This was a precursor to the standard computer manipulation commonplace in modern musical composition. "I always do a lot with resonance and with placement of the sound in specific areas in the face and head, focusing on specific bones such as cheekbones, the forehead, and of course, the wonderful nasal resonance where one can make extreme sounds."[4]

La Barbara has influenced several generations of singers and composers. In 2015, Golden Globe–winning Danish composer Jóhann Jóhannsson incorporated parts of La Barbara's work "Erin" [from her album *As Lightning Comes, In Flashes*] in his score for Denis Villeneuve's science fiction film *Arrival*. Jóhannsson paid homage to La Barbara by recreating her repetitive vocal incantations during the teaching montage, which provided an amazing lengthy aural backdrop to the scene. The piece is heard again over the closing credits, taking the viewer into an incredible paralleled sound and visual experience. Jóhannsson said, "The film is about language and communication and how language affects the way we think and experience time. Therefore I wanted to pay homage to this avant-garde legend."[5]

B. WENTZ: You've always used your voice as an instrument. Did you learn music on another instrument, or have you always been attracted to singing?

JOAN LA BARBARA: I started singing very, very young in churches, but I also studied piano. I started when I was about four years old and played piano very consistently until I was about fifteen or sixteen, and then switched over to voice—mostly because piano playing made me so nervous. My hands got cold and clammy, and it was hard to keep my fingers on the keys. So I went to something that, for me, was easier, which was singing.

B. WENTZ: Have you always been working with contemporary music, or do you sometimes do some traditional singing and more arias with opera?

JOAN LA BARBARA: Not anymore. I've been doing contemporary music for about fourteen years, and I just found that when I was studying Western classical music, that although I did enjoy it, and it's a perfectly wonderful art form and period of music, I just found that I wanted to do something different. I wanted to discover new uses for the voice, and I wanted to engage my brain in this discovery.

And I found that contemporary music was an area that I could get into and find out new things, find out new sounds, work on pieces that were being written right now instead of pieces that were written so long ago. And I like the idea of being able to talk to a composer and discuss what his or her ideas are about any particular sound that they're interested in.

B. WENTZ: When did you begin composing your own works?

JOAN LA BARBARA: My own composing started around 1973 when I realized that the kind of improvising I was doing was developing into real pieces, into compositions. And I felt that it was really necessary to get into composing so that some of the sounds that I was working on could get out into the public and perhaps interest other composers in writing for those sounds.

B. WENTZ: A lot of your recent music heard on "Winds of the Canyon" seems to go back to the old ways of singing, meaning a more traditional ethnic music.

JOAN LA BARBARA: We look at sort of ethnic traditional music and then change and alter and develop a different kind of style. It's just something that I'm interested in at the moment because I feel like I've gotten to a point where I really don't think I'm going to discover any new sounds on my own, so I'm going to other cultures, and I'm listening to their vocal sounds. Because there's a lot of interesting vocal work that's done in other cultures that is not part of our tradition. Like the Native Americans, like the Inuit Eskimos, like Pygmies in Africa.

There's just a number of different cultures that have really fascinating vocal sounds, and I'm not imitating them because I have no idea how they do what they're doing. All I'm doing is to go to these other cultures for inspiration.

B. WENTZ: Do you actually visit these communities?

JOAN LA BARBARA: In the case of the Native Americans, yeah, I've gone to the Southwest and visited reservations or pueblos where they're having ceremonies, so I can hear what they're doing. When I do a piece like that, it's not as if I'm trying to do the same sounds. I'm just trying to get an impression of what it is that they enjoy. I don't think I'm singing the way they sing. I'm using my own techniques in a kind of imitation of but more of an homage to what they're doing.

So "Winds of the Canyon," which is a piece that I did in 1982, was an homage to Native Americans. And right now, I'm fascinated by the Inuit Eskimos, who are throat singers. And again, I'm not trying to imitate their style. I'm just fascinated by the sound that they get.

B. WENTZ: How would you describe their sound?

JOAN LA BARBARA: It's very difficult to describe. It's like rhythmic breathing. It's done, generally, by two women who stand facing each other and sing directly into each other's—almost into each other's mouths. But directly face-to-face. So they're getting a lot of resonance between the two of them, not just their own head resonance, but some sound waves that are bouncing back and forth between the two of them. So they get a lot of interference in different tones. And they're also circular singing so that they're singing on the inhale and exhale. And it's just a very complex series of sounds that they're producing.

B. WENTZ: Is there any aspect of vocal technique that you especially like to work with? I mean, do you like the manipulation of vocal pitch and harmony more than the repetition or rhythm of vocal incantation?

JOAN LA BARBARA: There are some people who have worked with the voice, who seem to be focusing on one aspect. For instance, David Hykes in the Harmonic Choir is focusing completely on this very particular technique of isolating overtones and has really focused on that very particular area.

I'm sort of working in a broader spectrum. In investigating the voice as an instrument, I'm really developing a new vocabulary so that when I write pieces for even my own voice in layers on tape or for a choral group, I really orchestrate with the voice so that there are, for instance, a number of sounds that I would consider percussive sounds. There are a number of sounds that are more horn-like or more string-like.

Recently I've been reorchestrating a piece I did called "The Solar Wind," which was scored for a voice and ten instruments. And I've reorchestrated it for a mixed chorus and about three instruments. So I've had to translate a lot of those sounds back into the voice, which is almost coming full circle because when I started working with the voice, I was, in a way, translating from instruments to voice. And now I'm going from voices to instruments and back again.

B. WENTZ: But you perform a lot with tape.

JOAN LA BARBARA: I do. I started performing completely solo with no accompaniment. Then I started using some electronics; when I had the opportunity, I would use other instruments. And it's, in a way, sort of an economic necessity to be able to perform solo. So when I had pieces in mind that needed more than the simple solo voice, I went to the medium of tape and to multitrack tape so that I could layer the voices and get a richer texture to work with.

B. WENTZ: I find with your singing, it's sort of like what in visual art is called sound painting or sound work. Your voice becomes sort of like the paint, the way you manipulate it and the way you use it. I know that some visual artists have worked with you, like Rolf Julius in Germany. Do you ever think of the voice in that sense?

JOAN LA BARBARA: I do. In fact, sometimes when I'm singing, what I'm really doing is I'm singing a kind of illustration. I'm singing the pictures that are in my mind. So I am, in essence, painting with the voice. A couple of the pieces that I've done, let's say, "Twelvesong" from 1977 and "Klee Alee" [from 1979], I think of as sound paintings in that, when you go and look at a painting, generally what happens is you take in the whole painting, all at once. You get a general impression, and then the longer you stand there and look at it, you begin to see details, or you'll see certain aspects of the form. Just different things come into focus and become clearer. So with these sound paintings of mine, you get most of the material all at once. You get a general impression of the piece. Then over a period of time, which we can deal with in sound, I direct the way in which you listen. I'm focusing your attention on certain aspects of that sound. So I'll bring things forward in the mix to draw your attention to that particular sound at that point in time.

B. WENTZ: Is it something you can do easier on record rather than live?

JOAN LA BARBARA: What I can do live, if I've got one of these pieces that is done in layers, is to do live what I do on tape, which is to bring out certain aspects of the piece. So I'm developing another layer on top of what already exists. So instead of just bringing it up in the mix, I'm drawing your attention to it because of the presence of the live voice and what that live voice is doing at that point in time, whether it's doing material from the tape exactly or whether it's doing a sort of counterpoint to that material.

B. WENTZ: Your most recent record is on a label called Wizard. Is it true that you're going to be moving to Nonesuch?

JOAN LA BARBARA: Well, Wizard is my own independent label.

B. WENTZ: How long have you had that?

JOAN LA BARBARA: Since '76, and as most of us in contemporary music who are interested in the record medium, I've brought out my own label to get my work into—not really into the marketplace because it's certainly difficult to get records into the marketplace but to be able to make my music available to a wider audience than just those people who are able to come to the concerts. So that by listening to the record, they can get a reasonably good idea of what I'm working on.

As far as the move to Nonesuch is concerned, I will be doing one record for Nonesuch next year, and I'm very excited about that because I'm hoping that they'll get better distribution than what I can get as an independent, which is not to say that New Music Distribution is not doing a wonderful job. They do, and they're really remarkable, and the only distributor for independent records. The problem is that it's really a vast area, and we're dealing with commercial outlets, meaning the stores, and they're interested in products that move. And contemporary music sometimes will sit around for a month or two before that person who's really interested will come into the store and pick up the record.

So it's important to have the records in the stores, and I hope that record stores will be able to keep stocking contemporary music. It may be that at some point that we'll have to have specialty stores that are just dealing with contemporary music where the people in charge are more patient and are more interested in a quality selection of music rather than just things that move quickly.

B. WENTZ: What are you working on right now?

JOAN LA BARBARA: On the Nonesuch record, there will be three pieces of mine. One is "October Music: Star Showers and Extraterrestrials," which I'll be performing at Symphony Space Saturday afternoon. It's part of the composer's forum series of concerts. So "October Music: Star Showers and Extraterrestrials" is for quadraphonic tape and amplified voice. And the material on the tape is all vocal.

So when I put it on record, I'm going to have to remix it from quad to stereo. And in this particular case, I designed the quad tape so that I was placing the audience almost as if they were underneath a nighttime sky, and you can see shooting stars, or feel or imagine stars shooting across the sky, and see little twinkling lights. So it's going to be a major production to try to get that same feeling on stereo.

B. WENTZ: Can you do it digitally?

JOAN LA BARBARA: I don't know whether we'll be able to do it on digital. But the whole idea of the sounds that, in the quad tape, are moving from behind you, over your head, from left to right and right to left, and all around, I'll have to figure out some way of getting that same impression. Maybe it will be like watching a movie of the night sky.

Also on the record will be two ensemble pieces, one called "Vlissingen Harbor," which is for voice and seven instruments. I premiered that last season, in '82, at the Monday Evening Concerts in Los Angeles. I had been doing some concerts in Holland, and I went to a town called Vlissingen, which is on the coast. It has huge beaches, but they were all deserted because it turned out that the ocean floor drops off very, very quickly, and the tides are very strong. So that big tankers can come in, within, I'd say, about 50 yards of the shore. So it's a very bizarre kind of contrast between this sleepy little town with very tiny houses and these huge tankers drifting right offshore. Which doesn't tell you an awful lot about the sound, but that was my image that I was looking at.

B. WENTZ: Have you ever given voice lessons?

JOAN LA BARBARA: I do classes and workshops, mostly on extended vocal techniques. I teach the kind of warm-up exercises, but I do exercises for the body so that you can relax, and your body works for you instead of against you. And then I start working on isolating overtones and teaching multiphonics and inhaled singing and a number of different techniques that are fairly standard once you get into extended vocal techniques.

B. WENTZ: Extended vocal techniques? Is that a more nontraditional vocal style?

JOAN LA BARBARA: It's sort of the catchall phrase that we've come to use for anything that goes beyond normal melodic singing; using the voice to make other kinds of sounds. Some people call them sound effects. I don't think they're sound effects. As far as I'm concerned, it involves using the voice more as an instrument than as a means to deliver a message.

Tim Berne
Artist

I lived in Brooklyn, and was pretty new to the scene because in the eighties I was more a participant than a player. I worked at the Soho Music Gallery and later Tower Records. I remember going to someone's living room in the Lower East Side to see music with John Zorn. I'd go to Roulette, Studio Rivbea, and Ornette [Coleman] studio. I wasn't a "downtown" musician. I was more into the scene with Hank Roberts, Bill Frisell, Joey Barron, and Herb Robertson.

New York City had so much going on; everyone lived there. I never lived in Manhattan. I've always lived in Brooklyn where, at the time, it was cheaper, bigger space to make more noise and people like Julius [Hemphill], Oliver Lake, Lester Bowie, Pharaoh Sanders, and Cecil Taylor lived.

PART VI

————

THE DISSENTERS

Modern Jazz Innovators

FIGURE 25.1 ANDREW CYRILLE
SOURCE: MICHAEL WILDERMAN

25
ANDREW CYRILLE
September 1986

Andrew Cyrille took up drums when he was a child. By seventeen, he was recording with Phillie Joe Jones, and by nineteen, he was accompanying singer Nellie Lutcher. He studied percussion at the Juilliard School but was more interested in jazz. He did what all musicians in New York do—hang out at clubs and talk shop with other musicians. Around that time, he struck up a relationship with avant-garde composer and keyboardist Cecil Taylor and played with his group for more than a decade. He's collaborated with countless artists—including Walt Dickerson, Butch Morris, and Bill Frisell, to name just a few—and formed a trio with Oliver Lake and Reggie Workman. Throughout it all, he's become a force in contemporary drumming and percussion, reimagining the idiom again and again.

With his laid-back, graceful demeanor, Cyrille is a joy to hang out with. In typical WKCR-FM fashion, our afternoon interview was cut short because John Cage arrived at the station, and I had to give both composers precious air time.

B. WENTZ: We just heard some tracks by Andrew Cyrille and his group Maono from the 1975 album *Celebration*. That album has a pretty wide-ranging group of musicians.

ANDREW CYRILLE: That particular album had about nine people on it, but not everybody played on all of the tunes. I mixed it up. There's a duet with singer Jeanne Lee and poet Elouise Loftin, and then in comes a Haitian drummer named Alphonse Cimber. Then there's a quartet/quintet with Donald Smith on piano, Stafford James playing bass, David Ware on tenor saxophone, and

Ted Daniel playing trumpet. And then, on the side that we just heard, some of the synthesizer work was done by Romulus Franceschini.

Maono is just a name I use to introduce material I've written or conceived of, and I get musicians who understand the music and want to play it to perform it as a group.

B. WENTZ: Are you working with a particular group now?

ANDREW CYRILLE: I do a number of things. Like the day after tomorrow, I'm going to be in Canada to do a percussion performance with some Canadian drummers. Then I'm going to Cambridge, Massachusetts, to play with [jazz composer and saxophonist] Henry Threadgill and [double bassist] Fred Hopkins.

B. WENTZ: So, that's considered a trio, then.

ANDREW CYRILLE: That's a trio. It doesn't have a name like Maono or anything like that. I don't use that name a lot because I find Americans have difficulty pronouncing two vowels together. They kind of don't know what to do with it. It's a Swahili word for feelings. Maybe I'll use it again.

B. WENTZ: You've brought up a few tapes we're going to listen to. What are we going to hear first?

ANDREW CYRILLE: This is something that I did about two or three years ago at a festival in Moers, West Germany. I played with Famoudou Don Moye, a drummer with the Art Ensemble of Chicago. And a drummer from Guinea named Fodé Youla. We had never played before, and we didn't have any rehearsals. We just came out and started cooking together. And this was in front of an audience of about four thousand people. I think you'll enjoy it because we did.

B. WENTZ: I read that you played with another African drummer, Babatunde Olatunji of Nigeria.

ANDREW CYRILLE: Olatunji was the first African musician that I played with here in the U.S. I also played a lot with Joe Mensah, a singer from Ghana who was here on your program. And I've done some things with people like Ladji Camara, another drummer from Guinea, and then, of course, there was James Hawthorne Bey, who was also a part of a number of formations that I've played with.

B. WENTZ: What's it like for an American drummer who, perhaps, has been brought up on the jazz tradition, to play with, say, an African percussionist who is coming from an entirely different background?

ANDREW CYRILLE: I don't know if it's entirely different. There are a lot of similarities in terms of improvisation and feeling. So if you know how to assign rhythms, if you know how to layer them, if you know what will work in certain contexts, then it's not that difficult.

Of course, you have to learn these rhythms, and I listen to a lot of things. Growing up in New York, you find yourself in situations with musicians that you wouldn't ordinarily find yourself in. Like, I've worked with musicians from the Caribbean only because they're here in New York, and I make myself available to that.

And there's a certain common denominator. When you think about jazz, you have to remember that people like [Cuban composer] Chano Pozo played with Dizzy Gillespie. People like [Cuban percussionist] Mongo Santamaría do jazz pieces written by people like Herbie Hancock. So it's not as disparate as one might think.

I love playing with African musicians. Because some of this is so basic, but at the same time, it's so complex. And the beauty is, it's just astounding, that feeling of levitation, being able to kind of rise out of your body, or have the whole body move, that sensuousness of the rhythm. It's just fantastic. I mean, they do it in a very, very special way, and it just exalts me, you know? I just love African music.

B. WENTZ: Let's talk about some other things you love. You have a cassette here of you playing with Richard Teitelbaum, an American composer who's been a pioneer in electronic music, especially with regards to improvisation. In your own music, how do you approach improvisation?

ANDREW CYRILLE: There are a couple of ways that you can approach improvisation. You can have some thematic material that you can improvise on, which simply means composing variations on it. Another way of doing is the act of playing the music and following the sound, whereby the music becomes a composition itself. So a lot of people do it that way.

B. WENTZ: When you were eighteen years old, you met the pianist Cecil Taylor and went on to play with him for over fifteen years. How did he influence your ideas about improvisation?

ANDREW CYRILLE: With Cecil, I could play just about anything I wanted. So I can relate that experience to other musicians. In other words, the sky's the limit, and I can do and play with whomever and whenever I want. I would even do some stuff with Indian musicians if it were possible. So having that kind of attitude just kind of gives me a license with humanity, you know? If I can find people who respect me and I respect them, and we want to do something together, then we can reach out through the vibration of sound and have something to say to each other and relate to. That's one of the powers of music. And I really have to thank Cecil for giving me that kind of confidence to be able to play in any context, with any musician, simply because I feel that it's right.

B. WENTZ: So, how does improvisation work with someone like Richard Teitelbaum? He's playing electronic keyboards and synthesizers while your instrument—primarily drums—is entirely acoustic.

ANDREW CYRILLE: When Richard and I play, we have rehearsals, we think about ideas, we talk about certain ingredients that we're going to use here and there, and we just move in and around that. But when I play with musicians like [saxophonist] Peter Brötzmann or [bassist] Peter Kowald, for instance, we just do what we do. Sometimes it really turns out great, and sometimes it turns out not so great. It doesn't ever really turn out terribly because we have so much experience with the music, so we know what to do at certain times to make certain things happen. But that's the name of the game, too. We expect spontaneity.

Yale Evelev
Producer

I moved to NYC in 1977 and worked at the Soho Music Gallery, a record store two blocks from my house. At that time, NYC was an easy place to exist in. I was the buyer for world music, jazz, and twentieth-century classical. We hired a lot of musicians in the store: John Zorn, Anton Fier, Anthony Coleman, etc., and a lot of the neighborhood musicians like David Byrne and Brian Eno came in as well. Zorn and I would hang out in the empty store and talk about music. It was during this time that he and I started to discuss him doing an album of Ennio Morricone pieces.

After work, we would go to a small space with Wayne Horvitz underneath the Exotic Aquatic pet store on Bleecker Street, they called it Studio Henry or 1 Morton Street. There would be performances there of people from the improvising

scene, some ticketed and some just happening.
There was a Yugoslavian guy, that would record
all of Zorn's performances. Anton Fier's band,
the Golden Palominos, formed there.

I worked at New Music Distribution, distributing
albums made by musicians considered avant-garde.
We had albums on Phil Glass's label Chatham
Square, John Zorn's Parachute Records, and then
thousand albums by the Residents, Don Cherry,
John Cage, the Pyramids, Anthony Braxton, Harry
Partch, Sonic Youth, and many more. Most were
in editions of one thousand, and most sold very
poorly and are now quite valuable. One album I
produced was the one I had talked to John Zorn
about so long ago when we both worked in the
record store, *The Big Gundown: John Zorn Plays
the Music of Ennio Morricone.*

FIGURE 26.1 BILL FRISELL

SOURCE: STUART NICHOLSON

26

BILL FRISELL

September 23, 1986

Jazz guitarist and composer Bill Frisell cut his teeth in downtown New York in the early 1980s, playing with avant-garde musicians like John Zorn, Tim Berne, and Julius Hemphill. Yet when renowned jazz drummer Paul Motian set out to form a trio, he recruited Frisell and his Berklee College of Music classmate, saxophonist Joe Lovano. The resulting album, *Psalm*, was released on the German ECM label in 1981—around the same time ECM released Steve Reich's *Octet/Music for a Large Ensemble/Violin Phase*, Art Ensemble of Chicago's *Full Force*, and Meredith Monk's *Dolmen Music*—which made jazz heads take note of Frisell's virtuosic guitar playing. "Frisell brings something of an edge to his playing here that is the province of youth and rebellion; something that is as appealing and satisfying as it is challenging," wrote jazz critic Doug Payne.[6] The downtown scenester became the in-house guitarist for ECM. In 1982, the label released his solo debut, *In Line*, which incorporated both electric and acoustic guitars.

Soft-spoken and modest, the congenial Frisell joined me at WKCR to speak about his fifth album, the upcoming 1984 *Rambler* release. He opened up about his childhood, training, fellow performers, and how Pat Metheny's words of encouragement helped fuel Frisell's passion. We filled up the two-hour Afternoon Music show, discussing how difficult it is to straddle both the jazz and avant-garde worlds and how his early work with ECM initially pigeonholed him as a jazz artist. At the time, he aligned himself more with the experimental music scene bubbling up in New York's Lower East Side. Regardless, he believed his music shouldn't be categorized. "I am playing the same thing," Frisell told me, referring to the slidey, almost-dreamlike guitar sound that would become his trademark. "I don't put labels on it, but others do."

B. WENTZ: I read that you learned clarinet as a child at your mother's suggestion. Mothers usually want their kids to learn either the piano or the violin.

BILL FRISELL: There was a program at the elementary school, I guess, when I was in fourth grade. That was when they sent a flier home with all the kids saying now's the time, you can sign up for these music lessons. My parents liked the clarinet, so I got stuck with that.

There was a guitar sitting around the house, and I would play it more for fun. Whereas with the clarinet, I had to practice it every day. The guitar was more recreational. I still try to have fun playing it.

B. WENTZ: So did you ever study guitar?

BILL FRISELL: Around the time I was finishing high school, I found a teacher in Colorado, where we were living. I was able to apply a lot of the technical information that I had learned from playing the clarinet. That opened me up to the whole jazz world, which really didn't exist in Colorado. There was one radio station that played Wes Montgomery or John Coltrane once in a while, but it was hard to find that kind of music out there.

B. WENTZ: You eventually made your way to Boston's Berklee College of Music and began playing in New York, where you met the jazz drummer Paul Motian.

BILL FRISELL: I met Paul through Pat Metheny, who had done a few things with Paul. I actually had taken a lesson with Pat years earlier, and he'd always been really encouraging and seemed to like the way that I play. So he gave my name to Paul, who at the time was looking to put a group together with a guitarist. When Paul called me, it was a couple years after I moved to New York. At that point, I was scuffling around playing all kinds of strange gigs just to make a living. I had even moved with some friends from school to a small town in Belgium, hoping to get work. So to get a call from Paul was a huge break. I wound up joining his trio, and I still play with them.

B. WENTZ: Another person you studied with early on was jazz guitarist Jim Hall.

BILL FRISELL: He had a huge influence on my playing. The first teacher I had in Denver growing up introduced me to his music. There were a few years there where I just sort of worshiped him. I listened to nothing but him and the people he played with, like Sonny Rollins and Bill Evans. I got to do a concert with him just a couple days ago. That was an honor and really fun.

B. WENTZ: Were you playing acoustic guitar when you started out, or have you always been playing electric guitar?

BILL FRISELL: Mainly electric, but I try to play acoustic. There are a few recordings where I play acoustic. Like on my first solo album, *In Line*, I played quite a bit of acoustic music.

B. WENTZ: That record seems so different from what you do now.

BILL FRISELL: It's a more subdued side to what I do, I guess. But that's definitely something that's in me, that's quiet and more relaxed. Although I wasn't that relaxed when I was making that record.

B. WENTZ: The playing in some of your solo pieces has been called "nuanced," and that the dissonances we hear give off a "shimmering and vibratory effect." This auditory effect is what listeners like to talk about in your music: how the way in which you use the electric guitar is different from what one might hear in rock or jazz. What sort of effects do you use to get those sounds?

BILL FRISELL: I use a volume pedal so I can mess with the "attack" of the guitar or the normal picking sound of the instrument. I can take that away and have the notes come out in ways that sound more like a wind instrument. I try to get a kind of a breath going through the note. But sometimes, I try to get a real clear, clean attack. I also use a digital delay that has a real long span of time, like sixteen seconds, which will record what I play. It's almost like having a little tape recorder that I can play live and sort of manipulate things that I played. Speed it up or slow it down, play it backwards, play along with it, things like that.

B. WENTZ: Certainly, you're not the first person to do this kind of stuff.

BILL FRISELL: Everything I do, I stole from everyone else. Starting with Jim Hall. A lot of what I do comes from him. The way he plays with other musicians, the way he listens to people, or the way he voices chords or develops his ideas or whatever. A lot came from him. And as for that tape loop thing, Robert Fripp did that a lot.

B. WENTZ: You've played with a lot of different people—from the Paul Motian Trio and Tim Burns to the rock guitarist Vernon Reid. You're also on three of John Zorn's records.

BILL FRISELL: There are a lot of things that haven't come out yet. There's a piece he wrote called *Cobra*, which will come out this fall. Then there's a tribute to the French filmmaker Jean-Luc Godard. And then, just recently, he did another sort of tribute thing to the crime novelist Mickey Spillane. I'll probably do some more things with John, I hope.

B. WENTZ: Do most people consider you a jazz musician or a new music musician or something else?

BILL FRISELL: I guess it just depends on whom I'm playing with. Different people hear different things, even if I'm doing the same thing all the time. If I'm in a jazz club playing a standard tune, then I'm a jazz musician. But if I'm playing at King Tut's Wah Wah Hut on the Lower East Side with John Zorn, then I'm new music. Or if I'm playing somewhere else, then I'm a rock and roll musician. Or if I'm playing a wedding, I'm that. I don't think of myself as one thing or another. I try not to put labels on what I do.

B. WENTZ: You've brought a tape of music you've done with your own newly formed group, which I've just been told does not have a name. So if any listeners have a wonderful name, give us a call here. The four people in the group are Bill Frisell on guitar, Hank Roberts on cello, Kermit Driscoll on bass, and Joey Baron on drums. And do any of these songs have titles?

BILL FRISELL: These songs aren't really titled. So if anyone has any names for these songs, for the band or for the songs, that would be great!

Gerry Hemingway
Artist

In 1983, I was in Anthony Braxton's quartet. Naturally, this experience was central to this period of time, and certainly, his music had a great impact on me. I also was a regular at The Kitchen. I spent a lot of time in dance and theater since my wife was a dancer. But the major influence in the eighties in New York City was film. We were addicted to cinema; regulars at the Public Theater cinema (often curated by Jim Hoberman), the Collective for Living Cinema, Anthology Film Archives, and the Film Forum, which had a very progressive program back in those days.

I also frequented The Kitchen, the Performing Garage, the place where Richard Foreman performed at the Ridiculous Theater Company, CBGB's, Beacon Theater, seeing James Brown at the Palladium was amazing, and Funkadelic at the Apollo Theater.

Seeing Dorothy Love Coates at SummerStage along
with Five Blind Boys of Alabama was amazing,
and seeing Merle Haggard with Earl Howard at the
Westbury Music Fair on Long Island was completely
outstanding.

I listened to WKCR all the time, collected
music, read a lot of William Faulkner on the
subway to work, and began crafting a solo music
that would make up my first solo release,
"Solo Works," on Auricle Records that was first
presented live at The Kitchen in 1980. I did all
of this in my apartment in L.I.C., Queens. It
was a time where I began to refine my personal
ideas and my conception as a musician. It was a
crucial transition.

FIGURE 27.1 RONALD SHANNON JACKSON
SOURCE: DEBORAH FEINGOLD

27
RONALD SHANNON JACKSON
May 1987

Avant-garde jazz drummer and composer Ronald Shannon Jackson wrote classical suites, dance songs, improvisational compositions, and jams. He was a sideman, bandleader, and arranger. A student of pianist Cecil Taylor, Jackson culled his sound from working with saxophonist Ornette Coleman, Taylor, and guitarist James Blood Ulmer.

Jazz musicians always scared me a bit. They were erudite, witty, and complex, and I hadn't grown up listening to their music. But Jackson seemed approachable. He'd traveled to Africa, where I had just been. He'd incorporated worldly rhythms that I had a passion for and understanding of. He'd been grounded in Buddhism and meditation, a practice I had incorporated into my life.

We met at his Upper West Side apartment, where we sat on the floor of a sparsely furnished room. Jackson referenced the Buddhist chant "Namu myōhō renge kyō" numerous times throughout our interview, impressing the importance of this tradition in his thought process and attitude towards life. He had just released *Barbecue Dog*, a 1983 Antilles label release with his ever-growing free-form funk group Decoding Society, which included guitarist Vernon Reid, bassist Melvin Gibbs, and bassist Bruce Johnson. Ronald Shannon Jackson and the Decoding Society melded together numerous genres of music, including Central African, Polynesian, and Middle Eastern rhythms. Members of the band moved in and out. The music was open, improvisatory, yet accessible. "We play with as much life as we can!" said Jackson.

He grew up in Texas, entrenched in the music of Guitar Slim, Howlin' Wolf, Freddie King, and Lightnin' Hopkins. His parents were musical; Jackson's mom played piano and organ, and his father ran one of the only Black-owned record stores in Fort Worth, Texas. He attended college in Missouri, and near there, he met trumpeter Lester Bowie and saxophonist Julius Hemphill (the latter of which went on to form the Art Ensemble of Chicago). Eventually making his way to New York to attend NYU on a full scholarship, Jackson stayed in the city, studying composing and, of course, working with Ornette Coleman and his group Prime Time. In the late seventies, he formed the free-form funk group the Decoding Society and later joined Melvin Gibbs and Bill Frisell in a trio called Power Tools.

B. WENTZ: You've worked with free jazz pioneers like Ornette Coleman and Cecil Taylor, as well as James "Blood" Ulmer, who leans more towards funk and blues. What sort of influence did they have on you?

RONALD SHANNON JACKSON: I learned a lot of things from Ornette Coleman. I learned things like composing from Cecil Taylor. But the ideas and my own music basically existed before I met these people. A lot of things I do, I was first exposed to them in public with Albert Ayler. The music I'm playing, it's the music I've always heard. I knew that I had this music in my life. But I didn't know how to get it out of me. I had bought a piano back in the sixties, and so I had to write from a piano. And I just didn't have the discipline to do that.

And before I went to music school, I wasn't really interested in the theoretical aspect of training and learning to write classical music because it wasn't my forte. A few years later, I ran into Ornette Coleman. And after we did a long stay in Europe, he used to listen to me play all the time, and he said why not get a flute and write down the melodies I was playing on the drums.

And that was the major influence Ornette had on my life. To actually help me do what I'm doing now. It's not that I went into that group and came out with something. It was like I went into that group with something, and after I met Ornette, I learned how to bring out what I was hearing.

B. WENTZ: But Ayler was probably the first person to allow you the freedom to—

RONALD SHANNON JACKSON: To play, to just totally play. He was the first person who said just play music. Play what you feel we're doing, as opposed to playing background. At the time, I'd been working the bebop scene, and I had enjoyed that. I'd worked with people like Jackie McLean, Kenny Dorham, and Betty Carter, and people in that genre.

But when I started working with Albert, I realized that the things I'd been practicing at home, I could do in public. I could do the things that I'd been hearing and was doing on the drums, but I would only do those things when I was playing by myself. I love playing drums, and it's been very difficult for me to actually synthesize that as a pure, true feeling because I've always wanted to play other instruments. I go to my studio now, and I can spend twelve hours at a time just playing drums. So many fascinating things come out of that, and that's basically where I write the music from.

I don't constantly sit down and write music. I'm playing the drums, I'm working out rhythmic patterns and rhythmic ideas, and if I work on them long enough—it's just like a snare drum, when you play it long enough and you stop playing it for at least half a minute, you can feel electricity come out of the drum. If you put your arm by the drum, it will raise all the hairs on your arm, you know? Because it has this electricity that you have been injecting into it.

My point is that if you play enough rhythms with enough concentration, the melodies emerge, just like a bubble. All you have to do is remain in that concentrated state and remain almost as blank as you possibly can and write the music.

So that when I do hear a melody, I block everything out and focus on writing that melody. Because it's not something that belongs to me. I'm just given the responsibility of making it manifest in the environment, you know?

B. WENTZ: So you write parts down, and those are what the other instrumentalists in your group play.

RONALD SHANNON JACKSON: I write out the composition and I work on it. I'll write the composition first at the bottom of my music manuscript paper, especially when the music is coming from rhythm. That's maybe one of the problems I have . . . or virtues. I think it's a virtue that I don't have mass pop appeal or anything like that. I'm much more satisfied playing rhythms with melody as opposed to taking the melody and trying to make it match the rhythm. Today, people are listening to basically the beat on one, or two and four. The melodies I hear [as a drummer] and work with are a little more complicated. As a result, most of my compositions incorporate different rhythms and varying melodies.

B. WENTZ: Much of your music seems to be based on repetitive themes or a theme that comes in and goes out. Are there any styles of music that have influenced you? Or is it just your general knowledge of different types of world music that you incorporate?

RONALD SHANNON JACKSON: My first response is, basically, I don't set out with a form. Some of the compositions I personally enjoy most are not on my recordings—mainly because record companies find them too inaccessible.

So most of the compositions I've recorded were made so they can get some sort of radio play. That means the pieces have to be shorter and more compact. But the compositions I enjoy most are the ones that are much longer, more extended. I'm just not allowed to put those on a record.

On the new recording I have coming out, *When Colors Play*, the composition I enjoy most is a suite I wrote that we could only put on the CD. Now to me, I think that's one of the most fantastic things that happened for this music. Because with CDs, I can play extensive compositions since there's more room. And that's another problem I encounter with this music is that it's so dense that it could never sound like, say, like a Michael Jackson record or a U2 record or a Prince record because I'm feeding too much information. And modern technology is not geared towards the amount of information I'm trying to put on tape. Now that seems ironic since you have classical music being recorded and so forth.

Another problem I had is that to create music with intensity and drive, I use two basses, and they eat up all the tape. So I can't make records that are twenty and twenty-one and twenty-two minutes long. Because when I make a record like that, if you play it on the radio and they play another composition from another artist, my record will sound very tinny. You wouldn't hear the bottom because the bottom is being eaten up by all that information. And CDs allow you to do that for seventy-two minutes instead of thirty-eight minutes. So now I'm gearing my music more toward the CD, which allows me to do what I want to do.

B. WENTZ: You formed your own group, the Decoding Society, in 1979. Can you talk about the ideas behind the group and what you're trying to achieve?

RONALD SHANNON JACKSON: What I'm doing with the Decoding Society is playing music that is the spirit of music itself. Music is spiritual as well as emotional and physical. But the spiritual aspect, and what I mean by *spiritual* is the spirit in which the musician wants to play, and the spirit of what you hear in most instrumental music is almost totally different from what happens with a singer who's able to totally express their emotions.

With instrumentalists, we're expected to play more background, and I think this has played havoc in what we hear. With the Decoding Society, we just do what is natural to do with the music. In other words, I'm not trying to make the music commercially viable because I know that there's a large audience of people who need the spirit of the music and the spirit of music played the way the music is itself, as opposed to people who are mass-moved, you know? So that's what I do. I have to remain true to myself, so I have to remain true to the music that I'm playing.

So we play the music with as much life at this moment, in the eighties, as we possibly can. We just interpret the music—the same way as when the original jazz and bebop was formed, it was something that arose out of the environment. Same with Decoding Society. We're not trying to make a hit record. When you consciously try to do that, it immediately takes away creativity. It takes a person to another state. And I don't want to be in my old age thinking, I shoulda, or if I woulda, or if I coulda. I prefer to make the music I want to make now and live with whatever I'm able to create and to make manifest in my life.

B. WENTZ: You've recently been playing electric drums. How has that affected your playing? How has technology come into play?

RONALD SHANNON JACKSON: I think technology is beautiful. I think it's necessary. I will always play the original drums because it's the heartbeat of man, it's the pulse of man, and it's the feeling of man. But I think electronics are beautiful. I think the creativity that goes along with electronics is sadly lacking.

Technology has totally out-advanced musicians. The creativity is not at the same pace. Which I think is great for me because I'm going to use it to the max as soon as I can get enough of it.

B. WENTZ: Where do you see Black music going today? It's certainly not going back to bebop or jazz. It's moving on in different directions.

RONALD SHANNON JACKSON: That question conjures up a lot because there's a lot of pure Black music that won't be recorded. You can go from here down to South Carolina and other parts of the South where there are Black communities and hear some music that is so inspiring and so spiritually strong that you wonder why nobody records it or plays it.

But when you talk about Black music in New York City, one of the problems I see with that is that most of the Black musicians here don't understand their own heritage. So how can you take something somewhere when you don't—it's one of those philosophical sayings, you know, those who don't know history are condemned to repeat it.

I hear and see, and musicians who I think their intentions are great, but when you ask that question, the question conjures up Black music, a Black audience. And if you're talking about instrumental music, there's basically no Black audience for instrumental music. The kind of music I do [with Decoding Society], there's a very, very small amount of Black people who listen to this music.

Black music is always going to move. Black music is the foundation, basically, of this country. Nowadays, you've got people like Robert Cray, who represents the rhythm and blues for the yuppy crowd, but if those people could have heard Jimmy Reed and Howlin' Wolf and Guitar Slim and the musicians I heard playing the blues as a child down in Texas, that's a different experience because those people were playing from their life. It was like, this is what was needed on the weekend after working your ass off all week from sunup to sundown.

People danced with more vigor, and it was the event of the week. You couldn't go bowling or watch TV during the week. You relied on music. And that was the blues as I know it.

And you have some young musicians trying to do a Black rock thing. Rock basically came out of the blues. Today there are some young R&B singers I enjoy listening to, like Anita Baker, and Chaka Khan is my favorite. I couldn't say where Black music is going. I'm not a soothsayer. . . . I can only say that I'm going to continue doing the music I'm doing with all the strength I possess to do it, and hopefully, people will enjoy it.

I have an album called *When Colors Play* that will be out on Caravan of Dreams. It should be out about the time this airs [on the radio]. Some of the compositions I wrote while I was in Africa. "March of the Pink Wallflowers," [from that 1986 release] was inspired by my trip to Africa. One afternoon, I was watching this ceremony that takes place on Friday. In some Muslim countries, in the afternoon, there is a field of people doing their vows, and traditional dancers with all their vivid, colorful costumes sing and play drums. When I saw this, I made a mistake going up trying to take pictures. The drummers came up and let me know "no pictures," but it was alright to record it. So the next morning, I woke up and wrote that composition, "March of the Pink Wallflowers." My room had pink wallflowers, and it seemed like the right mood.

That whole album has that kind of spirit about it. I wrote the composition "When Colors Play" about a day before I left to go to Africa because, as a Black man going to Africa by myself for the first time, I had chosen the most adventurous country I could at the time. Kinshasa in Zaire was my jump-off point, so I figured I was, you know, a little perplexed about it. I didn't know if I was going to be able to return to the States [due to the ongoing civil war in the Congo], so I wrote this composition. This whole album has that feel about it, you know Decoding Society playing music, I wrote while I was in Africa—all the vividness of the colors and the things I experienced there.

The new album we recorded last month, in April, has a lot more electronics than I've ever used before. And it will be my responsibility now to actually coordinate the reasonable input, which is the musicians and the music themselves playing and what the new technology can add to it as opposed to taking away. But I look forward to it.

Robert Longo
Artist, former video curator at the Kitchen

For me the eighties in New York City was like a flash forest fire that started simultaneously with the *Pictures* show at Artist's Space in 1977 and the music scene—the Ramones, the Talking Heads, Joy Division, the Clash, the Contortions all within less than a ten-year period. A new world emerged, burned bright, and then crumbled in the nineties.

In the late seventies and early eighties the minimal and conceptual art on the white wall galleries of Soho was dying. A new art was coming, one that existed in the darkness of night, in performance spaces and in rock clubs.

Downtown seemed to be divided by Broadway: the cliques of punks in leather jackets, dyed hair, and safety pins on the east side and film noir, No Wave artists and musicians on the west side. I felt more aligned with the latter.

All the music at Max's Kansas City was incredible. I played in a few bands there. The downtown art and music scene was raging, and experimental art rock was the best with the emergence of Rhys Chatham and Glenn Branca. They were like the Philip Glass and Steve Reich of my generation.

FIGURE 28.1 EVAN PARKER
SOURCE: LONA FOOTE

28

EVAN PARKER

November 30, 1986

The British saxophonist Evan Parker has been revered as the father of "free jazz." An experimentalist and improviser, Parker has played tenor with fellow improvisers Derek Bailey, Fred Frith, and John Zorn. His irreverent style contributed to the music of jazz legends Cecil Taylor, Anthony Braxton, George Lewis, and Dave Holland. In the mid-eighties, he contributed to the Charlie Watts Orchestra. Even minimalist new music icons like Michael Nyman and Gavin Bryars were drawn to his intriguing amalgam of harmonics and polyphonic fingering.

Born in Bristol, England, Parker never had any formal music school training. He picked up the saxophone at fourteen and listened obsessively to his heroes Paul Desmond, Lee Konitz, Charlie Parker, Eric Dolphy, and John Coltrane. Eventually, he took private lessons and later met guitarist Derek Bailey, with whom he would play in various groups, including the groundbreaking free-jazz outfit Spontaneous Music Ensemble.

Parker made an impact in New York in the early 1980s, coming here for the first time with his free-improvising group that included Derek Bailey (guitar), Barry Guy (double bass), and Paul Lytton (percussion).

B. WENTZ: It's been a while since you've played here in America.

EVAN PARKER: Not that long. I come here when there's some work to do. I've been here with the Globe Unity Orchestra, a free jazz ensemble formed in the sixties by the German pianist and composer Alexander von Schlippenbach. I've played here with Derek Bailey, the jazz guitarist. And before that, I played here solo. But this is the first time I've come here with a group of my own.

B. WENTZ: Who are the members of your group?

EVAN PARKER: The bass player is Barry Guy, who's a very versatile player. He plays baroque music, contemporary, or what they call "serious music," and also plays improvised music. And the percussion player is Paul Lytton, who pretty much specializes in improvised music.

B. WENTZ: Is most of your music improvised?

EVAN PARKER: When you play with people for so many years, you come to know what they're doing, and you have a pretty good idea of what to expect from them. But in formal terms, everything we do is improvised. There's no fixed thematic material at all. We start from silence and see what happens. But like I said, we have good ideas about what kind of gestures will provoke what kind of responses from one another. So we'll start from something relatively simple and move to something more complex and perhaps back again, which is kind of like a variation on a theme. But none of the material is fixed or arranged beforehand.

B. WENTZ: You grew up on the outskirts of London, near Heathrow Airport. How did you come to play the saxophone?

EVAN PARKER: I began taking lessons at the age of fourteen from a man named James Knott. He had an eclectic approach towards music. He could teach you jazz, but he also wanted you to know about classical music, like Tchaikovsky. I never went to music school. Gradually, I got to know one or two more established musicians who helped me become a little more established myself.

B. WENTZ: One of those people was the drummer John Stevens, a British pioneer of free improvisation, who recruited you in the mid-sixties to join the Spontaneous Music Ensemble. Is that how you met Derek Bailey?

EVAN PARKER: I met Derek for the first time in about '66 or '67. We played together in the Spontaneous Music Ensemble. It was an important early group for me—it's where I met a lot of musicians. Trumpeter Kenny Wheeler, Barry Guy, who plays in the trio with me now, trombonist Paul Rutherford. Those are probably the names that would mean something to people here.

I continued to work with Derek on various projects. We played for a few years in a kind of collective called the Music Improvisation Company. And we've done occasional duo concerts, and I've been involved in different versions of a group he calls Company. We also formed a label called Incus Records with Tony Oxley, a very fine jazz drummer, in 1970.

B. WENTZ: Incus focuses mainly on improvised music?

EVAN PARKER: Well, right now, it focuses even more specifically on the music of Derek Bailey and Evan Parker because it's not really a sanely organized commercial activity. It's very much an extension of our lives as working musicians. So we can't do justice to representing other artists on the label. We can barely do any kind of job for ourselves. At different times, we've attempted to broaden the catalog. But for the last few years, it's gotten really narrow.

B. WENTZ: So musically, you came of age in sixties-era London. Who were your early influences?

EVAN PARKER: Well, my whole reason for playing the saxophone has to do with American musicians, principally John Coltrane and Eric Dolphy. If it weren't for their music, I wouldn't play at all. I was not only influenced but also totally inspired and motivated by them to take up music. And by certain parts of the American jazz tradition.

As far as the direction my music ultimately took, in terms of improvisation, the avant-garde of the early sixties served as a springboard—the work of composer and theorist George Russell, the compositions of Carla Bley, the groups of Paul Bley. I could go on and on, but I think that gives you a rough idea of the principal sources.

B. WENTZ: Why don't you tell us a little bit about the group you're working with now?

EVAN PARKER: This specific trio has one record out. I've got two duo records out with Barry Guy. And I've got two duo records out with Paul Litton. So it's very extensively documented already. Whether or not we'll do another trio record remains to be seen.

B. WENTZ: How do you record improvisational music? Do you take recordings you've done from live performances?

EVAN PARKER: It's a mixture. I actually prefer to record the way they record classical music, which is to use a slightly more ambient studio space. Or a church. Just a big acoustic environment that suits what you're doing, and then record that directly to a two-track master. I find it very difficult to recreate the specific dynamic detail of free-group improvisation in a multitrack, mixed recording.

B. WENTZ: What's it like for you to listen to your recorded material?

EVAN PARKER: Well, I have to listen to it so much before the thing actually comes out as a record that by the time it's released, I'm probably trying to clear my head for the next project. So I don't spend a lot of time listening to the older records. Every so often, I'll have a crisis of confidence and think, "Can I really play? Does this really mean anything?" Then I'll go back to the records and pick some things out and see if it makes sense to me or if it still has some power or strength or vitality. But most of the listening gets done when I'm deciding which material to use.

Graham Haynes
Artist

I was intrigued by several people at the time but one in particular, who I would work with later, was Butch Morris.

Although I really liked Danceteria, I remember Steve Coleman, Cassandra Wilson, and I went to see Kim Clarke play with Defunkt at the Peppermint Lounge. Quite a vibe and quite a show!

Listening to WKCR had very, very profound influence on music that I got into later—experimental electronic music, contemporary classical composition, and various styles of jazz. At that time (since there was no internet) the only way to hear this music was by living in New York City.

MUSICA ELECTRONIC VIVA—FREDERIC RZEWSKI, RICHARD TEITELBAUM, STEVE LACY, ALVIN CURRAN, GARRETT LIST—KNITTING FACTORY, 1989

SOURCE: COURTESY OF THE ESTATE OF LONA FOOTE

ARTHUR RUSSELL & PETER ZUMMO, THE KITCHEN

SOURCE: PHOTO BY TERRI BLOOM

JESSICA HAGEDORN, NTOZAKE SHANGE, THULANI DAVIS FROM TENEMENT LOVER AT THE KITCHEN, 1981

SOURCE: PHOTO BY © PAULA COURT

Turn Up for New Music on Your Radio

New Wilderness on Transfigured Night
5 Live Concerts on WKCR 89.9FM
10:00–11:00PM   December 12–16

Brooke Wentz, Host

Mon: Morton Subotnick "Music from the Dance Orgone"
David Garland "Control Songs"

Tues: Tom Buckner "Full Spectrum Voice"
Judith Martin "Release the Mighty Flame of Cosmic Peace"

Wed: Glen Velez "Doira" for tambourine and voice
Annea Lockwood "Slow Drift Downstream", the Hudson River in the Adirondacks

Thurs: Steve Rathe, w/Leslie Peters "Annie Sprinkle in My Dreams"
Alice Eve Cohen "Street Song" and "Manu and the Fish"

Fri: John Guth "New Works for Radio"
Peter Schumann, w/the Bread and Puppet Theater "First Insurrection Oratorio"

Special Thanks to Connie Kieltyka and Peter Darmi

For information: 212/807-7944

This program is made possible by MEET THE COMPOSER, the NATIONAL ENDOWMENT FOR THE ARTS, WKCR–FM & WNYC–FM

NEW WILDERNESS RADIO FESTIVAL ON WKCR-FM POSTCARD, 1983

SOURCE: COURTESY OF THE AUTHOR

MPOSER MILTON BABBITT AT COLUMBIA PRENTIS 318

URCE: COURTESY OF COLUMBIA UNIVERSITY COMPUTER MUSIC CENTER

CHRISTIAN MARCLAY AND ELLIOTT SHARP AT THE SKI LODGE, 1983

SOURCE: PHOTO BY CATHERINE CERESOLE

THE PERFORMING GARAGE VISITING ARTISTS SERIES PRESENTS

CHRISTIAN MARCLAY

DEAD STORIES

A NEW MUSIC SPECTACLE FOR RECORDS AND VOICES

RENE CENDRE

DAVID GARLAND

SHELLEY HIRSCH

DAVID MOSS

SHEILA SCHONBRUN

SUSIE TIMMONS

THE PERFORMING GARAGE   33 WOOSTER STREET

MARCH 21-22-23

9 PM $8

RESERVATIONS 966-3651

This presentation is made possible in part by the NEA and Meet the Composer,
it is co-sponsored by Artists and Audiences, a public service program of the
New York Foundation for the Arts.

CHRISTIAN MARCLAY, DEAD STORIES FLYER, 1986

SOURCE: COURTESY OF THE AUTHOR

CHRISTIAN MARCLAY, 1987
SOURCE: UNKNOWN

IKUE MORI AND CHRISTIAN MARCLAY AT TIN PAN ALLEY, 1983
SOURCE: PHOTO BY CATHERINE CERESOLE

IOTT SHARP IN STUDIO, 1982

RCE: PHOTO BY JOACHIM RIEDL. COURTESY OF ELLIOTT SHARP

XTC (DAVE GREGORY, ANDY PARTRIDGE, COLIN MOULDING, TERRY CHAMBERS) IN NYC, 1980
SOURCE: PHOTO BY VIRGINIA TURBETT

SQUEEZIES (ZEENA PARKINS, BILLY SWINDLER)

URCE: UNKNOWN

COMPOSER & SOUND ARTIST CHARLIE MORROW

SOURCE: COURTESY OF CHARLIE MORROW

THE RAINCOATS AT THE KITCHEN, 1982

SOURCE: PHOTO BY © PAULA COURT

MARITIME RITES, ALVIN CURRAN, RADIO FLYER, 1982

SOURCE: COURTESY OF THE AUTHOR

BOOSTY COLLINS, MACEO PARKER AT GROOVE ACADEMY AT SOB'S, 1990

SOURCE: PHOTO BY ALICE ARNOLD

JERRY HUNT AT ROULETTE, 1985

SOURCE: COURTESY OF THE ESTATE OF LONA FOOTE

Hal WILLNER

Vernon REID -
"LIVING
COLOUR"

HAL WILLNER, VERNON REID POSTER, 1987
SOURCE: UNKNOWN

MONDAYS AT DIANE BROWN

JANUARY 20   ELLIOTT SHARP

MARCH 24   PETR KOTIK

APRIL 21   JOHN CAGE

PERFORMANCES TO BE HELD AT DIANE BROWN GALLERY
100 GREENE STREET (212) 219-1060

MONDAYS AT DIANE BROWN, 1986
SOURCE: COURTESY OF THE AUTHOR

ROBERT ASHLEY PERFORMING *PERFECT LIVES (PRIVATE PARTS)*, 1980

SOURCE: PHOTO BY ROBERTO MASOTTI. COURTESY OF MIMI JOHNSON

GANG STARR (KEITH ELAM, AKA GURU, ON MIC AND DJ PREMIERE ON TURNTABLES) AT GROOVE ACADEMY, SOBS, 1991

SOURCE: PHOTO BY ALICE ARNOLD

DAVID BEHRMAN, POSTCARD ANNOUNCEMENT
SOURCE: COURTESY OF THE AUTHOR

RONALD SHANNON JACKSON AND THE DECODING SOCIETY (REV. BRUCE JOHNSON, MELVIN GIBBS, ZANE
MASSEY, RONALD SHANNON JACKSON, HENRY SCOTT, VERNON REID), 1982
SOURCE: PHOTO BY DEBORAH FEINGOLD

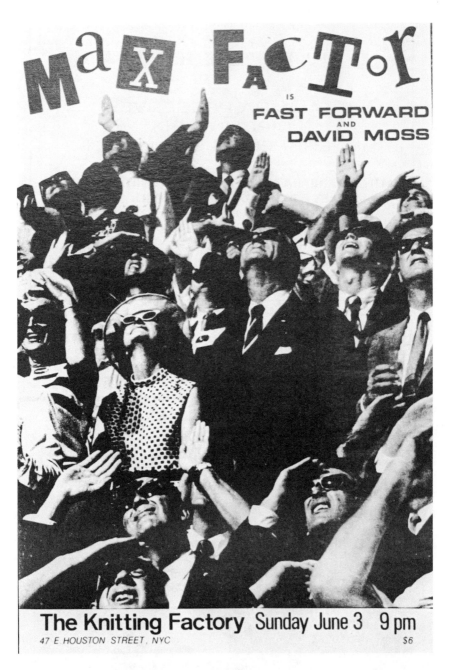

MAX FACTOR (FAST FORWARD, DAVID MOSS), THE KNITTING FACTORY, POSTER
SOURCE: COURTESY OF FAST FORWARD

la monte younG

festival

WKCR 89.9 FM

24 hours

Sat. Oct, 20 midnight - Sun. Oct, 21 midnight

WKCR-FM LA MONTE YOUNG FESTIVAL POSTER, 1984

SOURCE: COURTESY OF THE AUTHOR

ROBERT LONGO, WHARTON TIERS, RHYS CHATHAM, JULES BAPTISTE—APRIL 17, 1981

SOURCE: PHOTO BY © PAULA COURT

PART VII

THE POPULAR
AVANT-GARDE

Pop Idiom Crossovers

FIGURE 29.1 LIVING COLOUR

SOURCE: ANTHONY BARBOZA

29

LIVING COLOUR

July 24, 1990

L iving Colour was one of the first bands signed by New York City's Black Rock Coalition (BRC), an artists' collective dedicated to fighting the music industry's bias against Black rockers. Their debut release *Vivid* became one of the top rock albums in the United States in 1988 and paved the way for other BRC bands such Eye & I, Kelvinator, and Fishbone. With production help from Mick Jagger, an early champion of the band, the album stayed on the charts for fifteen weeks, thanks in part to "Cult of Personality," which landed in heavy rotation on MTV—a first for a Black rock band. By the time the album won a Grammy for Best Hard Rock Performance, the group had already become a bona fide pop phenomenon.

I had gotten to know the group's guitarist Vernon Reid, one of the founding members of BRC, on the city's club circuit, where he could be seen tirelessly promoting fellow bands—many of which I played on WKCR. When I met with the group at the station, all four shared Reid's deep knowledge of music and a commitment to opening doors for Black rockers in the city.

B. WENTZ: The four of you formed Living Colour in 1986. How did you all meet?

MUZZ SKILLINGS. I met Vernon at a Block Rock Coalition meeting in New York. A friend of mine, the manager and producer Bill Toles, was involved with the organization, and he kept trying to get me to come to meetings every other Saturday. They were held at an art gallery in midtown owned by Linda Goode Bryant, who was a major supporter of Black artists. Toles said, "Come to this meeting, meet Vernon, he's looking for a bass player." So I came down to the gallery one Saturday and checked it out. Vernon and I spoke briefly, and I think it was a couple weeks later he asked me to play a gig for the Vietnam Veterans War Memorial.

B. WENTZ: The group had previous iterations under the name "Vernon Reid's Living Colour."

VERNON REID: Yeah, the band actually started around the end of 1983. It went through a bunch of different lineups. I met Corey around 1985 at a birthday party. He was singing "Happy Birthday." It's the only birthday party I've ever been to where just one person sang "Happy Birthday" in a room full of people. We started talking, and it turned out we had similar interests in music and stuff. I met Will [Calhoun] at a gig in Soho. Delmar Brown's band Bushrock was playing. Will and I had some mutual friends, and we hit it off. I ran into him again in Brooklyn at an African street festival, and we exchanged numbers. Sometime after that, our drummer, J. T. Lewis, just disappeared the day of a gig. So I called Will, and he literally had to learn the music the day of the gig. He came in that Saturday, and we rehearsed, and that night we played Maxwell's in Hoboken.

B. WENTZ: What was it about this current lineup that worked so well?

VERNON REID: I think this was the lineup of Living Colour that really worked because everyone had the same sense of commitment, and we all had our heads in the same place regarding what we wanted to do with the music. But we played gigs for almost two years before we got signed to a label. There was a lot of disappointment. We got rejected by everybody.

B. WENTZ: You guys were sending music out to everybody.

WILL CALHOUN: We were sending music out to everybody. One of the interesting things for me was how so many people at the labels were excited about the music and the band, but when it came to the final decision, it was like, well, you're too this, you're too that, no way it'll sell. Things like that. I didn't get upset, though. I felt like we were doing something special. I could have pounded the pavement with this band for the next five to ten years. A lot of people were coming out to see the band at clubs like CBGB's and Tramp's, and they were flipping out about our music. That was a sign for me that this was something different.

B. WENTZ: Corey, how did you feel? Before joining the band, you were pursuing an acting career. You appeared in the film *Platoon* and hosted some shows on VH1. You could have gone back to that.

COREY GLOVER: When I first heard the songs that Vernon played with earlier versions of the group, I was like, this is what I want to do. This is the kind of music I want to play. This was the kind of music I wanted to be a part of for a very long time.

So when the four of us got together, there was a real commitment to playing. We all wanted to give 200 percent to the music because we just thought it deserved that much. We never backed off something. Even if I didn't particularly like a song, I still gave it my all. There was a passion that went into putting it together. And just the energy we felt for each other. That translated to the audience. And to record execs, for the most part. But the whole package was not palatable to them.

B. WENTZ: You've said that Mick Jagger ultimately played a role in helping the band get signed. How did that come about?

VERNON REID: Mick was looking for musicians to play on his second solo album, *Primitive Cool*, and I was invited to audition. So I went up to this studio in midtown. Corey was there at the audition.

COREY GLOVER: I had just left my job at Tower Records. I was horrible at it because I would always let people steal records.

VERNON REID: The audition was . . . I don't even want to get into that. It was a trip. But afterward, Mick walks right up to me and shakes my hand, and says, "I heard that your band is really good. I'm gonna come check you guys out sometime." He probably heard about us from Doug Wimbish, who had played bass on the Sugarhill records and was playing with Mick back then. Anyhow, Corey and I told him that we were playing CBGB's that weekend. We never imagined he would come, but he did! He showed up with Jeff Beck, and they stayed for the whole set.

MUZZ SKILLINGS: We had a really good night. We were tight. And a lot of people turned out because, by that point, we had built up a local following.

VERNON REID: Not long after that, Mick offered to produce a couple of demos for us while he was mixing his album. Again, we didn't have a record deal at that point. We recorded "Which Way to America?" and "Glamour Boys." Mick was a really good producer, very attentive. He has a lot of experience making records. He produced those demos around May '87. That fall, we signed with Epic.

B. WENTZ: That album, *Vivid*, didn't take off until nearly a year after it was released, when MTV began airing the video for your second single, "Cult of Personality." At the time, there were hardly any Black artists in heavy rotation on MTV.

COREY GLOVER: "Cult" had been on MTV for about two months before it really got some sort of recognition. People were calling up and saying, "What's that song? We want to hear it again." By that point, we were playing in clubs all over the country. We visited radio stations. We played in record stores. Everybody had a good feeling about the band. Things just started to sync.

B. WENTZ: When you play outside of New York City, what type of crowds do you get? Is it mostly young white guys?

COREY GLOVER: It changes depending on where we are. I would say that more Black people come out for this rock than come out for other kinds of rock.

B. WENTZ: Is it a real young crowd?

MUZZ SKILLINGS: As we've gotten more popular, we've seen more older people come out. People between twenty-five and forty-five.

VERNON REID: It's interesting. At in-store appearances, you'd see older people who would bring their teenage son, and they would both want to get things signed. Sometimes people would come up to us who you could tell were rockers back in the sixties and seventies, and they'd pay us a great compliment. They would say, "You guys remind me of a time when rock music was sincere and people would try things differently and there was like a real energy behind it, as opposed to nowadays when a lot of bands are more based on a visual image."

B. WENTZ: Right. When you come out, you just play and do your thing.

VERNON REID: When we were on the Stones tour, we had a guitar tech named Larry Chapman, and his twelve-year-old daughter was there while we were doing soundcheck. We were playing an instrumental fragment of "Memories Can't Wait," and she was dancing to it. She told Larry, "That's 'Memories Can't Wait.'" Her father didn't even know what it was. That was heavy for me. She recognized the song without any words. That means she was *really* listening to the album. It wasn't just a passing thing.

B. WENTZ: And she's going to remember your lyrics more when she gets older than her father ever will.

LIVING COLOUR: Right.

WILL CALHOUN: Because as kids sometimes, we focus a lot on the images surrounding the music. We focus on hair or the way someone looks holding a guitar. When I saw James Brown as a kid, I was amazed by the band. But I didn't relate to the lyrics, honestly. I related to James Brown jumping on his knees and rolling over and doing the splits and all that kind of stuff.

COREY GLOVER: I couldn't relate to James Brown at all. He moved around too much. He was screaming, yelling. . . .

WILL CALHOUN: Now look at him.

COREY GLOVER: . . . and doing everything I'm doing now.

VERNON REID: Part of it, too, is a sense of continuing what music did for us. Like when "Family Affair" came on the radio, that was different. Or like when "Black Dog" came out. That was really different. That's a magical thing. And I think it's something that still needs to be in music. Our music shouldn't just tell people stuff they already know or think they know about themselves. Part of it is revealing something different. I think that's what "Cult" did. People never thought about how Mussolini and Gandhi are somehow similar, you know?

It fascinated people. We need to keep that magical element of revelation. That sense of wow. But it's really to keep it for ourselves as well.

B. WENTZ: Do you think that your success will help other Black rock bands? I read that other Black Rock Coalition bands, which are really great, are having problems getting signed. They're getting told that they sound a lot like Living Colour.

VERNON REID: That's a cop-out. That's lazy listening. Michael Hill's Blues Mob is an amazing band. He's an excellent songwriter who's carrying on the blues tradition, and it really bothers me when I hear the same sorts of things being said about Michael that were being said about Living Colour. And now that Living Colour is successful, everybody says, "Wow, you guys really stuck to your guns." But at the same time, these other bands aren't getting a shot. And none of the bands in the coalition sound like Living Colour.

MUZZ SKILLINGS: It's very diverse.

VERNON REID: The one thing that we're trying to promote is the idea of diversity in music. There are a lot of white rock-and-roll bands. And nobody says, "You know, there are too many white rock and roll bands." We don't say that either. We're just saying that it wouldn't hurt rock and roll for there to be ten or twenty Black and mixed rock bands or even more than that.

In fact, it's because of diversity that rock and roll actually even exists. Because of all the different types of people playing the music. So If there's a backlash against that, then it just proves what we've been saying more than ever about race and racism in the business. It just burns us up.

One thing that's real hopeful is that we're seeing now people of different races playing together. That's a really good sign. Arista just signed the mixed Dutch band Urban Dance Squad. And Follow For Now, a Black rock band that opened for us in Atlanta, just got signed to Chrysalis Records. So it's the beginning of a trickle. But we want to see much more happen in terms of increasing diversity in music.

Frank London
Artist

I moved here in 1985 and immediately started
playing with Jemeel Moondoc [sax player]
at Neither/Nor on East 6th Street and with
[composer, conductor, musician] Gerry Eastman
at the Williamsburg Music Center. There were
these squatted and alternative spaces presenting
cutting-edge art like CHARAS/El Bohio, La MaMa,
and the GAS STATION on Avenue C and Houston Street.

Everything in New York connects and is about
connections. I got a gig with my group, Les
Misérables Brass Band, at The Public Theater.
I invited trumpeter Lester Bowie (who I had
studied with) to be our guest artist. Lester
also lived down the block from me in Brooklyn,
and through this, I became a member of his
group, Brass Fantasy. That changed my life. In
addition, the booker at The Public, Nancy Weiss,
introduced me to Kip Hanrahan, which led to me
touring Europe with his group. Through Kip, I
got introduced to the music of Astor Piazzolla,
who I heard twice in one weekend—outside in
Central Park and then in the more intimate space
of SOB's. It was a musical highlight!

The group I cofounded in 1986, the Klezmatics,
transformed Yiddish music and, at the time, the
only Jewish music group to win a Grammy. We were

founded because of the vibrant interchange of
musicians and social action and AIDS activism in
downtown New York in the eighties. That downtown
New York scene became a strong part of our reputation and identity internationally.

FIGURE 30.1 PETER GORDON AND ARTHUR RUSSELL

SOURCE: JOEL SOKOLOW

30

PETER GORDON AND ARTHUR RUSSELL

April 1986

When I met Peter Gordon, the composer and saxophonist was best known for his Love of Life Orchestra, a loose assemblage of musicians that took shape in downtown New York in the mid-1970s. Gordon had set out to create a "populist" outfit where musicians and artists from various backgrounds could perform together. The result was a joyously raucous big band that trafficked in funk, minimalism, jazz, and rock, sometimes within the same song. Their music captured Downtown's free-form aesthetic, and the group's lineup included, at various points, many of the scene's luminaries, such as percussionist David Van Tieghem, guitarists Rhys Chatham and Arto Lindsay, and writer Kathy Acker, to name a few.

Gordon was born in New York City, but he spent his childhood in Virginia, Munich, and Los Angeles, where, while in high school, he met Don Van Vliet (aka Captain Beefheart), who introduced him to the idea that music could be simultaneously raw and intelligent. He got his bachelor's degree in the early seventies at the University of California, San Diego, under the tutelage of experimentalist Roger Reynolds. He earned his master's at Mills College, where he studied with Terry Riley, one of the founding fathers of minimalism, and electronics pioneer Robert Ashley.

Gordon moved to the East Village in the 1970s. Since then, he's collaborated with seemingly everyone in his orbit, working on projects with Laurie Anderson, video artist Kit Fitzgerald, and composing a score for the choreographers Bill T. Jones and Arnie Zane.

One of Gordon's closest friends and collaborators is Arthur Russell, an avant-garde cellist, composer, and sometimes dance-club staple. Intense and whimsical, Russell defies categorization. He's released all kinds of music under a variety of names (and on a variety of labels). Russell appears on several tracks by the Love of Life Orchestra, the most memorable of which is "That Hat." On it, Russell's delicate vocals hover over a skittering drum beat, punctuated by Gordon's funky, squawkin' saxophone. "Arthur said it was about a hat that focused the positive energy of the universe directly into one's consciousness," Gordon told me. The song appears on Gordon's 1986 solo album, *Innocent*. He and Russell graced the WKCR-FM studio to discuss the release and how they met.

B. WENTZ: Welcome Peter and Arthur to Afternoon Music. Peter, you've performed for years in New York with your own group, but this is your first solo record, correct?

PETER GORDON: Yes.

B. WENTZ: The album is called *Innocent*, and it's being put out by CBS's FM label. What does FM mean?

PETER GORDON: Fucking Masterworks.

B. WENTZ: You're not supposed to say that on the radio! We hope no one from CBS is listening. The album includes music from a dance score you wrote called *Secret Pastures*.

PETER GORDON: Yes, the premiere was done by Bill T. Jones and Arnie Zane a couple years ago at the Brooklyn Academy of Music. There are a few things from *Secret Pastures*, and there are a number of new pieces which were made specifically for the record. There's also one cut, "Diamond Lane," that I wrote in 1980 for a film directed by the conceptual artist Barbara Bloom. So the songs on the album cover a spectrum of work.

B. WENTZ: Let's listen to the track "The Day the Devil Comes to Getcha." Who provides the rousing backing vocals on that song?

PETER GORDON: That's Clarence Fountain, Sam Butler, and some of the Blind Boys of Alabama. I worked on "The Day the Devil" with Laurie Anderson, and we had been talking about incorporating a male chorus. Laurie had seen the Blind Boys perform in Lee Breuer's musical *The Gospel at Colonus*, and she said let's call them up. They're great!

B. WENTZ: About two dozen musicians appear on the record, including your frequent collaborator, pianist "Blue" Gene Tyranny. It seems many of them have also played with your Love of Life Orchestra, which you formed in the mid-1970s with percussionist David Van Tieghem. You've said the group is an attempt to create a "democratic music" that includes people from all sorts of backgrounds— classical music, rock, funk, poetry, visual art. That seems like a pretty good reflection of the city's downtown scene.

PETER GORDON: It's been an evolution. I was born in New York, but I studied at the University of California in San Diego and then at Mills College. There are people who I work with now, such as [composer and musician] Ned Sublette, who I met in San Diego. Arthur was one of the first people I met when I came back to New York in 1975. So there's a group of musicians who have been working together under their own auspices or in different configurations. I think what I've been doing in the Love of Life Orchestra is representative of that. I mean, Arthur might use the same group of musicians and call it the Arthur Russell Band, or [composer and trombonist] Peter Zummo might use a similar configuration. But the music is all different.

B. WENTZ: Arthur is looking very remorseful in the back.

ARTHUR RUSSELL: Looking what?

B. WENTZ: Remorseful. Or, I should say, attentive. Arthur, you brought up a recording of your own, which you and Peter produced, correct?

ARTHUR RUSSELL: Right, we had a chance to do something together in the studio. It's called *Clean on Your Bean*. For the vocals, we wanted a bunch of guys doing raps. And these guys we found, they would do raps and they also had a tumbling troupe. So we were going to have a big circus of our own, and they came in and we did some raps, and we had several songs going on at once. But it turned out really good because [producer] François Kevorkian came in and remixed it and made it into a real rap record.

B. WENTZ: So this is rap music by Arthur Russell, produced by you and Peter, right? On your own label, Sleeping Bag Records.

ARTHUR RUSSELL: By Dinosaur L. That's the name of the group. It's a 12-inch.

B. WENTZ: A 12-inch by Dinosaur L. All these names!

ARTHUR RUSSELL: Right, it's like names of bands or names of poems, or names of songs or ideas. And you make up a new one each day, and you try to write them down, but you only get one chance a year to use one, sometimes two.

B. WENTZ: The next recording we're going to hear is something very rare that you brought with you.

ARTHUR RUSSELL: I had a record that was on [Les Disques Du] Crépuscule called *Instrumentals*, which is maybe unavailable now. And they printed the wrong information on the cover. Well, the information was right, but they put the wrong tapes on the record and didn't check the cover. So this is the right groove. The only time you get to hear it is right now.

B. WENTZ: And this is recorded live at The Kitchen with Peter and who else?

ARTHUR RUSSELL: Yes, April 27, 1975, with Peter Gordon, Ernie Brooks, Rhys Chatham, John Gibson, Garrett List, Andy Paley, me on cello, Jon Sholle, and Dave Van Tieghem on percussion.

There are so many versions of *Instrumentals* because the idea of *Instrumentals* is to have a core melody which has no form but which assumes a form gradually and that unites the stream of events of a group of musicians. Not unlike the Love of Life Orchestra. The melodies take on a visible form in the form of concerts. These concerts are recorded, in some cases, and that's why they're put on the record, and they're different versions. But this is the first concert of *Instrumentals*, and it's one of my favorites. The Kitchen has a great room sound.

PETER GORDON: The recording is hard to find since Crépuscule is a Belgian label. So if you can't find it, go to Belgium.

B. WENTZ: How did the two of you meet in New York?

PETER GORDON: I think we ran into each other at the St. Mark's Poetry Project?

ARTHUR RUSSELL: I think the first time I ever saw you was when [English experimental composer] Cornelius Cardew was answering questions after his concert. That's when I talked to you for the first time.

PETER GORDON: That was at The Kitchen, and you were music director of The Kitchen from 1974 to 1975.

ARTHUR RUSSELL: Right.

PETER GORDON: And that was the first time I was at The Kitchen. And it was a very cold day in January.

ARTHUR RUSSELL: Yeah. It was a good concert, and you had some good things to say. I remember.

PETER GORDON: I was probably obnoxious.

ARTHUR RUSSELL: Yeah, you were leaning against the pole.

PETER GORDON: I actually met David [Van Tieghem] through Arthur.

ARTHUR RUSSELL: Yeah.

B. WENTZ: The track "That Hat" is one you both wrote together?

ARTHUR RUSSELL: Yeah. I bought a hat just for the occasion.

B. WENTZ: Oh. So the hat's why you're wearing the pointed hat? Is this the hat that inspired the piece?

ARTHUR RUSSELL: No, the piece inspired this hat. I got it at a place on Atlantic Avenue in Brooklyn. That's where they made the hat.

B. WENTZ: Okay, so let's listen to the extended version of Peter Gordon and Arthur Russell's "That Hat." Thank you guys for coming up.

Mikel Rouse
Artist

Some of my fondest memories were seeing Robert
Ashley, jazz at Barry Harris's place [Jazz
Cultural Theater], Sonny Sharrock at Peppermint
Lounge, James White at Danceteria, and DNA's
farewell show at CBGB's. I saw Phil Glass's
ensemble perform "Spaceship" from *Einstein* [*on
the Beach*] at Peppermint Lounge at rock volume.
It felt like the whole place was lifting off.

All the music I was involved with, from my
pop band, Tirez Tirez, to my chamber ensemble,
Mikel Rouse Broken Consort, to my media operas,
Failing Kansas, *Dennis Cleveland*, and *The End of
Cinematics*, were reflections of everything I was
absorbing in NYC.

FIGURE 31.1 JOHN LURIE
SOURCE: STUART NICHOLSON

31

JOHN LURIE

February 16, 1987

J ohn Lurie, the leader of the quasi-jazz group the Lounge Lizards, is a busy visual artist living in the Caribbean. Although he hung out with the art crowd in 1980s New York—Keith Haring, Jean-Michel Basquiat, Francesco Clemente, and Julian Schnabel—he was impossible to pin down: He was an actor, an artist, a wildcard. But above all, Lurie was a musician. He founded the Lounge Lizards in 1978 with his younger brother, Evan. When we met in 1986, the group was on its third iteration. Prolific avant-garde guitarist Arto Lindsay had joined for a while. Drummer and producer Anton Fier was in the group for a few minutes. Bassist Erik Sanko and singer Oren Bloedow were also in the mix. The only constant members were Evan, the group's keyboardist, and Lurie, who played lead saxophone.

Groomed yet disheveled, slightly arrogant, a constant cigarette smoker, and an avid music buff, Lurie speaks in a low, Brooklyn-tinged accent, even though he was born in Minneapolis. Tall and lanky with sharp features and witty comeback phrases, his movie-star looks and I-don't-care attitude captured the attention of the era's downtown press—arguably more than his music did. "I've been declared hip for so long it makes my skin crawl," he told the *Village Voice* in 1984. "When somebody says, 'John Lurie is hip,' it's like sticking worms on my back."

At the time, Lurie was instantly recognizable around lower Manhattan, thanks to film director Jim Jarmusch, who had cast him in the cult films *Stranger Than Paradise* (1984) and *Down by Law* (1986). Wim Wenders included him in *Paris, Texas* (1984). Despite his notoriety as an actor, Lurie told me he wanted to be known strictly for his music with the Lounge Lizards.

I met Lurie at his downtown apartment to discuss the Lounge Lizards' new album, *No Pain for Cakes*. His girlfriend was moving about, the phone kept ringing, and I felt like I should turn around and hop on the train home. But shortly after he found me a place to sit among the newspapers and magazines littering his apartment, he opened up, and I learned that he had a passion for all kinds of music.

A self-taught musician, he got excited talking about the music he listened to—Astor Piazzolla, Naná Vasconcelos, The Meters, Muddy Waters, Charles Mingus, Béla Bartók, and Vernon Reid. He seemed to enjoy going to hear live music more than he enjoyed performing himself. "I'd rather be spending my time paying $15 to see music at SOB's, Area, or Nell's," he said, referring to some of the popular clubs of the era. Perhaps, having already reached a level of fame on his own, he wanted to relax and listen to others—or maybe leave New York altogether and just paint pictures.

B. WENTZ: You got into music as a kid, playing harmonica in Massachusetts.

JOHN LURIE: I played harmonica for a long time, and I played classical and electric guitar. Then I switched to the saxophone. Harmonica seemed limited, and, at the time, I was trying very quickly to become an adult. I was like eighteen or seventeen, and I couldn't imagine a grown man playing guitar. The saxophone seemed like a more sophisticated instrument to me. It's also sexier, I think.

B. WENTZ: Did you teach yourself, or did you study somewhere?

JOHN LURIE: I never studied. I didn't jam with people or play gigs. I kind of have an aversion to most musicians. I saw all these people going to study at the Berkeley School of Music in Boston, and I didn't like their theory of what music was about, so I kind of avoided the whole thing.

B. WENTZ: When you came to New York around the mid-1970s, did you connect immediately with the scene that was happening here?

JOHN LURIE: I was more hooked into film at the time. Artists like Vito Acconci were making these Super 8 films and video installations that I was very impressed with when I came to New York. In terms of music, the two things I saw around that time that kind of blew me away were [free jazz group] the Revolutionary Ensemble and [no wave jazz act] James Chance and the Contortions. Other than that, the music scene for me was kind of dead until the late 1970s. That was when all these people who weren't really musicians started playing, and I came across some strange stuff that I hadn't heard before.

B. WENTZ: So, were you playing around the city at that time?

JOHN LURIE: I was making Super 8 movies back then. Nobody knew I played.

B. WENTZ: So your passion has always been film?

JOHN LURIE: No, my passion is music. I think music is a purer art form than film. I feel a bit more deeply, at least emotionally, about music than I do about film. But music's very hard to get across: If you make an album, no matter how great it is, if people can't buy it, can't hear it, then what's the point? Film is more accessible.

B. WENTZ: Early on, you called the Lounge Lizards' music "fake jazz." Why was that?

JOHN LURIE: For our first gig, we took this music I had written for a movie and manicured it to be done on stage live. It just sort of came together and was actually very good. We didn't even think of it as a first gig—it was really just a jam. And suddenly, we got all of this attention. So I called the music fake jazz. It was meant as a wise-guy remark. It wasn't jazz, it wasn't rock, so I thought "fake jazz" sounded good. What does that even mean? It means nothing. The press has such an incredible ineptness in talking about things usually—I thought fake jazz was just, like, kind of obscure enough. It ultimately backfired on us, but I didn't want the media calling us fusion or something idiotic like that.

B. WENTZ: So, how would you describe the new record?

JOHN LURIE: I can't explain the sound.

B. WENTZ: Yes, you can.

JOHN LURIE: No, I can't.

B. WENTZ: Why not?

JOHN LURIE: I don't know—I can't really describe the sound. There's a couple tangos, there's—there's no way to explain it.

B. WENTZ: Is there a horn section? On the lastest album, you have a piece called "Carry Me Out," which sounds very Southern in style.

JOHN LURIE: [Gestures at promotional tape I have by my side.] That's the new record. You have it, so you can explain it. Wait, let's see this. [Picks up the tape and examines the labeling on it.] These song titles are wrong. This one isn't called "Carry Me Out." And the title "Cue for Passion" is spelled wrong. They shouldn't be giving this out. It's all fucked up. Where did you get this?

B. WENTZ: I went to Island Records' office and picked it up.

JOHN LURIE: When did you get it?

B. WENTZ: On Friday.

JOHN LURIE: Shit.

B. WENTZ: So, ignoring the promo tape for a moment, let me put the question this way: How would you describe your music today?

JOHN LURIE: I think it's just kind of like an entity. The sound is like jazz or rock: It's got a very hard edge, like rock, but a lot of the time, the rhythm is syncopated, and the lead voice is a saxophone, which makes you think of jazz. But the conception of the music is more like classical music. Because what we're trying to do is more about texture than about soloing—which is how a jazz band works—or about dancing.

B. WENTZ: It's music that's hard to market.

JOHN LURIE: What's good musically is bad commercially. It seems the only record store in the entire world that carries our last record is Tower Records in Greenwich Village. That's it.

B. WENTZ: That goes back to what you were saying before about getting people to hear your music.

JOHN LURIE: It's a little frustrating. At this point, everybody knows who I am from acting in these movies, like *Stranger Than Paradise*. Which is really not a major concern of mine. What I work on most of the time is my music.

B. WENTZ: Well, it takes a lot more for a person to go out and hear music than it does for them to go see a movie. Maybe it's especially frustrating for you because, given your experience in both music and film, you understand how much more of a struggle it is to be a musician than it is to be an actor?

JOHN LURIE: That's not really true. Actors have just as horrible a time as musicians do. But I would much rather be a musician than be an actor. Life is just better, you know? At least it's more fun.

Pheeroan akLaff
Artist

The music of my mentors Sun Ra, Rashied Ali, Sam Rivers, Milford Graves, Reggie Workman, would mix with African diaspora music. Afro beat, tropicalia, reggae, zouk, and the many types of music we didn't know the names of were palpable for those of us with wide lenses. King Sunny Ade, Tania Maria, Milton Nascimento, Fela Kuti, Salif Keita, and many international musicians would have my very divided attention.

One night at Bradley's I ran into Hermeto Pascoal. I was thrilled to get a chance to sit and talk with him at a table for two. We talked about things in music, and I expressed how much I enjoy his composing. After a modest retort he went on to say, "Yeah, Miles likes my compositions too, and he said he might like to record one of my compositions. But I told him, 'I'm not so sure if I want you to record one of my compositions, Miles.' I could not hold my guffaw or the cognac in my mouth." That must have been a humorous if not lofty conversation.

FIGURE 32.1 ANDY PARTRIDGE

SOURCE: VIRGINIA TURBETT

32

ANDY PARTRIDGE

April 19, 1981

When I met with Andy Partridge in the spring of 1981, his band XTC was one of the most intriguing new-wave acts around. They sounded like the Beatles on crystal meth, merging pop with punk to create songs that were noisy and agitated, danceable enough to get the crowds going at CBGB's but also whimsically artful, thanks to Partridge's interest in the sort of minimalism and avant-garde experiments that could be heard at The Kitchen and Limelight. Though XTC was from southwest England, their sound was tethered to New York.

The group was in town supporting their new album, *Black Sea*, their fourth and catchiest yet, filled with avant-pop nuggets disguised as earworms like "Generals and Majors" and "Towers of London." The album had put XTC squarely on the map in the United States, peaking at number 41 on the Billboard chart. But Partridge seemed unscathed by his newfound pop stardom. He was personable and approachable over an Easter breakfast of scrambled eggs and bagels at the Gramercy Park Hotel. It seemed no one at the hotel knew he was.

B. WENTZ: How would you describe XTC's music?

ANDY PARTRIDGE: To be blunt, it's pop music with all the trappings. We'd like our music to be popular, and we'd like to make some money from it.

B. WENTZ: But your music is more sophisticated than most current pop bands. You use avant-garde elements, and your arrangements seem more complex.

ANDY PARTRIDGE: We have this unspoken code in XTC that we don't break the pop format. It's like being inside a plastic bag, and you're allowed to push it in any shape you want to, but if you break the bag, that breaks the spell. As youngsters, we all liked the Beatles. I especially liked the odder pop songs where they pushed their little plastic bag as far as they could, like with "Blue Jay Way," or "I Am the Walrus," or "Baby You're a Rich Man." But when they broke the bag on things like "Revolution 9," it broke the spell.

I like the restrictions of our code. It's nice. I enjoy being a slave to a certain style or in a certain house that I know I mustn't break from. If you limit yourself to an area, then you can discover every square inch of it. I don't think we've discovered every square inch yet of our format of two guitars, bass and drums, and a couple of voices. I honestly feel that we're pushing it in some shapes it's never been pushed before.

B. WENTZ: The vocals aren't particularly pop-y. They're used more like another instrument.

ANDY PARTRIDGE: When we started playing in the early seventies, I was scared I was going to be a very bland singer. So first, I had to learn to get rid of my American singing accent. Which is how most British rock singers sang until David Bowie came up with this entirely new way of singing. Then it was alright for everybody to sing in their normal British accents. Once I did that, I thought, "Well, I'm not a good singer in the singing sense," so I quite intentionally began singing in a way that was a cross between scat singing and vocal acrobatics. It felt good to do. And it just stuck over the years. So, I suppose I'm sort of a clumsy vocal acrobat.

B. WENTZ: A few months ago, you released *Take Away/The Lure of Salvage*, a collection of dub-style remixes of songs that appeared on XTC's 1979 album *Drums and Wires*. Is this a solo album? All of the songs are credited to "Mr. Partridge," which is you.

ANDY PARTRIDGE: It's me acting as a producer and reattacking some XTC tracks. When you record an album, you put music down on a huge multitrack tape, and then you put that through the mixing desk. However you have the levels set, you make a different landscape each time with the song. What I did was take those original songs and rearranged the mountains and the hills to create different landscapes. So, it's not strictly a solo album.

B. WENTZ: The album also includes a remix of an outtake from the 1978 album *White Music* that was initially called "Refrigerator Blues" but appears here as "Commerciality." The lyrics sound like you're reading a list of charges against capitalism.

ANDY PARTRIDGE: Most of the lyrics for these versions are what you might call freefall association prose. I have these mental menstruations and write down whatever comes to my brain. I write pages of this stuff and just toss it in the cupboard. Then I pull out the ones that might work for a three-minute song.

"Commerciality" is just about a maniac selling stuff. The song "Shore Leave Ornithology" is about a sailor in the 50s waiting in a bar for somebody to turn up, and Charlie Parker just happens to be playing in the bar. It comes from the Charlie Parker track "Ornithology."

B. WENTZ: Where do you get the idea to reimagine XTC songs? This is the second time you've done something like this. You previously put out an EP of dub remixes of tracks from XTC album *Go*, called *Go+*.

ANDY PARTRIDGE: I was first exposed to radical studio altering when I began listening to dub music in the seventies. The first dubby record I heard was called *Ire Feelings* by Rupie Edwards. It was a top-ten hit in Britain. It's just him going "skanga, skanga, skanga," and the vocals are heavily echoed and lots of different bits come in and out. And I thought that was excellent. And somebody said, "You know, it's just existing music that they fed through a mixing desk and carved it up." I got quite fascinated with it. To think that when you went into a studio and made music, it didn't stop there. You could go back in and alter it. I find that quite exciting. It's like stripping down a car and building something else out of the bits of metal, like a sculpture.

B. WENTZ: So, moving forward, you'll be working solely with XTC?

ANDY PARTRIDGE: Oh no! I do lots of side projects, but that's what makes the XTC marriage quite interesting. I'm allowed to cheat on the side, as it were. The problem is time. So much of the music quotient inside my brain and body is taken up by XTC. But if I do have time, I'd like to try some other things. I mean, I do need money. Maybe I can do an album very cheaply and sell it to our label, Virgin. I'm very broke at the moment.

B. WENTZ: You must have made money with XTC? "Making Plans for Nigel" did well in the UK. And the group's most recent album, *Black Sea*, had some popular singles.

ANDY PARTRIDGE: Oh no. I'm not making any money with XTC. Part of the problem is, we embarrass some people in England because we're so English hammy. It's like a member of your family who does stupid things that embarrass you, but to outsiders, they're quite entertaining. It's like we're a little too close for comfort. We don't have any street credibility. We don't do drugs or anything perverse. We're just very quiet people from a quiet town. We do what we do, and we're rather unassuming about it. And I think that provokes people because it's sort of personal.

B. WENTZ: But the response in America has been good. *Black Sea* reached Number 40 on the album charts here.

ANDY PARTRIDGE: Because Americans have no preconceptions as to what we should be. Musical tastes here aren't dominated by the music papers like they are in Britain. So people in the U.S. either like us or not. Whereas in Britain, they tend to theorize too much.

B. WENTZ: At XTC's recent gig in New York City, before the group came on stage, the club's sound system played a piece by Philip Glass. Was that your idea?

ANDY PARTRIDGE: I'm particularly fond of his music. He reminds me of Terry Riley, whose music reminds me of being in the womb or something like that. Philip came to see our earlier gigs in New York.

B. WENTZ: One of your songs I've played on this show is from the remix EP *Go+*. It's called "A Dictionary of Modern Marriage," and for a long time, I had been playing that on 33. And when I first put it on the air, people said, "You know, you're playing it at the wrong speed! It's supposed to be at 45!" But I enjoy it at 33.

ANDY PARTRIDGE: That's the thing about several of the tracks on *Go+*. People tell me you can play them at different speeds and still enjoy them. You were being creative in your own way. I used to do that all the time. As a kid, I would buy Kinks records with my pocket money and play them at 78. It was much more exciting. I used to play my dad's Sarah Vaughan LPs at 16, so she sounded like old blues.

B. WENTZ: Did those experiments influence your music?

ANDY PARTRIDGE: Literally! Everything I've ever done in my life has influenced me. Everything other people have said to me. Every film I've seen. Every book I've read. All those records I played. They have all influenced me. I've modeled myself on other people. Not so much nowadays. But everything that goes through your sensory organs influences you.

Mark degli Antoni
Artist

Three nights a week, I was at The Knitting Factory, upstairs, on Houston Street; my band Soul Coughing started there.

Then at my Harmonic Ranch Studio, on Franklin, I worked with Christian Marclay and Brooks Williams. We recorded, produced, and wrote with Spalding Grey, Richard Prince, Bebe Miller, Karole Armitage, William Wegman, Shelley Hirsch, Anthony Coleman, and more. Using Pro Tools 1.0, we could overdub eight tracks of turntable and then begin "sculpting & carving" the recording like it was a slab of marble; we'd chisel away to reveal something unheard before. It was a very new way of working.

The first time I played in John Zorn's "Cobra," at The Knitting Factory, I was positioned right next to Arto Lindsay. I had met him several times but never performed with him. It was a thunder shock working with him because he played with such exciting force. Marc Ribot was part of the group, and Zorn conducted; it was all very new and transformative for me.

PART VIII

THE GLOBAL NOMADS

International Superstars
of Western Thought

FIGURE 33.1 BAABA MAAL
SOURCE: FRANS SCHELLEKENS

33

BABA MAAL

July 1988

fter promoting and delving into "new music" over the last decade, I decided to take a trip to the continent of Africa to explore the "new" sounds and rhythms in parts of both East and West Africa. In 1988, I ventured on an ambitious two-month trip alone after stopping at Sterns Africa record shop at 74–75 Warren Street in London. I purchased about thirty or forty records and had them sent back to New York City just before flying to Nairobi. My musical adventure didn't officially start until I landed in Abidjan, Ivory Coast, and I started meeting up with artists and music folks whom colleagues in New York had helped introduce me to.

One such artist was Senegalese guitarist and vocalist Baaba Maal. His album *Wango* was on the verge of being released on the Stern's label when I visited him in his home in Dakar. Sung in Senegalese Peul (or Pulaar) language, not in Wolof like his contemporary Youssou N'Dour, Maal's groove-based rhythms, high-pitched vocals, and tiny thumping of the cradled hand drum were all new sounds to me, and ones I wanted to explore and know more about.

Maal grew up in a small village on the Senegalese River. He received a scholarship to study in Paris at the École Beaux-Arts. Upon returning to Senegal, he continued his tutelage with renowned Senegalese guitarist Mansour Seck before recording on his own. I had seen Maal perform at the world music festival WOMAD, founded by Peter Gabriel, and his voice was heard on Gabriel's *Passion* soundtrack. Maal's first U.S. recording on the Mango Record label, a world music sublabel of Chris Blackwell's Island Records, was the 1989 acoustic release *Djam Leelii*, which put him on the international music map. Critics have deemed this recording of Maal and his idol Mansour Seck to be in the top "100 Records to hear before you die." Understandably so, with his passionate soaring voice over simplistic reverberant acoustic guitar. Consisting of songs he'd written five years earlier, the album was a beautiful culmination of Maal's unique Peul style, and the rhythms appeal to all.

I had a chance to meet Maal at his home in Dakar in 1988 during my travels through Senegal. It was toward the end of my trip, and I was simply waiting in Dakar for a one-way ticket back to New York. Maal's warm smile was welcoming to this white female traveler in a sea of dark-skinned broken-French locals. His statuesque and elegant demeanor was amplified by the gold and brass jewelry he wore over his smooth skin. We sat on the floor of his home and conducted the interview in French.

The relevance of including this in the book stems from my pursuit of new music and sounds, and how New York City's panoply of cultures influenced the musical landscape at the time.

B. WENTZ: Your new album, *Djam Leelii*, was recorded in London with a group of musicians you've worked with for a while now. Are all of them from your native country of Senegal?

BAABA MAAL: One is from Mali, and another is from Gambia. Otherwise, the rest come from every corner of Senegal. The Senegalese have many ethnic groups. There are the Wolof in the Northwest, the Toucouleurs in the north, and the Bambaras in the south. So the musicians come from almost every ethnic group in Senegal.

B. WENTZ: You're from the Senegalese River valley in the north. What language do you sing in?

BAABA MAAL: I sing mostly in Pulaar, which is the language of the Peuls. It is a language that is found almost everywhere in Africa, even south of the Sahara.

B. WENTZ: Is there a difference between the music of northern Senegal and southern Senegal?

BAABA MAAL: Yes. In the north, it's the Toucouleurs and the Peuls who live there. They have a cultural tradition that is not the same as the people of the south. There are also the effects of the landscape, the assets of the locality itself that come into play. For example, when you go to Dakar, the capital on the central coast, you go to the sea, whereas in the north, it is more of a savannah landscape. There is agriculture, livestock, and nomadism. And in that region, we make music that is turned towards the interior of Africa. Even the musical instruments we use are not the same as those in the south. But in the music I make, I want to be able to synthesize all the music of Senegal—the north and the south.

B. WENTZ: Your current group plays modern-sounding music. But you're a student of traditional African music as well?

BAABA MAAL: Before setting up this modern electric group, I played for ten years in a traditional group where I played with traditional instruments. With that group, I visited all of West Africa. We went from village to village, we did research on the tradition of music, on the history of Africa itself. How was the music started? Who made the music, and under what circumstances? Why this or that instrument in African music? What is the role of such and such instruments in African music? For example, in African music, to make the arrangement of a piece, you might use a kora, which is like a lute or a harp, with twenty-two strings. Or a ngoni, which is more like a guitar. And you have to know what role the ngoni plays in African music to be able to give it a very beautiful score and a very big role.

B. WENTZ: Around that time, you left to study music in Paris.

BAABA MAAL: I lived in Paris for almost three and a half years to attend the international conservatory. I studied only Western music. As I knew more or less what was going on in African music, I tried to make a connection between the two, to understand the similarities and differences. To know what is missing here and what is missing there.

Africa does not have conservatories. But it has something much greater. It has these families of musicians, or *griots*. I realized in Paris that it was the families of griots that I had left in Africa—*that* was the real conservatory. So when I came back to Senegal, I gave much more importance to African music.

B. WENTZ: When you were in Paris, you invited your local griot in Senegal, Mansour Seck, to join you and play music in the city's Senegalese immigrant neighborhoods. The two of you have played together ever since?

BAABA MAAL: Yes.

B. WENTZ: He's a great guitarist. The rest of your current group is very good as well.

BAABA MAAL: Thank you, they are very good musicians. I am very, very happy to work with musicians like them. They are very human. A musician can have great popularity, but if you still want to be a musician, you have to stay human, to stay natural. When I work with them, the music comes naturally. That's important.

B. WENTZ: When I saw you perform, you were wearing a gorgeous colorful bobo which complimented your dance movements. They are not only extraordinarily colorful but fashionable as well. It was quite stunning on stage. Who makes your costumes?

BAABA MAAL: Sometimes it's me who wants to put on a costume according to my personality. Sometimes there are people who make my costumes. There are four parts that make the concept of African music. There are the gestures up to the expressions of the face, the expression of the hands, the expression of the body, the clothing that one wears. Because we can understand the personality of the musician in relation to his dress. And the colors in our costumes show that Africa is very optimistic.

We know that Africa is going through a lot of things like drought, famine, there is not much money. But despite this, the African is very smiling. They say that things are going well. And this is shown by the costume. People do not like to wear sad things. Even if they don't have any money in their family, they wear something nice. That's very African.

B. WENTZ: Are you recognized on the streets of Dakar, and are griots considered famous here in Senegal and get mobbed on the streets like a rock star might?

BAABA MAAL: Now I don't dare hang out in the street. [Laughs.] No, I know that Senegalese musicians, even if they are very, very famous, are a part of society. So they have to be with the society, in the streets, in the markets. Even if sometimes people come up to say, "There is Baaba Maal," it does not prevent me from walking down the street because it is in the street that I can see what I sing. And it is in those people that I find inspiration.

B. WENTZ: In Zaire, the focus of the music is the guitar. In Nigeria, it's a lot of drums. But in Senegal, it seems everything revolves around the singer. And it seems there are a lot of singers here.

BAABA MAAL: When people listen to a piece of music, first of all, what they listen to is, "What does the singer want to say?" Because the lyrics of the songs come directly from the spoken language of society. It's how we educate society, from infancy to old age. It's like if you want to know something, you open a book to see what this philosopher or others have said. And here, there are no books. There is nothing but singers. Very often, you can hear someone say, "I don't do that because the singer said such and such," or "That's not good. The singer said we have to be united." So the song makes a very big reference.

B. WENTZ: What are your songs about?

BAABA MAAL: Everything.

B. WENTZ: Everything?

BAABA MAAL: Very often, we speak with proverbs and we tell a story. But most often, it is about social life. Like, for example, the cohabitation between people. And what to do so that people can live well together. Then comes the politics, feelings. Everything.

B. WENTZ: What sort of Western music do you like?

BAABA MAAL: Everything that goes through my ears, I like it. Not necessarily for the music at first. For example, if it's an American musician, I try to understand the person who makes this music, his feelings, and so on. Because, for me, it's through music that you externalize your feelings. So I try to understand the personality of someone, what he wants, what hurts him, what makes him happy. I try to understand all that. That's why I listen to all kinds of music.

I don't know jazz very well, but I know it brings me a lot of balance. I like it. I also like Don Cherry. I like how his music opens towards other musical currents in the world. I also like reggae and the message of reggae. The way to assert oneself as a person, as a human being. Music can help a lot, in this sense, to help the person who is a little frustrated, who wants something. It can give you courage.

I think that it is the dynamics of African music as well. It is music which pushes people to think. It educates people. It helps people live better.

Verna Gillis
Ethnomusicologist, producer, Soundscape

NYC was the multicultural haven from which
I programmed during those years. I opened my
venue Soundscape on West Fifty-Second Street in
1979, which remained open till 1984. The venue
put me on the map because it became the first
multicultural presenting space. In 1981 when
the Mariel boatlift occurred, all of the Cuban
musicians ended up at Soundscape because of Andy
and Jerry Gonzalez. They were leaders of the
band Manny Oquendo & Libre.

FIGURE 34.1 ASTOR PIAZZOLLA
SOURCE: DOM SLIKE

34

ASTOR PIAZZOLLA

May 1986

Late one warm spring night, I visited a midtown Manhattan recording studio to meet one of Argentina's greatest musicians—tango composer, arranger, and bandoneon player, Astor Piazzolla. Famous for creating nuevo tango, or new tango, his reinterpretation of the classic tango, Piazzolla was in town to perform for three nights at the Public Theater—his first time in ten years playing to a live audience in New York City. Piazzolla greeted me right as I got off the rickety, scissor-gate elevator and, with a very calm demeanor, escorted me to a high-top table to chat. The sixty-five-year-old was kind, polite, and excited about playing for his ardent fans in New York.

Raised in lower Manhattan in the neighborhood known as Little Italy, a teenage Piazzolla joined a local gang that included future boxing greats, Rocky Graziano and Jake LaMotta, to learn how to fight. This, he explained, is how he prepared himself to "fight in life," and, ultimately, "fight for my music." Piazzolla wrote his first orchestra piece at twenty-five. Around this time, he began experimenting with the traditional sounds and structure of the tango. Five years later, he won a composing competition that took him to Paris to study with Nadia Boulanger, one of the most influential music teachers of the twentieth century. She encouraged his experimentation, giving him the support and encouragement he needed to reimagine the tango.

Although rooted in the rhythms and 2/4 tempo of the tango, Piazzolla's style melds local folk, classical, and jazz music, elevating tango, the ballroom dance music of Buenos Aires, to a new level and incorporating the saxophone and electric guitar. His sumptuous signature style influenced numerous musicians and choreographers.

B. WENTZ: You were born in Argentina but moved here when you were a young boy. Why did your family come to New York City? And how did you discover the bandoneon here?

ASTOR PIAZZOLLA: The story is very simple. My father and mother wanted to come to the States to work very much. When I turned nine years old, for my birthday, my father brought me a strange big black box. Inside was a bandoneon, a typical tango instrument used in Argentina. The instrument was invented in a small town in Germany because the local church didn't have enough money to buy an organ. So they created the bandoneon. German sailors brought the instrument to Argentina in the late nineteenth century, and today, you can't play tango music without it. The bandoneon makes this sad, melancholy sound, which is why the tango is so dramatic.

B. WENTZ: Did you study bandoneon in New York?

ASTOR PIAZZOLLA: There were no bandoneon teachers in New York. This was 1930. So I started playing alone. I used to play the harmonica. I was listening to Borrah Minevitch and his Harmonica Rascals—I loved American music. I had nothing to do with tango.

At the time, a concert pianist lived next to my house, and he would play Bach all day long. And Bach got into me, into my music, and I told my mother I wanted to study with that man. He was a student of the Russian composer Sergei Rachmaninoff, who had emigrated to New York years earlier, and this man taught me how to play classical music on the bandoneon. I played Bach, Schumann, Chopin, Mozart. I didn't play my first tango on the bandoneon until I was fourteen years old. I had no intention to play tango music, but the great Argentine singer, Carlos Gardel, came to New York, and he needed somebody who played the bandoneon. So I played with him and the NBC orchestra. For most Argentines, the most important moment in my life was when I played a bandoneon with Carlos Gardel. But I always explain to them that I think what's important about Astor Piazzolla is *being* Astor Piazzolla. It took me more than forty years to be what I am today. I am what I am today thanks to Bach, to Mozart, to Schumann, and all those great composers.

B. WENTZ: One could add that you're also who you are today because of tango music.

ASTOR PIAZZOLLA: When I was sixteen, my family moved back to Argentina, and I began hearing the great Argentine tango orchestras, and I got a tango attack that really sank into my skin, into my blood. I began playing that music. I was the only musician in Argentina that played the bandoneon and also played classical music and even jazz. I played "Rhapsody in Blue" by Gershwin. I played the music of Duke Ellington. Other musicians looked at me as if I was some strange creature. Tango people are like a sect. They are born for tango, they live for tango, and they die for tango. That's why I left the world of tango when I was thirty-nine years old. I wanted to study classical music and be a composer and a conductor. In Paris, my teacher was Nadia Boulanger. I think she was one of the most important music teachers in the world. She was a professor of Leonard Bernstein, of Aaron Copland, and all the great American composers.

B. WENTZ: What did Nadia Boulanger teach you?

ASTOR PIAZZOLLA: When I brought Nadia Boulanger my music, she said, "This is very interesting. It is very well written music, but I would like to know who is Astor Piazzolla because I can't find him in this music." And eventually, she made me play a tango on the piano. I played just eight bars, and when she heard those eight bars, she discovered that I was Astor Piazzolla in that music and not in the symphonic music. She made me believe in myself. I never believed in myself before. She said, "This is the music you have to follow."

B. WENTZ: So you returned to Argentina.

ASTOR PIAZZOLLA: I went back. This was 1955. Two very important things happened that year. They threw Juan Perón, the president, out of Argentina. And at the precise moment, tango was dying. The music of Bill Haley and Elvis Presley, as well as the Bolero from Mexico, came to Argentina. And all that music, all that rhythm, kicked the tango out. It was rock and roll music that young people wanted to hear.

B. WENTZ: So this was when you began developing your "new tango"?

ASTOR PIAZZOLLA: Yes, I started with an octet at the university in Buenos Aires. The dean didn't want me to play there because tango was considered a dirty word, but when three thousand people showed up to hear me and my group, he said, "Something is happening here." He asked me to play at the university again two months later. At that second concert, we began a kind of revolution. I was changing tango from a crying type of music—the Argentines like to cry very much, they always think of people who are dead—but my music doesn't speak the language of the dead. My music speaks the language of people who are alive. Young people, who liked rock n' roll, came to hear Astor Piazzolla because it was exciting, it was aggressive, it was violent, it was new, romantic—it spoke the same language as rock n' roll.

B. WENTZ: How much of your music is written, and how much is improvised?

ASTOR PIAZZOLLA: Ninety-nine percent is written, and 1 percent improvised. I give my band members the liberty of expression. If they want to improvise or do a different kind of phrasing, they can do it. It's a very curious quintet. I just look at them, and they know what I want. Or if they look at my head or my ears, they know where I'm going to move or what kind of a rhythm I'm going to make—they know everything.

B. WENTZ: What in your music do you find is most important: rhythm, structure, or tempo? All of your pieces are extremely different. You play with tempo: the music moves fast, it moves slow, even within one piece.

ASTOR PIAZZOLLA: I think there's something very important in my music. I don't like to say because it's myself I'm speaking about, but I'll say what other people say. There's a great writer in Argentina called Ernesto Sabato. He says there's tango before Astor Piazzolla, then there's tango after Astor Piazzolla. And the most important thing about Astor Piazzolla's music is Astor Piazzolla, that I don't imitate anybody. And that's why the rest of the musicians, they imitate me.

B. WENTZ: How has your music changed since you began writing tangos?

ASTOR PIAZZOLLA: I change every time I have to do new arrangements, new recordings. I'm crazy and enthusiastic about this new record I made called *Tango: Zero Hour*. It's not only a new way of writing, of composing, it's also a new way of playing, a new expression. I'm sixty-five years old now, and each time I'm playing on stage, I get so happy. I think I've never played how I'm playing right now. How I feel music now, I never felt it in my life. Every day it's a new experience, and the arrangements are different. The harmonies, the chords, could be absolutely different. Every day it changes.

B. WENTZ: So you won't be writing any more symphonies.

ASTOR PIAZZOLLA: I will, but I changed my way of writing classical music. Now I write symphonies as if they're a continuation of the music I perform with my regular quintet. They're symphonies with a popular feeling. That's what Nadia Boulanger taught me, and that's what I'm doing today.

B. WENTZ: Did you coin the term *new tango*?

ASTOR PIAZZOLLA: Yes, I called it new tango because it's a new way of playing tango. In Argentina, they say that most of my music isn't tango. It's good music, but it's not tango. But I always tell people, "What is tango? It's the music of Buenos Aires. And my music is the music of Buenos Aires." Every time you see on television or in a film the city of Buenos Aires, my music is used on the soundtrack because it's the sound of the city. So if people think my music isn't tango, let's not call it tango. Let's call it new tango.

B. WENTZ: What I find so interesting about your technique is how you dampen the sound of things. Like your string players, they dampen the sound.

ASTOR PIAZZOLLA: That's not an invention of mine. What I invented is another type of rhythm. I mean, you can play the violin and imitate a guiro instrument and go *chu . . . chu . . . chu . . . chu.*

We have someone who bangs the violin with his ring, he hits it, and then he imitates a drum doing a pizzicato with his fingernail underneath the strings. With my instrument, I bang my instrument with my left hand, and it sounds like a bongo. And the bass player bangs the back of his instrument, and it sounds like a bass drum. We don't have drums in the quintet, but we always make use of new types of noises.

B. WENTZ: Can you talk about your new record?

ASTOR PIAZZOLLA: I think sometimes when there's a record out, everybody speaks so much about the record, but I always speak for the people who like music. If the people love music, I think they will love my record very much.

B. WENTZ: Can you do me one more favor? This is for one of our station promos. Can you say, "This is Astor Piazzolla."

ASTOR PIAZZOLLA: My name is Astor Piazzolla. I'm sixty-five years old, and I play the bandoneon. This instrument is the sound of Buenos Aires and the sound of tango.

Ikue Mori
Artist

In early eighties, after my no-wave band DNA finished, I met John Zorn, who introduced me to the improvising world of musicians and scene, which opened up whole other possibilities. With DNA, I played CBGB, Max's Kansas City, Squat Theater, Danceteria, but later in the improvising scene, we played the Saint, Studio Henry, Chandelier, where John Zorn organized concerts before The Knitting Factory opened.

FIGURE 35.1 RAVI SHANKAR
SOURCE: JACK VARTOOGIAN

35

RAVI SHANKAR

October 1983

The most profound cultural shift in 1956 was Elvis Presley's appearance on the *Ed Sullivan Show*. But that year also saw a flashpoint that would prove nearly as influential: The release of Ravi Shankar's *Music of India (Three Classical Rāgas)* album. Recorded in London while the Indian sitarist and composer was on a world tour, it introduced Indian classical music to Western ears. Within a decade, Shankar's presence could be heard across the musical spectrum, in concert halls and at stadium shows, from rock to pop to jazz to classical.

Shankar, born Ravindra Shankar Chowdhury, grew up in a family of dancers and musicians in northern India. After mastering the droning, melodic rhythms of the sitar with the help of legendary Bengali music teacher Allauddin Khan, he became increasingly interested in merging Eastern and Western musical currents.

That drove Shankar to tour extensively outside India, helping build a Western following for the sitar. George Harrison picked up the instrument in 1966, a year before he met Shankar in London. Their relationship catapulted Shankar to pop stardom. He performed at the 1967 Monterey Pop Festival, slotted into a bill featuring Jimi Hendrix and the Grateful Dead. His appearance at the three-day festival led to Shankar recording a live album that, remarkably for an Indian musician, landed in the Billboard Top 50.

When I met Shankar, he was in New York City to discuss an upcoming performance at the Lincoln Center. His influence in the United States was going through its second or third iteration. He had been nominated that year for an Oscar for Best Original Music Score for his work on the film *Gandhi*. His imprimatur could also be heard in *Satyagraha*, the most recent opera composed by

Philip Glass, who had worked with Shankar as his assistant on a film score in the late 1960s. Dressed in a traditional *kurta* and *churidar*, Shankar was thrilled to be back in the city, where he lived part-time. Comfortably sitting in a big armchair, Shankar exuded a sense of unforgettable calm and reverence.

B. WENTZ: What do you think has been your main contribution to music here in America?

RAVI SHANKAR: I really think that it should be said by someone in the West because for me to say seems too difficult. But my music, or rather Indian music, has had quite an influence in the West starting around the time that I began touring this country in 1956. Initially, it had much more of an impact on jazz musicians, and then gradually on classical and pop musicians, and now it influences all different kinds of music.

John Coltrane took lessons from me, and he planned to learn much more about Indian music before his death. And jazz trumpeter Don Ellis was a student of mine. Then there were many other great musicians that I composed music for, like flute player Jean-Pierre Rampal and the violinist Yehudi Menuhin. Menuhin is a great man. He is a great musician and also very humble, which is rare.

B. WENTZ: Did most of these people approach you?

RAVI SHANKAR: It was spontaneous. I mean, we met and it just happened.

B. WENTZ: Who were some of your other students?

RAVI SHANKAR: George Harrison stands out, of course. Everyone knows about that. After he became my student in 1966, there was this big sitar explosion, and all the young people discovered me. But it had two sides to it. It was good in a way because the exposure to the music brought such a large audience, but on the other hand, because much of that audience was very young and immature, the whole thing was more like a fad. The attitude was very superficial in the sense that they took it in the same manner as rock or pop music. Not respectful like it should be, the way you would listen to Bach or Beethoven or Mozart, for instance.

Audiences were mixed up with the drugs, and it became very . . . difficult for me. It took about eight to ten years of being in a position to tell them to stop smoking and behave themselves. But it was good in a way because about 5 percent would remain, and they became some of my best students.

B. WENTZ: Can you explain for our listeners what a raga is?

RAVI SHANKAR: It's the hardest thing to explain! A raga is not a composition, it is not a melody, it is not a key or a tune, but it consists of all this, plus it has to be based on a scale. There are seventy-two principal full octave scales in our music, and a raga has to belong to one of the seventy-two structures. It has to have its own ascending and descending structure. A raga can be a five-note, six-note, or seven-note scale or a permutation or combination of any of these. It has to have a special feature, a phrase by which you can recognize it. Like how you would recognize the face of a human being. And it is all these rules and regulations, dos and don'ts, that you have to follow all the time.

It's only possible to understand it after years of practicing those rules, until it becomes a system within you, and when you start playing a raga or singing a raga, you don't think anymore about those do's and don'ts. Then you *can* improvise. I improvise up to 95 percent at times, and that's why many people compare our music to jazz—because of the improvisation.

B. WENTZ: In many of the pieces that I've heard, the tendency is to start slow and build up to a climax. Is this a typical, traditional structure?

RAVI SHANKAR: In India, we have two different systems of music. Hindustani of North India and the Carnatic of South. I belong to the Hindustani system of the north, and ours is exactly as you said. You start from a very tranquil, peaceful mood, which is called a raga, which is an ascending mood and is in all our art forms. So we develop into this tranquility, using pedals, and gradually build up to a dignified bravery, you know, and it goes to the Singara, the romantic and playful, exciting, happy, joyous thing. But sometimes, we might just take a piece that starts very fast. This is, again, the Hindustani system. Others may not follow that system and don't start with the slow thing always and may have the main raga at the end.

B. WENTZ: What can we expect to hear when you perform at Carnegie Hall in October?

RAVI SHANKAR: I cannot tell you the exact raga, but I can tell you that it will be in North Indian style.

B. WENTZ: Who else will you be performing with?

RAVI SHANKAR: The main focus in our music is the tabla, the drums. Alla Rakha is our drum accompanist. He's my friend and colleague who has been performing with me for almost twenty-eight years. I then always have the background drone, which is the supporting instrument called the tanpura. In our country, the tanpura maintains the drone of the tonic note. Their status is almost like a piano player in this country. I mean, they are there, and they're necessary, but anyone with a little experience can play the tanpura.

B. WENTZ: Also, you have a new record out.

RAVI SHANKAR: Yes, a new record I made in New York of sitar music, which is one of my own creations of a new raga. The other recording I've made, which hasn't been accepted yet, was done completely on the modulator and synthesizer. I find it very interesting, and people who've heard it are very excited.

David Soldier
Artist

The Cuban musician scene in New York which
included [Orlando] Puntilla Rios, Ignacio Berroa,
Paquito d'Rivera, and the American Gene Golden,
who knew orisha chants and drumming, was changing
Latin music in the city.

It was an active time. The scene around Giorgio
Gomelsky was exciting for me, including the
benefit for the Plastic People at the Kitchen,
which helped open up the Iron Curtain. Early
hip-hop like the Sugar Hill stuff with Sylvia
Robinson and Tommy Boy [Records] with Tom
Silverman changed the music world as well.

The late Scott Johnson deserves a lot of
credit for making people think differently, as
did Glenn Branca, Robert Ashley, Phill Niblock,
and the artists from the Lower East Side including the Swans, the Ordinaires, and Microscopic
Septet. All these scenes influenced my string
quartet.

PART IX

———

THE PERFORMANCE ARTISTS

Art Meets Movement

FIGURE 36.1 ERIC BOGOSIAN
SOURCE: DEBORAH FEINGOLD

36

ERIC BOGOSIAN

June 30, 1982, and February 18, 1986

One of the most memorable shows I hosted was with actor and monologist Eric Bogosian. He's a voice guy, a character imperson- ator who reveres the oral tradition. When I first met Bogosian in 1983, he had already been a performance artist, curator, and impersonator. In his one-man shows, his chief objective often was to make the audience uncom- fortable. He addressed topics that, in early eighties New York, generally weren't spoken about on stage—issues like race, poverty, and substance abuse. When we played excerpts from his performances on air, listeners phoned the station to complain.

Bogosian arrived in New York with a background in theater but soon left the world of "plays theater," as he calls it, for solo productions. He aligned himself with storytellers like Spalding Gray and the avant-garde actors coming out of the Wooster Group, such as Willem Dafoe, and eventually found a home at The Kitchen, a well-known experimental arts center, where he began staging his one- man shows. He played in downtown clubs like CBGB's as well as in venerated off-Broadway theaters, jumping around stage, and bursting with manic energy as he channeled a panoply of characters, many of them based on people he encoun- tered around the city's Lower East Side.

Bogosian visited my show twice in the 1980s. Affable and bushy-haired, he liked to banter using our "radio voices" ("We should have a war of mellow voices. Let's see who can get the mellowest"), play with the audience, and verbally spar back and forth—even at one o'clock in the morning. "You don't have to ask me any questions," he said. "I'll just keep talking, making things up, going off on tangents. Very exciting."

B. WENTZ: You're one of the rare people I interview on this radio show who is not a composer or a musician.

ERIC BOGOSIAN: I'm a composer. I compose the word things—these monologues that I make up. Then I put them together the way you might put together an album. Like when I was a kid, the Beatles or Jimi Hendrix would put out albums with twelve cuts, around some kind of theme. They were called concept albums. That idea stuck in my head, and now I do the same thing. My shows have around twelve segments, and each of them is around three or four minutes long, like a song. And they come together as some kind of idea.

B. WENTZ: How would you describe the theme of your recent show at the Public Theater, *FunHouse*?

ERIC BOGOSIAN: The show is about all the stuff coming out of people's heads these days, namely the funhouse that we all live in. I play about twenty different people. They tend to be either very normal Americans or real outsiders, like killers or perverts or maniacs. The show is pretty funny and black. Not black as in people who are Black, but black as in humor that's black.

B. WENTZ: A lot of the characters are very New York characters.

ERIC BOGOSIAN: I'm from a town outside of Boston called Woburn. But New York is my adopted city. I live in a very culturally rich part of New York, where the Bowery and Little Italy and Chinatown and fifteen other sick neighborhoods all sort of converge. I find a lot of good people to play down there. A lot of bums and winos and people like that. They get under my skin, and then they sort of pop out as these different characters. If you've got a guy sitting on your front stoop for a couple of weeks, he starts to invade your consciousness. Generally, whoever I'm running into ends up getting into my stuff. You don't want to hang around me too long.

B. WENTZ: You went to Oberlin College in Ohio. Did you study theater there?

ERIC BOGOSIAN: Yeah. I was in the theater. My first role ever was in high school at Woburn. I played Juliet's father, and I screamed and yelled and broke a lot of furniture on stage. That's basically what I've been doing ever since. But after a few years, I didn't want to be in theater anymore, or at least not plays-type theater because that's very depressing in New York. Early on, I put on some plays and worked with some really nice people. But I was working a full-time job just to pay for those pieces, and then you kiss the money goodbye in one weekend. And if no one in the press writes about it, then it's like the old tree falling in the forest—it's like it didn't happen. It was very debilitating.

So I said, "Look, you can't do this, you can't afford it. Just do a solo show and go into a hole somewhere and do it." I really didn't care as long as I was making something. I wanted to have nice rehearsal periods with people, and when it was just myself, then I could always get myself to show up for rehearsal. That's the way I thought about it. So I began hanging around The Kitchen in Soho and did performance art. That was around 1981. Now I'm somewhere in between performance art and theater. *FunHouse* is being performed at a theater—the Public Theater on Lafayette—so I must be making theater. I guess that's one way of looking at it.

B. WENTZ: What were you doing at The Kitchen that is so different from what you're doing now? Or what would you distinguish as performance art, as compared to what you're doing now? Some people might view what you're doing as stand-up comedy in the sense that you do solo shows and impersonate people.

ERIC BOGOSIAN: Like I say, I'm in the theater now, and what I did at The Kitchen isn't substantially different. I always wanted to make performances that were not boring. That is exciting and fun to watch and interesting and about something. When I got involved with performance art, there was a lot of stuff that was very boring and also real conceptual. And I thought that there could be something more done with it or at least different done with it. And since I had theater skills, I would bring those to it because it made sense. But I wasn't going to make theater.

As far as being a comedian, I make people laugh, but that isn't my first objective. And I think that's the difference between me and a comedian. The first thing a comedian wants to do as soon as you walk in the door is to get you laughing, and he wants to keep you laughing through the whole thing. It puts him in a very vulnerable position because if you don't laugh, then there's nothing going on.

What I'm trying to do in my work is to make people laugh and then think about it, and then get scared, and think about why they got scared. And still have a good time—not a good time in the traditional sense but have a very exciting and engaging time. Basically, what I put on the stage is what I would like to see on that stage if I walked into the theater and it was just one person. If I were working on a larger thing, then I would imagine something else up there. But being one guy, I want to see somebody tear ass around the stage for an hour. And that's what I do. I think, right?

B. WENTZ: Yeah, you do it very well. We have an album of yours here called *Voices of America*, which is a recording of a performance you did in 1982. It's like an extended radio show: There are over-the-top imaginary advertisements—one's for a weight-loss drug that's basically speed—and grimly funny news reports, including catastrophic headlines like how the model "known only as the Coppertone girl" goes on a shooting spree on Fire Island. Where did that idea come from?

ERIC BOGOSIAN: *Voices of America* is the voices of TV and radio that bombard us twenty-four hours a day. The idea hit me when I was trying to get voiceover work for commercials. You had to make a demo tape to send around, and since I'd never done any ads, I made up my own ads. I didn't get any work, but everybody thought it was a real riot, and eventually, I started doing it in front of an audience. Then we did it in England, where the album was recorded. Over there, they think we're barbarians walking around on our knuckles. So they think it's really funny if you can show that.

B. WENTZ: Like putting down your own culture.

ERIC BOGOSIAN: Yeah. I mean, I'm mainly addressing Americans, and I want to talk about American hypocrisy and American this and American that—you know, the same old stuff that Lenny Bruce talked about.

B. WENTZ: Did you listen to a lot of Lenny Bruce growing up?

ERIC BOGOSIAN: I read his books. I used to do a piece called the Ricky Paul Show at places like Danceteria and the Mudd Club in downtown Manhattan. Ricky Paul is a similar name to Lenny Bruce, and people used to say that show was just like Lenny. And I thought, "What was Lenny Bruce like?" So I started listening to a lot of his recordings. And Ricky Paul was not like Lenny Bruce, but I think Lenny Bruce is fantastic. Because he tried to expand the way people look at things. And underneath it all, that's what's important. If you have to talk dirty to do it, or whatever you have to do to do it, well, that's hip, to use Lenny's term.

B. WENTZ: How do you approach your work?

ERIC BOGOSIAN: What I want to do is get people really comfortable with a character I'm playing on stage, almost to the point that they can identify with that character. Like it's someone they think they know and can relate to. Then they find out this person is an incredibly ugly character underneath it all. And they go, "Hey, I'm like that in some way." Or take a perverse character and find something about that character you kind of like. Like the guy that starts off *FunHouse* is a rubber fetishist, and I think he makes a pretty convincing argument for what's good about being a rubber fetishist.

The main thing is to flip things around and look at it from two angles. That was the whole point of the Ricky Paul show. I was playing this incredibly sexist, misogynistic, racist, homophobic character, and what I was trying to do was get the audience to see what a crass individual this guy was and how he could make them laugh. If you can laugh at a sexist joke or a racist joke, then obviously, you still have some parts of you that are sexist or racist.

I mean, I'm not out to preach either, which is what Eddie Murphy says. I'm there to get people cooking and enjoy something a lot. But personally, I enjoy things that make me think. But I don't only enjoy them if they make me think, but I like it if they do that too.

That's why I like Lenny Bruce, because he plays around with how much I like violence, or all those, like, edges. Those edges are important.

And the thing that bugs me is people who say some of my best friends are Black, as Lenny Bruce would say. And then when there's no Black people around, they tell Black jokes or whatever. That's not even the point. The point is, are you going to move out of a neighborhood that a Black person moves into?

It's even more complex than that, but the main thing is, now that we've gone through the sixties and the seventies, and everybody thinks they know everything they need to know about everything that's liberal, I think it's a good time to, like, maybe go back and look it over again. Because I don't think we ever really know that stuff as well as we think we do.

And in the middle of all this Reagan stuff—really, you've got to choose sides. You've got to really decide whether you want to be, as my character in *FunHouse* says, you're either part of the problem, or you're part of the solution. That's an old one too, right? But it's got to be done. Nowadays, it better be done in a way that's going to get people into it because I'm not going to get on a stage and start waving some flag or start preaching to anybody because they'll just turn it off. They'll walk right out.

What you've got to figure out is, how do you feel about power? That's a much more interesting thing. How do you feel about fucking over your next-door neighbor over a job or something because this kind of stuff is much more important right now. People are being broken apart, and it's every man for himself. And the only way to fight it is to laugh at it and think about it at least a little bit. Geez, that was pretty heavy.

B. WENTZ: The station's phone is ringing.

ERIC BOGOSIAN: Can I get it?

B. WENTZ: You can if you'd like.

ERIC BOGOSIAN: Excuse me.

[Eric steps away, then quickly returns.]

B. WENTZ: What did the caller want?

ERIC BOGOSIAN: They said they're going to send this station a very nice hate letter.

Zeena Parkins
Artist

Every aspect of my work would have never come
about had I not lived in NYC and participated in
the vibrant, multifaceted scenes of the mid-late
eighties. Working with Fred Frith and Tom Cora
in Skeleton Crew was life-changing. I worked and
recorded with Butch Morris's ensemble for ten
years, was invited to play accordion in a big
piece by Pauline Oliveros, and John Zorn brought
me in to play his game piece "Darts" with dancers
and improvising musicians.

I had a short-lived duo, OWT, with drummer
David Linton, using mainly my electric harp, and
I had another duo, the B.Z. Squeezies, with the
brilliant accordionist Billy Swindler. We put on
accordion nights (Accordion-O-Rama) at PS122 and
Darinka.

Living in NYC was a place where we didn't have
to work full-time to cover basic expenses. The
lifestyle was simple and focused. . . . Playing
all the time, going to rehearsals, going to hear
friends play . . . going to hear strangers and
idols play, or see Dancenoise in small apartment
performances, or the Wooster Group or Richard
Foreman and his Ontological-Hysteric Theater
performances, or Anthology Film Archives, Film
Forum, Collective for Living Cinema. For a
moment, I helped run a tiny, once-a-week venue

in a basement space on East 9th Street called A
Mica Bunker with the improvisers collective.

NYC was a total feast, an immersion into
worlds that were brand new to me, and I loved it.
Friends, lovers, collaborators I made then still
resonant deeply to this day. The streets were
dirty, dark, and, yeah, sometimes dangerous. It
was a moment of heaven before the AIDS crisis
emerged in the early nineties.

FIGURE 37.1 KRONOS QUARTET. FROM LEFT: DAVID HARRINGTON, JOHN SHERPA, JEAN JEANRENAUD, HANK DUTT

SOURCE: NORMAN MASLOV

37

DAVID HARRINGTON

June 3, 1984

ontemporary classical music has generally been performed by the composers, with groups of trained musicians who know the author and are familiar with their idiosyncrasies. In the 1980s, it was rare to encounter performing groups that intentionally decided to tackle and bring new music to wider audiences, exposing odd tonalities, strange tunings, and disparate aural colorings. The Kronos Quartet, a string quartet, was one such group, and they became internationally known simply because they enjoyed the challenge. As their reputation grew, the group began commissioning composers to write for them.

Founded by violinist David Harrington in 1973 with initial members John Sherba on violin, Hank Dutt on viola, and Joan Jeanrenaud on cello, the quartet is based out of San Francisco. I had the chance to meet and talk with Harrington in New York just before a performance.

B. WENTZ: Are all of you from the Bay Area originally?

DAVID HARRINGTON: None of us are from the Bay Area. I formed Kronos in Seattle, in 1973 and at that point, we performed there and really started our foundation for the group. We were there for several years, and then we were invited to upstate New York to teach at SUNY Geneseo for two years. Then the call of the Wild West was so strong we moved out to San Francisco. And it's really at that point that Kronos became what it is now, both in terms of the membership and the vision we have of music.

B. WENTZ: How did you come up with the name?

DAVID HARRINGTON: I was looking through a Greek dictionary with my wife one night in the bathtub, and we were thinking, "Wow, what do you name a quartet?" The quartets I truly admired, in terms of their music, were the Beatles and the Modern Jazz Quartet. I saw that the Greek word *chronos* stood for time and the way time passes. I thought, "That's a good name for a quartet." But I didn't like the spelling. I thought that C-H-R was not nearly as dramatic as K-R, so I changed it. With the K-R, it means something totally different, too. Kronos, with a K, was the god of mayhem.

B. WENTZ: You've performed works written for you by a number of contemporary composers, including John Cage, Terry Riley, and even Frank Zappa. Do any of you compose pieces yourself?

DAVID HARRINGTON: Not really. None of us are composers in the traditional sense. But when we work with composers, oftentimes we improvise, and certain sections are created in a compositional way.

B. WENTZ: What sort of music do you like to focus on? Contemporary? Chamber music? Has the group gone through phases since it came together more than ten years ago?

DAVID HARRINGTON: Well, in '73, the composers that are writing for us now didn't even know about us. So I think the development of the quartet has a lot to do with the people that are writing for us. And I feel we're in a position now to work with some really wonderful composers.

B. WENTZ: Do they approach you?

DAVID HARRINGTON: It works differently with every composer. John Cage's manager called us and said, "Would you accept a dedication to John's new quartet?" It didn't take me long to say yes because I'd always wanted him to write another string quartet. So that was a wonderful pleasure and a great high for me. With Terry Riley, we were artists in residence at Mills College for about two years before we ever really met him. This was in the late seventies, and he was teaching there at the time. We started talking with him about a new quartet, and then, about three years later, the piece got done. Now he's doing another big piece that we'll be playing soon.

B. WENTZ: Who else was at Mills at the time?

DAVID HARRINGTON: The composer Robert Ashley was there, and the whole new music group of the late seventies. At that point, it was a really thriving part of the music community in the Bay Area. It's not right now.

B. WENTZ: What is the scene like in San Francisco now?

DAVID HARRINGTON: I love it because I feel close enough to what's happening in so many different kinds of music. I kind of feel involved in music as a whole in a way that I don't in a lot of other places that we visit. It's probably only a subjective feeling, but it's a nice one to have.

B. WENTZ: Since those of us here in New York don't necessarily know what's happening on the West Coast. Who are some upcoming musicians out there that you like?

DAVID HARRINGTON: Recently, we did a collaboration with the Rova Saxophone Quartet. In terms of bridging what most people see as two different worlds of music, I think that was the most significant thing that we've done. That collaboration is something we definitely want to bring to New York. The idea of a string quartet playing with a saxophone quartet sounds fairly odd. But when you amplify the string quartet, it's an incredibly new sound that's not in the vocabulary of most listeners.

B. WENTZ: Tell me about the piece you're doing with John Geist.

DAVID HARRINGTON: John Geist's quartet, "Fall From Grace," is written for nineteen different quartets. Eighteen of those are prerecorded on tape, and the nineteenth we play live, amplified. We've performed that piece several times on the West Coast, and this summer, we'll be presenting the Europe premiere at the annual festival in Darmstadt, Germany. It's a ten-minute piece and right at the very end, the sounds of mayhem and hell come through with a chorus of voices. So it's very dramatic.

B. WENTZ: What else are you performing at Darmstadt this summer?

DAVID HARRINGTON: We're doing the world premiere of John Cage's "Thirty Pieces for String Quartet." Also, the world premiere of Terry Riley's "Cadenza on the Night Plain," the new quartet I mentioned. And a piece by Philip Glass called "Changes," and Ruth Crawford's "Seabreeze Quartet," from 1931.

B. WENTZ: Are a lot of people writing pieces for quartets these days?

DAVID HARRINGTON: I think probably more than ever.

B. WENTZ: Really?

DAVID HARRINGTON: It seems to me the medium is kind of at the center of European and American music again, as I think it was in Haydn's time, in the late eighteenth century. When you consider that people like Morton Subotnick are writing for us, Michael Hoening from Tangerine Dream, Frank Zappa again, and people like John Geist. The spectrum of interest in the medium shows its health, I think, and it's probably healthier now than it's ever been.

Guy Klucevsek
Artist

One of my favorite memories was meeting John
Cage for the first time. I created an accordion
arrangement of his solo piano piece "Dream" and
wanted his approval to perform and record it.
I mailed him a note, to which I received a lovely
invitation, by postcard, to come play it for
him at his loft in Chelsea, which I did. When I
knocked on the door, he opened the door, smiled,
and said, "Do you play chess?" Alas, I did
not, so I said, "No." My loss. Anyway, I played
"Dream" for him, after which he said, "That's
very nice. I just have one request: please play
this one chord more staccato." With his blessing
obtained, I recorded the piece for a solo album
of mine and have performed it dozens of times over
the years.

My first work in NYC was as a sideman in bands
at La Mama ETC playing for a dance/theater piece.
It was here that I met choreographer Maureen
Fleming and wrote my first solo accordion dance
scores. This was my introduction to the world
of composing for dance, which became my primary
creative outlet for the next twenty-five-plus
years.

From John Zorn I learned that great music can come from any source, and so I acknowledged to myself that I no longer need be embarrassed by my childhood/teenage years as a Slovenian American polka/waltz player, nor of my long-time unexpressed love for film scores, which I had previously thought of as a lesser form of music. I began incorporating these things into my music, much of which, heretofore, had been take-no-prisoners minimalism.

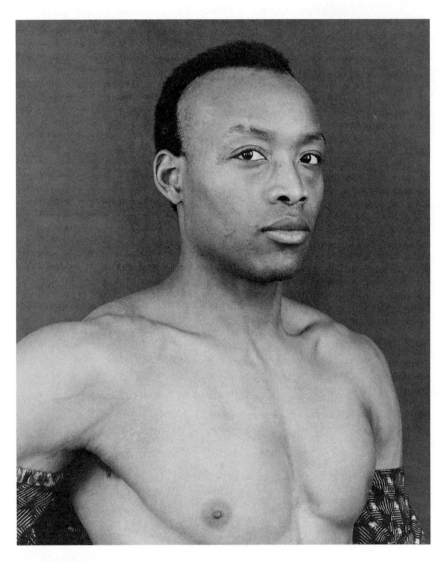

FIGURE 38.1 BILL T. JONES
SOURCE: PEGGY KAPLAN

38

BILL T. JONES

Unknown date, 1985

Dance and theater were vital strains of the avant-garde in 1980s New York. The Wooster Group theater outfit produced performers like Willem Dafoe, Kate Valk, and Spalding Gray. Its space was only a few blocks away from The Kitchen in Soho. Downtown dance companies took the stage at Dance Theater Workshop and The Kitchen before stepping up to present at the Joyce Theater in Chelsea. The Brooklyn Academy of Arts brought to audiences the bigger, more costly productions of crossover theater/dance/opera troupes, like the cerebral choreography of Pina Bausch; the dangling, powdered bodies of Japanese butoh group Sankai Juku; and the Philip Glass/Robert Wilson/Lucinda Childs collaboration, *Einstein on the Beach*. One burgeoning dance outfit during this period was Bill T. Jones and Arnie Zane, who performed together with their company, the Bill T. Jones/Arnie Zane Dance Company, at various dance and music venues throughout New York City.

One of twelve children in a migrant worker family, Jones was drawn to theater and sports early on. He earned a track scholarship to Binghamton University, where his interest in dance took off and he met his partner, Arnie Zane. Through dance teacher Lois Welk, Jones was introduced to the modern choreography of Steve Paxton and started creating his own style. During this time, he and Zane created movement pieces around the music of both modern jazz and new music composers.

Jones is a tall, strappy, strong-bodied Black man, and his partner Zane is a petite white guy. They were a strikingly odd couple. I spoke with Jones before his solo premier of "1, 2, 3" by electronic music composer Carl Stone, a piece by the visual artist Jenny Holtzer called "Holzer Duet ... Truisms," and Jones's solo piece "Make." Jones was deeply attuned to music and sound as well as to the city's art scene. Jones had worked with rock artist Peter Gordon since 1982 and continued their collaborative relationship over the decade. He presented dances to the player-piano works of Conlon Nancarrow, the eclectic drumming of Max Roach, the saxophone of Eric Dolphy, the experimentation of George Lewis, and the works of American composer Virgil Thomson. He was fascinated by the ideas that broke boundaries and how music could provide a narrative spine to his work.

B WENTZ: Can you tell us about the program of pieces you will be performing at the Joyce and what has led up to this moment?

BILL T. JONES: The last four years have been dedicated to changing the media image I had, which was that of a soloist, and as a member of a very dynamic and eccentric dance company I formed with my long-time collaborator Arnie Zane. Arnie and I decided, for various reasons, that we wanted to expand and have an ensemble of dancers, some of those reasons being that we wanted to use a kind of broader palette. We wanted to work with different personalities rather than have a dialogue between two old friends. And that's what we have now, and we're very happy with it. Of course, a good deal of my creative self is a private one, and it is best expressed in solo works. This is a collection of approximately six works. So tonight, I'll be performing six solo works, including a piece called "Everybody Works," which was the first solo I performed in New York in 1976. That piece sort of launched my career in this town.

The ensemble will also be doing a new piece called "Make," which reflects on the Judson Church. I don't know if you're familiar with the church on Washington Square, but it was an extremely active and exciting performance space for dancers and choreographers in the 1960s. The piece includes a text discussion, with Arnie and I looking at photos from that period.

Then there will be a piece called "Three Dances," which has to do with how sound and text can influence pure movement. The movement begins with that beautiful, almost kitsch, Mozart music for brass harmonica, followed by silence. Then you hear composer Peter Gordon's screeching, outrageously grand but very short reprise accompanied by the most foul, loud screaming that I can possibly conjure up while trying to do the movement as pure as I had done it in silence.

There's also a piece by saxophonist Eric Dolphy called "New Formalist." During the intermission, you'll hear music composed by Carl Stone. He calls the composition "1, 2, 3" because it includes parts of the Jackson Five song of the same name. And this brings me to the heart of how I feel about this piece of music and why I chose it. Because when I heard it, it was very intelligent and very witty, and very freewheeling. It was as if you took pop art, pop music, and put it through a Cuisinart of sorts and then rearranged it in a structuralist fashion. That, I found, was quite a wonderful thing that he did. You keep hearing bits of "My Girl," and the Jackson Five's "ABC," and other recognizable bits. And I've tried to construct a dance which draws on images of the Temptations or Michael Jackson or James Brown or Wilson Pickett or even Broadway show dancing. But in the same way in which Carl has chopped up this popular music. So it's extremely repetitive and jerky but full of all that personality. And it's done in a canary yellow suit with a fuchsia shirt. It should be very, very exciting and very beautiful.

The audience hears Carl's piece through the last eight minutes of a fifteen-minute intermission, so many of them won't even know what they're listening to, and then the curtain rises, and the piece comes right out of it because the piece of music is eighteen minutes long. I hope Carl likes it. . . . He's never seen it!

B. WENTZ: Oh really?

BILL T. JONES: Yes. The next piece will be a piece called the "Holzer Duet . . . Truisms." Jenny Holzer is one of my favorite artists who works with words. Kay Larson described her in *New York* magazine as one of our leading "moralists." And she has this way of stating truisms as if she were expressing the opinions of anyone in the world, from the most saintly to the most demonic, from the most conservative to the most leftist. This piece is done with Lawrence Goldhuber, who is a three-hundred-pound actor, and he and I partner each other. We dance, and he recites some of Jenny's words in this wonderful stage voice of his. In the background, there's ambient sounds playing that range from jungle sounds, like animals in a preserve, to beautiful Gregorian chants, to little snippets of popular radio, machine-gun fire, and it all winds up with a waltz by Debussy. So it's quite evocative.

B. WENTZ: You've been incorporating spoken-word passages into your pieces ever since the late seventies when you were performing at places like The Kitchen. What attracts you to mixing text with dance?

BILL T. JONES: Ever since I was about ten years old, I was involved in theater. When I went to college at Binghamton University in upstate New York, I initially wanted to be an actor and go to Broadway. But in college, I became deeply enamored of the abstract beauty of movement. I was an athlete—I ran track— and suddenly, I just put together the things I loved most, the rush and push of the muscles, the sweat. And it was a shortcut to the poetry that I was always looking for in words. Now, years later, I've come back to the words, hopefully in a more direct way, in terms of autobiographical storytelling, images, and descriptive bits of writing. The possibilities just keep explaining themselves to me.

B. WENTZ: How did you end up collaborating with New York composers like Peter Gordon and Carl Stone?

BILL T. JONES: Peter and I first worked together around 1982 on a piece called "Rotary Action" that premiered at the Vienna Festival. I respect Peter a great deal. When we did that piece together, it seemed like a kind of golden age of art—there were very, very smart people coming from the classical, avant-garde school who were turning more and more to the use of traditional instruments like saxophones and loud clanging guitars. And these were feelings that I had too. I was looking for a way out of some of the more abstract avant-garde experiments that I had been involved with. So that's how I met Peter. Artists like Robert Longo were important theoreticians in this way as well. They were kind of bad boys.

B. WENTZ: What were the abstract experiments that you had been doing before that time?

BILL T. JONES: I was doing things that were very strict and compressed. I was saying no to manipulation, no to charisma, no to illusion. And I began to think I could say yes, yes, yes to those things and still make coherent and challenging work.

And these artists were encouraging me. Keith Haring, Robert Longo. Running into Jenny Holzer's work plastered on a wall somewhere. Not understanding how could this person be saying this, and then saying this, and then saying this? And finally, it occurred to me that her writing wasn't about her, but it was about me, about how I felt about what I was reading and who I identified with. Spending time in Soho and the East Village, I have to admit that I was never nurtured as much by the dance world as I have been by the visual arts world or the world of music.

B. WENTZ: You've also worked with the Japanese composer Yoshi Wada. How did you come into contact with him? How did you also come in contact with Yoshi Wada? He is a man who tends not to get out in the public too often.

BILL T. JONES: I must admit, the first time I ever heard Yoshi's music, I was on an arts panel in 1981, and there were these tapes of a person yelling and singing along with the steam pipes. I don't even know if he was funded that year, but I was intrigued by the music. I wanted to know more about it. I had this vision of this person in some funky loft in Soho, plugged into his heating system and making music. I felt a great deal of empathy with it. Then sometime later, Arnie was making a piece called "Black Room." For music, we initially tried some Bach solo cello sonatas and some other things. By this point, I had my own tapes of Yoshi's music given to me by a friend from The Kitchen. And Yoshi's brought this space and ambiguity into the music. Is it Eastern music or Western music? What is this music about? Is it music? Is it sound? Is it aggressive? Is it extremely passive? Those qualities were really attractive to us, and so we chose to work with him on "Black Room."

B. WENTZ: So, you hear the music and then you find sort of similarities or you connect with the music and feel that you're able to dance with it?

BILL T. JONES: Three strong composers sent us music recently. I haven't listened to it yet, but after this, I'm going on tour for a month on the West Coast. Somewhere in Portland, I'll be on a bus and I'll have my Sony Walkman on, and I'll just put on this tape that I received, and I'll just lay back and I won't expect anything to happen. And I might hear one passage.

Then when we're back in the studio, I'll be working on movement one day, and I'll suddenly say, "Hey, what about that passage? What would it be like if I put that passage of music I heard on my Sony Walkman outside Portland and put it together with this movement?" Sometimes it works, sometimes it doesn't. There's a constant cataloging process that goes on. I love to hear new things. Whenever I meet a composer, I always say, "Please send me something." Because if not now, maybe in a year, they'll be the right vehicle for it. Our friend, the composer Julius Eastman, used to say to me, "You don't know anything about music." Then he would laugh that incredible laugh of his. And I used to get a little upset when he said that, but quite frankly, I don't. I'm naive. But I think, in certain ways, I can sometimes surprise a musician by how I respond to what they do. Because I have young ears in that way. We can take the music and show it in a way that's never been seen before.

B. WENTZ: When you choreograph pieces, especially to contemporary music, is it actually notated dance, or is there much improvisation involved?

BILL T. JONES: Let's take "How to Walk an Elephant," which is the first piece I worked on with Arnie. It's also one of his most difficult pieces. I put on the video recorder, and I just went at it, doing a jumping pattern and trying to see how long I could keep up with the music. I captured it all on videotape, but I could never have performed it like that again.

Then I have dancers, Amy Pivar, Heywood McGriff, Janet Lilly, who are very good. They would look and see everything I did, every arm gesture, and learn it [from the videotape]. And it was built with the music but built improvisationally, and they could teach it to a core of dancers. As a matter of fact, that core of dancers taught it to the Alvin Ailey dancers. And that's how the rights are given to a work.

Some works are built completely in silence, like "Black Room." Later Yoshi Wada's music was laid on top of it.

B. WENTZ: As a Black dancer, do you ever feel the need to use in your pieces genres of music that are almost exclusively Black art forms, like African or jazz music?

BILL T. JONES: Well, like I said, we're doing a piece in this performance to music by Eric Dolphy. I need to think carefully, as I don't know as much about jazz as I should. And quite frankly, I'm a product of the rock generation. I like classical music, but I'm more a product of the new music, "serious music," generation. I feel a great affinity for the "1, 2, 3" piece because so many of those artists that Carl Stone has used are Black artists. That's important to me.

B. WENTZ: I ask because a recent *New York Times* piece said racial attitudes figured as themes in your previous work.

BILL T. JONES: They have, particularly in my solo work. But those attitudes are just part of my personality now, they're more integrated and at peace with themselves and in the art I make. I am a Black man. When a Black poet writes, his voice is that of a poet, but it's also the voice of a Black poet. That's how I like to think of what I do.

Bob Wisdom

Actor, music and performance curator,
former music director at the Kitchen

I worked at The Kitchen as the music director
during the early eighties, and my take on
programming took me into all of New York's
big gumbo . . . the Black Rock Coalition, Butch
Morris, Phil Glass, Bronx/Harlem rap worlds,
pianist Borah Bergman, the Cuban musicians like
Orlando Puntilla Rios, Felipe Villamil Garcia,
and the rich Santeria/Lukumi worlds, John
Zorn, Christian Marclay . . . of course Ornette
[Coleman] and being introduced to jajouka master
musician Hassan Hakmoun and gnawa music, and
my teachers Randy Weston, the Art Ensemble of
Chicago, the Lounge Lizards, Vernon Reid and
Living Colour, Olu Dara, Henry Threadgill,
Sekou Sundiata, Terry Adkins, the Bad Brains,
Rammellzee, Thulani Davis, Jessica Hagedorn,
Jamalaadeen Tacuma, La Monte Young and Marian
Zazeela, and Terry Riley . . . it was an endless
swirl and my toes were in every tributary.

I can't begin to express how the time in
New York as undergrad at Columbia, WKCR, NPR,
an incredible New Music America series in
1983 Washington, DC, Laurie Anderson, meeting
writers dancers, pure experimentalists, unsung
musicians, painters, poets, hustlers and the
pop folks, funk and on and on . . . I was knee
deep and I'm still soaked to the bone!

FIGURE 39.1 MARGARET LENG TAN (WITH JOHN CAGE)

SOURCE: GEORGE HIROSE

39

MARGARET LENG TAN

November 1987

The father of contemporary music, John Cage, wrote compositions that could only be performed by very adept musicians. Realizing any of his pieces takes tremendous skill, over and above what any orchestral musician may have learned. Because of the nuances that avant-garde music requires, Cage greatly admired pianist Margaret Lang Tan, a wonderfully curious, classically trained, wunderkind musician.

I had seen Margaret perform numerous pieces of John's at festivals and concert halls throughout New York and always admired her upbeat, vivacious nature. Often, musicians of new classical music can be heady and erudite, but Tan is a ball of energy ready to tackle anything she desires to handle—and the works of John Cage are no joke!

Tan met Cage around 1981. She acquired an affinity for the prepared piano—a piano with objects stuck into and around the strings to create a tampered, resonating sound—and performing classical music with unconventional instruments, such as dishes, cans, and toy pianos. This unique exploration of sound and curiosity ran parallel to Cage's ascetic. Their friendship blossomed, and Tan continued collaborating with Cage until his death in 1992.

Born in Singapore, Tan studied piano from an early age and won the Singapore-Malaysia piano competition, which granted her a scholarship to the Juilliard School at age sixteen. She later became the first woman to receive a doctorate at the school. She continued her studies and fascination with prepared pianos. This passion drew her to seek out composers who crafted in that style. And of course, what better place to be than New York, where she ultimately was able to perform works by and collaborate with George Crumb, Henry Cowell, Tan Dun, Philip Glass, Somei Satoh, Morton Feldman, and Michael Nyman.

I got to know Tan during those early years when she performed Cage's works at New Music America and numerous venues and festivals around the city.

B. WENTZ: How did you get the title of "Queen of Toy Piano?"

MARGARET LENG TAN: I've amassed over eighteen toy pianos and have become a connoisseur in the joys the sound brings to audiences, both young and old. As long as it is not a gimmick, the world will listen to it.

B. WENTZ: Margaret, you have performed numerous premieres of works by John Cage, Alan Hovhaness, and Dane Rudhyar. You study different styles of performance and to learn the techniques used there in order to accurately perform the works in the United States. Just how did all this come about?

MARGARET LENG TAN: In 1986, I received a grant from the Asian Cultural Counsel to spend some time in Japan researching contemporary Japanese music. It was an opportunity to meet composers, including their performances, the styles of music composers were writing in, and the kind of collaborations people were doing in different disciplines.

B. WENTZ: What does new music in Japan really sound like? And where do the Japanese get their influences from?

MARGARET LENG TAN: New music is, generally, I would say, very much more out of an academic tradition. Much more out of the international style. A lot of people are writing in a minimalist vein in Japan, and they might come up with some very nice minimalist works, but minimalism was not a movement that was invented in Japan. It was adopted because it became a big thing in the West. So it naturally became a big thing in Japan too.

I see minimalism as an Eastern-derived Western phenomenon. After all, the music of La Monte Young and Steve Reich and Philip Glass, and Terry Reilly were all, to some extent, influenced by contact with non-Western music. I have been attracted to the works of three composers in particular—Somei Satoh, Ge Gan Ru, and Yoriaki Matsudaira—and will be performing pieces by these composers at the eighth annual New Music America festival in Philadelphia.

Joe Bowie
Artist

My fondest memory was opening for James Brown in
1989 at the Paramount Theater in Staten Island!
We opened the show and were in great form.
Russell Blake: bass; John Mulkerin: trumpet;
Bill Bickford: guitar; Kelvyn Bell: guitar;
Kenny Martin: drums. While we were performing,
James Brown watched closely from his dressing
room behind the stage. When we finished we felt
great. But when the James Brown stepped out on
the stage my band was now in the audience gazing
at the Godfather's show. Once James entered the
stage there was a metamorphosis in the band. The
music got super tight as they clung to James's
coattails. Wow!! The Defunkt Band was in the
audience on our knees praising "the Godfather of
Soul." I will never forget it!

I came to New York from St. Louis, MO, my
birthplace, by way of Paris, France, with the
Oliver Lake and the Black Artists Group. I met
Charles "Bobo" Shaw where together we mixed funk
and popular music with jazz and free jazz. In New
York I worked with James Chance with my brother
Byron on tenor sax. Soon, James asked me to bring
other musicians into his project. And eventually
I created Defunkt, a fusion of sounds new to the
scene—free jazz, funk, rock, a bit of bebop, and
music to inspire the audience to dance all night.
This would have never happened without the genre
mixtures and musical colleagues I met in NYC.

FIGURE 40.1 MICHEL WAISVISZ
SOURCE: FRANS SCHELLEKENS

40
MICHEL WAISVISZ
September 1985

I n my eyes, Dutch inventor and electronic experimentalist Michel Waisvisz was one of Holland's great innovative artists. Artistic director of
STEIM (Studio for Electronic Instrumental Music) in Amsterdam from
1981 until 2008, Waisvisz advocated for electronic musicians building and mod-
ifying their own instruments. His most famous invention, the Hands—a mag-
nificent pair of glove-like electronic gadgetry affixed to the upper torso—was
one of the first interfaces incorporating controllers to use sensors that converted
data into MIDI. He was a performer and composer, composing music using these
electronic contraptions in real-time onstage. Watching him perform the Hands
was like watching a magician perform a disappearing act. Facing the audience
straight on, he'd close his eyes and reach into the air with robotic gadgetry affixed
to his arms and strapped around his chest. He then jerked his body and slightly
moved like he was about to punch someone, all while his feet were stationary.
Gorgeous sounds would emanate and take you on a journey far away from the
performance space.

Waisvisz considered himself a composer of timbres, which included the
process of building instruments. As a child, he played with radio frequencies
through his father's shortwave receivers. He later entered the theater, but he
always considered composing like a performance where one had to be active and
involved. "Touch Monkeys" was an important piece he created at STEIM along
with the "Archaic Symphony." He was always developing new ways to combine
physical touch with electronic music instruments. You felt like he could touch
the electricity and beam the music into your body. "performance is separate
from the work of composing, so simply consider me a composer," he once said.[7]
So Waisvisz spent his many years at STEIM building instruments. One such

instrument was the cracklebox, a hand-held battery-powered electronic instrument. The instrument was attached to your body, becoming a living-wire circuit and making music. This new perception of composition working with sensors and MIDI attracted numerous artists-in-residence and visitors to STEIM as well as symphonic composers and instrumentalists.

Waisvisz was a very quiet and private man. You could sense he had a panache for eccentric electronics and was intent on how to use them and manipulate sound. Erudite, slightly reserved, yet cunningly jovial and intense, Waisvisz was a delight to be around. He loved his work, his students, and, most of all, explaining his work to interested parties. I met Waisvisz in Holland (in 1985) at the studio on the west side of Amsterdam after seeing him in the States at New Music America. I recall the studio as a bit out of the way but a fascinating place where "touch is crucial in communicating with the new electronic performance art technologies." When I met him, about five years after he started at STEIM, he'd already developed cracklebox and was deeply ensconced in his work and performance revolved around the Hands, which I had seen him perform.

B WENTZ: You're known for inventing electronic instruments that you can compose and play on simultaneously. What triggered your interest in creating instruments?

MICHEL WAISVISZ: In the mid-sixties, I was making music with shortwave receivers and strings, and also sometimes knitting needles and guitar pickups, so real old-fashioned mechanical sound production. My father was a ham radio person, and he had a lot of shortwave machines in the house, and when my brother and I were about four years old, we played a lot with the shortwave radio sounds, and those sounds really meant a lot to me. They sort of stirred up emotions and had very direct meanings to me—or at least I could feel it very strongly.

The problem for me was that you could dial and change the frequency but not really change the sound. And so, from the time I began playing around with radios when I was very young, I have always wanted to be able to touch sound, and I wanted to have an instrument that could give me the opportunity to manipulate sound with my hands. Through the years, I've built many different instruments. When I was around eighteen years old, I was confronted with a real Stockhausen-style approach at the Royal Conservatory in the Hague, where they had sine-wave generators, and you could just dial the knob and change the frequency. Musically, they were a bit primitive, and so I was thinking of other material when the first synthesizers arrived in Europe. Once they got cheap enough, I bought one, and I opened the back and started playing with the wires. Apart from being shocked now and then, what I discovered was that it was possible to change sounds by touching one point on the wires with one finger and like connecting that point with another point by touching another point on the wires with another finger. So you yourself would become a wire, like a thinking wire.

B WENTZ: It was around this time in the 1970s that you got involved with STEIM, a research facility in Amsterdam for composers and theater people to develop electronic music systems.

MICHAEL WAISVISZ: That was where I created an instrument based on the idea I had playing with those synthesizer wires. The instrument is called a cracklebox. There are contact pads connected to exposed circuits, and by pushing those pads, you can create direct sound—without being too much involved with the technology. Because the problem for me has always been, how can I make the sounds that I have heard all my life in my head without having to deal with a lot of technology? I'm not that interested in technology. I mean, I have to work with it, but I don't like it, and I'm very happy to have other people, very qualified people, help me with that, so I can focus on the ideas.

So we built the crackleboxes, and I did a whole series of concerts using them. At the time, I was very much interested in what was happening with improvisation, especially in Europe. And so I worked with a lot of improvisers, and I enjoyed having these little electronic instruments that ran on batteries and that you could just carry with you and then stick a microphone and a small loudspeaker in front of them, and that would be it. No big problems, no setup systems, nothing like that.

But after a while, it seemed like all the pieces we played sounded the same, and I sort of left the cracklebox behind. I also left the improvisation scene behind, or somewhere else. I started doing a lot of theater work and went in a completely different direction. But I continued using the technology that I developed with the crackleboxes. Like, I set up contact points on the stage, and by standing on those points, you could make music or trigger all sorts of sounds.

B. WENTZ: What got you interested again in creating electronic instruments?

MICHAEL WAISVISZ: When the first MIDI instruments appeared in the early 1980s, I got interested in how that digital interface used codes to synchronize an array of different electronic instruments and to control synthesizers from the outside. I began to think about creating a controller that you could just carry in a little case and unpack in a concert hall, and you could control as many MIDI instruments as you want. So in 1984, I developed an instrument called the Hands. Basically, they're small wooden constructions that you fit on each of your hands. On these devices are keys for each finger, as well as tilt sensors that sense the distance between each hand and also the tilting of the hands. I wear a small computer on my back that tracks how my hands are being held and how they move and which keys are being pressed. The computer translates that information into MIDI codes so I can play multiple synthesizers just by moving my hands and fingers. It also means that I can move freely around the stage, so I don't have to sit in a static way.

B. WENTZ: But you don't move around much during your performances.

MICHEL WAISVISZ: No. I feel like this instrument really is about the movement of the hands. The sensors don't detect differences in the position of my whole body, but your hands are sort of like aerials or outputs. So ultimately, it has a lot to do with the body, and I think that it's fine to just stand still and have all the energy concentrated on moving your hands. It helps me to concentrate, for sure.

B. WENTZ: So you can manipulate the volume of the sound and tonality through movement?

MICHEL WAISVISZ: When the Hands are very close together, the sounds can be soft. And when they're very far apart from each other, the sounds can get very loud. But you can add other functions to that. You can also control the timbre by changing the distance between your hands. You have very pure sounds when the hands are very close to each other, and as you move your hands further apart, the sounds start to modulate each other, so the rougher the sounds become.

And you can sort of reprogram the meaning of the movement. Like, I use a computer to shift functions with my thumb. With a computer switch in one position, I can just play notes with the keys on the Hands. But when I click that switch, then all the keys get different meanings, and I can reprogram what I'm doing, or I can get a completely different layout for the keys, like a different pre-programmed scale. Or I can even start sequences that begin running as an accompaniment to whatever it is I'm doing. But the Hands don't work like an ordinary sequencer. Once the sequence is run, you can change the speed or you can define a loop within the sequence or it can start repeating itself. And when it's repeating itself, when it's in a loop, you can, again, change the speed of the loop or the direction, or you can move the loop through a sequence that is stored in the computer's memory. So there are a lot of what you would call real-time control possibilities. Ultimately, about a year ago, I decided to stop the technical development of the Hands and really just play with this instrument for a while.

The result was the piece "Touch Monkeys," which we premiered last year at the Pompidou Center in Paris. The original version has eighteen instruments that are controlled directly with the Hands. Each instrument has its own PA system, so there are eighteen speaker systems on the stage. It's like an orchestra. It's like a six-voice piece, but each of the voices is doubled and tripled. And I've found that with electronic music, each sound should have its own loudspeaker.

So we're traveling the U.S. now with a six-voice sound system. But I hope when we premier a new piece here this winter, we can bring over the whole system.

B. WENTZ: What do you like most about working with the Hands?

MICHEL WAISVISZ: First, I really want to be able to play an instrument and not have the instrument play itself. I'm not interested in automated composition. I'm interested in having an instrument that reacts very intelligently to what I do. I'm interested in this funny thing where you can try to play notes in a very distinct rhythm, and then it turns out you make little changes, and you don't play it exactly right. In that area where you don't do it exactly right, there's so much information about yourself, about your musicality. It's in that area where our sensuality is probably stored. So I'm really interested in having a direct physical connection with the instrument.

And musically, I really like pieces that are not minimal. Like, I really want extremes to be in one piece, and I feel sometimes I haven't found a way to express it very well. It definitely comes back to Romanticism in the sense that it gets very emotional if you hook an instrument directly to your body. But I mix up so much different information in the pieces that it sort of doesn't get a chance to really develop in a very consistent way. And that's what I really want. I like these incredible changes and dynamics, like extremely loud and extremely soft. I don't like that simple idea of it being just very soft or just empty or just loud. But then you get this problem of how do you structure the piece, and you start really thinking about composition again. And what is new to me, with the Hands, is that the composition activity, the real labor, is now being done right on stage.

And it's possible, with the help of computers, to have prearranged structures that you can use, but while they run, you can also completely change them. So you can be a performer on stage, but if you have to play each note, then you're concentrated so much on the single notes that you're not a good composer any-more. That's the problem with real free improvisation music. You can see that all these pieces sound the same after a while.

But with the help of these machines, you can sort of prepare a structure, and you can control the structure at a very high level. But sometimes, you can also dive down and really control that single note. So in that sense, you can be a composer and a performer and a conductor at the same time, on stage or at home. And that's something that really is possible with this technology.

I'm aware that, in my case, I have to be a performer and a composer at the same time. Sometimes it works fantastically, but at other moments, it can be really hard to oversee the whole structure. It's impossible to stand in front of an orchestra and to tell them to play this note and to do this and to make it louder. With the electronic stuff, you can select a structure, and then the structure starts playing. And while it's playing, you can change the ingredients. And that's what I'm working on because it doesn't work as well as I'm trying to describe at this moment. There are still a lot of problems to figure out.

B. WENTZ: Do you see technology on the horizon that can help solve those problems?

MICHEL WAISVISZ: At this moment, you can see there is a sort of halt in the development of new synthesis systems, although people are working on it. You can see that there are these big samplers that are getting cheaper now. I'm afraid the industry will concentrate on having interesting systems become very cheap and widespread and that less development is going to be done into the area of really refining or thinking of new synthesis techniques.

Also, all these systems are getting so light and portable, people want to drag their stuff on stage. That means that people will need new controller systems, and the Hands could possibly contribute to that or other instruments that are developed in other places.

But the real thing I see is that composers and musicians are sticking to keyboards or, at least, to the instrument that they learned. And you can see, there are some really interesting controllers being developed, like Nyle Steiner's EWI, which can control woodwinds along with external synthesizers. So you sort of adapt to the old styles. At STEIM, we're happy that there's interest from Yamaha to develop a Hands-like instrument and to start using that in their schools with children. But anyway, I think that what will happen, there's a lot of interest in the academic electronic music world for a new input device, but you see a lot of composers that find it sort of horrible to see that their long labor in the studio or behind computer terminals gets sort of neglected and that there are people now that can just stick on some hands, go on stage and play all these sounds in a few seconds, where before they had to work for months to produce similar sounds.

And there are some people that really feel this is lowering the level of electronic music composition. And I don't believe that's true. I think it's a logical phase that you would want to get to the point with electronic music where you can compose and play it in front of an audience, that you want to be near them. I see what composers have done with electronic music in isolated studios, and I respect a lot of the people who do that kind of work. But music is something that is between people, and that should be alive, and that should be something that can alter itself in front of an audience. It shouldn't only be a formal study.

Jim Staley

Artist, artistic director, and cofounder, Roulette

The music of [John] Cage, [John] Coltrane, [Harry]
Partch, and Miles [Davis] intrigued me the most
during that time. I frequented The Kitchen on
Broome St. and Phill Niblock's Experimental
Intermedia Foundation and decided to start the
Roulette concert series in my loft.

One fond memory I have is playing at BAM's New
Wave Festival with John Zorn's The Big Gun Down.
It was a lot of work and pulling together of a
large number of talented musicians. It was fun
to do.

NOTES

1. JOHN CAGE

1. John Cage, *Silence: Lectures and Writings*, 50th Anniversary Edition (Middletown, CT: Wesleyan University Press, 2013 [2011]).

2. LA MONTE YOUNG

2. Abby Rooner, "Ragas and Ratios: 6 Things We Learned from Legendary Avant-Garde Artist La Monte Young," Vice.com, May 9, 2015, https://www.vice.com/en/article/4xqn33/ragas-and-ratios -6-things-we-learned-from-legendary-avant-garde-artist-la-monte-young.

14. JACOB DRUCKMAN

3. Will Robin, "New Horizons, Old Barriers," Newmusic USA, August 30, 2017, https://newmusicusa .org/nmbx/new-horizons-old-barriers/.

24. JOAN LA BARBARA

4. Tim Lawrence, "Ghost Story," *Journal of Music*, February 1, 2010, https://journalofmusic.com/focus /ghost-story.
5. Jóhann Jóhannsson, correspondence with author, 2017.

26. BILL FRISELL

6. Doug Payne, Sound Insights (blog), "Rediscovery: Paul Motian Band 'Psalm,'" April 8 2009, http://dougpayne.blogspot.com/2009/04/rediscovery-paul-motian-psalm.html.

40. MICHEL WAISVISZ

7. Volker Krefeld and Michel Waisvisz, "The Hand in the Web: An Interview with Michel Waisvisz," *Computer Music Journal*, 14, no. 2 (Summer 1990): 28–33.

INDEX